The New Design Museum

The *New* Design Museum

Co-Creating the Present, Prototyping the Future

 PARK BOOKS

Per Mara e Placido

TABLE OF CONTENTS

Design & Planetarity: Of World-Making and the Quest for Freedom

This editorial project revolves around one central tenet: that institutions of culture are essential parts of the social infrastructure we desperately need to invest in to ensure a democratic construction and inhabitation of the future. It is the conviction that the communities of knowledge connected across the capillary network of spaces and initiatives devoted to the production and preservation of culture are an invaluable and underutilized resource to rethink the organizational structures and deliberative methodologies we need to operate in a radically unstable, divisive, and unpredictable world. And that, in the face of the general collapse of systems capable of managing the polycrisis[1] we currently endure globally, they too need to transform to remain relevant assets of

1   The term was coined by complexity theorists Edgar Morin and Anne Brigitte Kern and was first used in their book *Homeland Earth*, Hampton Press, 1999. It refers to the entangled state of global problems which are not reducible to one single cause.

collective empowerment through which we can co-create values and ambitions for long-term futures.

What has design to do with this? Everything. Design is both imbricated in the modern constructs of normativity that regimented the territorial, spatial, racial, legislative, biological, and behavioral hierarchies that led us here, as well as the conduit to reconfigure the exasperated asymmetries they engendered—of access to financial and natural resources, welfare, safety, etc.—into eco-political frameworks of interdependence and co-constitution based on an "economics of the common good."[2]

The Western rhetoric of human-centered progress has always associated itself with notions and technologies of environmental control, measurement, and prediction. Preoccupations with anthropogenic climate modification and ecosystemic manipulation reach back to the territorial conquests of the 15th and 16th centuries, as empire-building became coterminous with processes of exploitation, improvement, and normalization of nature for the accumulation of wealth and geopolitical dominance. This manufacturing of Nature[3] as an externality to human society enlisted the dicourse around the climate and meteorology (the quantitative science of its observation) onto issues of colonial sovereignty and false imaginaries of civilizational superiority, the legitimization of warfare, the building of nation-states, the exploitation

2   On the economic theory of mission-oriented innovation and the common good see the work of economist Mariana Mazzuccato, particularly relevant are "Governing the economics of the common good: from correcting market failures to shaping collective goals", *Journal of Economic Policy Reform*, 27:1, 2003, pp. 1–24; her report for the Directorate-General for Research and Innovation of the European Commission *Mission-oriented Research & Innovation in the European Union – A Problem-solving Approach to Fuel Innovation-led Growth*, Publications Office, 2018; the books *The Entrepreneurial State: Debunking Public vs. Private Sector Myths*, Anthem Press, 2013, and *Mission Economy—A Moonshot Guide to Changing Capitalism*, Penguin Press, 2021.

of vulnerable people, and the monopolization of resources. Awareness of the environment, of the human effects of its perturbation, and the global scale of their extent are by no means a modern phenomenon, as historical climatology—that is, the study of accurate observation and reconstruction of weather events—is traceable over the past five centuries. The colonial literature of royal chroniclers, conquistadores' maps and journals of the 1500s, and memoirs and treaties produced by 17th- and 18th-century naturalists, experimental philosophers, botanists, and historians from European imperial societies and academies of science informed the establishment of the first state meteorological bodies in most Western countries in the 1850s, propelled by the advent of technological modernity [4]. This institutionalization and operationalization of weather forecasting intensified throughout the 20th and 21st centuries, aided by computerized modeling and satellite technology with the capacity to generate extensive information from global monitoring, which then prompted the emergence of global intergovernmental institutions for coordinated research and action. As the historian of science and technology Paul N. Edwards observes, "climate science [can be read] as a global knowledge infrastructure which has ushered in a massive perspectival shift that has helped promote an understanding of the world as a single physical system. [...] Building the weather and climate knowledge infrastructures spread a specific way of making global knowledge—one whose

3   On the dialectical construction and therefore alienation of nature versus the human as coterminous with the birth of capitalism see, among others, Jason W. Moore, "The Rise of Cheap Nature" in Jason W. Moore (ed.), *Anthropocene or Capitalocene? Nature, History and the Crisis of Capitalism*, PM Press, 2016, pp. 70–115.

4   There is a growing scholarship around the connections between climate study, imperial histories, and past societies. A significant list of references can be found in Jean-Baptiste Fressoz and Fabien Locher, *Chaos in The Heavens – The Forgotten History of Climate Change*, Verso, 2024.

techniques, values, and implications now extend not only throughout the sciences but far beyond."[5]

The legacy of this origin story is twofold. On one side, the constructs of the colonial project still virulently proliferate today in the socioeconomic asymmetries attendant to the biophysical deterioration of the planet and a still pervasive "boardroom politics" that favors dominant minorities. What sets our epoch apart is that the magnitude and rapidity with which we can effect irreversible change on life-supporting systems is unprecedentedly compounded by their complex interconnectivity and the multitude of challenges we humans are posing to them. The 2023 UNU report on Interconnected Disaster Risks individuates six critical tipping points—that is, the moment at which a given socioecological system is no longer able to buffer risks and provide its expected functions, thus resulting in collapse. They are: accelerating extinctions, groundwater depletion, unbearable heat, melting glaciers, space debris, and uninsurable futures. Among six categories of shared root causes and drivers, the two that are common to all are "insufficient future planning

5   Paul N. Edwards, *A Vast Machine—Computer Models, Climate Data, and the Politics of Global Warming*, The MIT Press, 2010, Introduction, p. xix. See also Hans-Joachim Schellnhuber and Volker Wenzel (eds.), *Earth System Analysis—Integrating Science for Sustainability*, Springer, 1999 and H. J. Schellnhuber, "'Earth system' analysis and the second Copernican revolution," *Nature*, 402:6761, December 1999, pp. 19–23. On the Gaia Hypothesis co-developed by James Lovelock, and Lynn Margulis which postulates a vision of Earth as a self-regulating system of co-evolving organisms see James Lovelock, *Gaia, a New Look at Life on Earth*, Oxford University Press, 1979.

6   Caitlyn Eberle, Jack O'Connor, Liliana Narvaez, Melisa Mena Benavides and Zita Sebesvari, *United Nations University – Institute for Environment and Human Security. Interconnected Disaster Risks: Risk Tipping Points*, United Nations University – Institute for Environment and Human Security, 2023.

7   Gaia Vince, *Nomad Century – How to Survive the Climate Upheaval*, Allen Lane, 2022.

and risk management,"[6] which means a lack of perception, preparation, and foresight to act in front of a problem. Climate change and extreme weather events have further exacerbated the phenomena of species migration across different habitats, from oceans to forests, and have particularly affected zones of the Global South where already vulnerable populations reside[7], thus fueling discriminatory border policies and deregulated labour practices connected to disaster recovery while producing a global epidemic of psychological malaise —or solastalgia—especially among the young. Evidently, we are living through an intertidal historical moment when the oper-ative frameworks of past world-systems—that is, systems of governance, information, life-sustaining production and supply, and of technological mediation—no longer hold, and new ones, together with their values, must be created.

On the other side, as the euphoric imaginaries of the "global" folded under their own radical provincialization by the turn of the millennium, another, more powerful construct emerged, countering the rhetoric of human dominance and centralized control. Enlivened by ecological scholarship probing the laws of scientific rationalization and technological determinism, the concepts of the "planetary" and "planetarity"[8] have increasingly and potently problematized a

8   The notion of planetarity was originally put forward by the literary theorist Gayatri Chakravorty Spivak who first used it in a paper presented at Stiftung-Dialogik in Zurich in 1997 entitled "Imperatives to Re-Imagine The Planet" and later expanded in her book *Death of a Discipline*, Columbia University Press, 2003. Various thinkers have tackled the implications of planterarity as a new operative framework of thought and method and its ramification across different disciplinary ambits, from systems of governance to techno-science and philosophy. An extensive bibliography can be found in Nils Gilman (ed.), *The Planetary,* Berggruen Press, 2024. Among others see also Amy J. Elias and Christian Moraru (eds.), *The Planetary Turn—Relationality and Geoaesthetics in the Twenty- First Century*, Northwestern University Press, 2015.

vast array of disciplinary discourses articulated around conceptions of "nature"' and what is "natural," intended as a normative attribute of conformity and authenticity. The various theoretical evocations of contemporary "planetary thinking," its "techniques, values, and implications," as Edwards would have it, mobilize the queering agency of ecological thinking by calling into question the epistemological and ontological frameworks of human exceptionalism, and, therefore, its Western origins, to reveal other cosmologies and notions of identity and collectivity as dynamically co-constituted in a relational and perceptual universe of biological, technological, and material diversity.

Tools and technologies make ideas possible. Maps, clocks, the printing press, microscopes, telescopes, and today's supercomputers have progressively enabled an augmented regime of sensing and knowing the world, from the scale of subatomic particles to the realm of the extraplanetary, placing man back into the web of living biosystems of which it was always a part, rather than its sole creator.

Post-natural studies, multi-species ethnographies, posthumanism, new materialism, pluriversal and many-world theories, non-Western concepts of embodied sovereignty, multinaturalism and rights of nature, planetary sapience, and synthetic intelligence—all energize an intellectual fieldwork devoted to cultivating a reparatory and regenerative imagination between man and world.[9] Relationality emerges here as a theoretical and philosophical position that, while empowering narratives of emancipation of the "global majorities" originating in Indigenous and place-based cultures, is also pragmatically rooted in a praxis of "designing," intended as a new politics of healing and remaking the web of life.[10]

Acting on this two-fold legacy is now taking on an irrefutable urgency as its layered impact is making itself visible in an epochal stigma of relentlessly changing and unstable environmental and geopolitical conditions. As observed by Indy Johar and Caroline Paulick-Thiel, "modern democratic institutions can no longer structurally make legitimate decisions at the necessary speed. [...] Dealing with uncertainty, shocks, and rapid change requires structures that increase organizational and societal adaptability. This means to center agency around learning instead of control and develop approaches that are systemically agile enough to respond to emerging challenges and at the same time resilient enough to withstand ongoing disruptions."[11] More fundamentally, this systemic shift speaks to the absolute need for thinking well beyond immediate temporal and geographical confines.

The methodologies and practices of systemic reconfiguration required for planetary survival are rooted in the disciplinary ecology of design: they are rituals of world-making.

In this light, today we encounter design on other avenues than those set by its modern foundations as a solutional apparatus engineered to serve the all-important human factor, perfecting spaces, objects, and machines to assuage users' needs, shape social mores, or fabricate desire. These instantiations of design certainly persist and continue laboring within the attention economy of ubiquitous platforms and the

9   This is a vast array of theories that covers studies from critical anthropology to artificial intelligence, as numerous thinkers, scholars, and practitioners have contributed to expanding and interconnecting the implications of 'planetarity' over the past 30 years. These bibliographies are widely available in relation to the cited concepts. It is also worth mentioning a more recently ascendant perspective encapsulated under the field of Earth Jurisprudence that centers around the concept of the Rights of Nature (which recognizes nature and natural systems as subjects of legal rights), emerging from countries of the Global South, which profoundly challenges the dominant political economy of Western legal knowledge. See Daniel Bonilla Maldonado, "Global Legal Pluralism and the Rights of Nature," *Max Planck Private Law Research Paper* No. 23/15, August 2023. Available at SSRN: https://ssrn.com/abstract=4510374.

10   See Arturo Escobar, Michal Osterweil and Kriti Sharma, *Relationality–An Emergent Politics of Life Beyond the Human*, Bloomsbury, 2024. For extensive references see also Arturo Escobar, *Designs for the Pluriverse. Radical Interdependence, Autonomy, and the Making of Worlds*, Duke University Press, 2017.

emotional capitalism of "good design" for smarter cities and happier individuals. But the aim of this editorial project is to detect how design reflects on the complexities of contemporary reality by producing a new politics and aesthetics of engagement with its transitional, often precarious, and fluid state, and therefore how this affects the mission and agency of the cultural institutions that have historically harbored it, as well as how it is simultaneously prompting new ones to emerge.

Design is an agonistic practice, to borrow an expression from the political theorist Chantal Mouffe;[12] it is somewhat never an accomplished state, but the investigative journey towards its fulfillment. Design is a form of future-thinking that constantly probes the rules that organize the "present"—the principles that govern its environments, the materials, mechanisms, processes, and formulas that hold them together and render them habitable constructs. This productive pull between contingency and intuition places design in an always emergent field of participatory observation which locates and maps the appearance of possible worlds into uncharted ecosystems of interaction—among disciplines, objects, technologies, living beings, and therefore different forms of intelligence. Both a science and poetics of relations, design is a collaborative enterprise through which we measure the extent of our "being human" and attempt to fathom what dwells beyond its reach.

11   "Designing Next Institutions," Version 2.2, paper by Indy Johar, Dark Matter Labs & Caroline Paulick-Thiel, *Politics for Tomorrow*, May 2024, https://darkmatterlabs.org/. Also see "A New European Bauhaus Economy, Designing Our Futures–An Invitation Paper V 01" developed by Dark Matter Labs as part of the New European Bauhaus lighthouse project, Desire–an Irresistible Circular Society, funded by the European Union and presented at the New European Bauhaus Festival in Brussels in April 2024. Available at https://www.irresistiblecircularsociety.eu/news/invitation-paper-a-new-european-bauhaus-economy-designing-our-futures – accessed 11/06/2024.

The theoretical and practical agendas of 21st-century design are cross-pollinated by three interconnected notions: biocentrism, decentralization, and hybridity. First, in the emerging Bio Age,[13] human-centric constructs are no longer viable if we are to sustain life on the planet for future generations, thus preserving biodiversity, championing bioregional approaches, and deploying nature-based methodologies that foster inter-species flourishing, address material scarcity, and combat moral apathy. Second, as hegemonic ideologies of domination—biological, racial, and political—are being vocally opposed by civil society at large, emancipatory practices valuing collaborative decentralized actions to support vulnerable territories, populations, and marginalized groups are emerging forcefully on a global scale. Third, we are already living in a fluid world of hybridity and post-binary agency, disaffected by rigid categorizations of materiality, class, or territoriality (digital/analogue, human/machine, centre/periphery, etc.), where planetary futures are inconceivable if not articulated in the encounter of human, natural, and artificial dimensions of existence.

These arguments confer new formal and temporal dimensions to the project of design; they enlighten a wider remit of its actions, but most significantly, they reveal trajectories for novel subjects and methodologies of knowledge produced under the planetary paradigm that support inclusive and egalitarian modes of coexistence. They also set forth new parameters for the role of designers and design practice, and therefore beg the question of whether the institutions of education and culture that contribute to fostering design's relevance and impact on contemporary and future societies are equally interrogating their methodologies and purposes during such a pivotal moment of change.

12 Chantal Mouffe, "Deliberative Democracy or Agonistic Pluralism?," *Social Research*, 66:3 1999.

13 See Wendy L. Schultz and Trish O'Flynn, *Law in the Emerging Bio Age*, Horizon Report for The Law Society, August 2022. Available at https://www.lawsociety.org.uk/topics/research/law-in-the-emerging-bio-age.

Institutions Revisited and Distributed Agency: Design and the 21st Century

The contents of this publication bring together people and ideas around institutional practice in the fields of design and architecture from two intersecting vantage points. The first group voices the perspectives of directors and chief programmers from traditional, established institutions which, however, do not represent or intend to project a comprehensive survey of museums (or their proximate variations) proclaiming authority on the subjects for their sheer longevity or the size of their artifactual endowments. The reader will immediately recognize ostensible omissions in this sense. What they offer are insightful viewpoints on how design is mobilized across narratives of public engagement with the urgencies of the present, and how these are translated, both conceptually and practically, into revisited programs, missions, and activities interrogating and building upon the institutions' histories. The selection features institutional typologies of varied nature—from those that bear design or architecture in their names, to those that sport dedicated departmental divisions, to others that inherently work with design as part of their research agendas and operations. The geographical expanse of these examples and their structural models are mapped largely onto Western regions and Western-inspired canons, with the dominant museological tradition being a product of the European modern project and its imperial powers. They are accompanied by a second group of case studies that instead highlights independent organizations and initiatives covering roughly the past decade, from a more widely situated network of distributed agency that traverses both physical and digital domains, sporting alternative methodologies of collaboration, funding models, forms of audience engagement, and investigative subjects expanding those emerging from the first cluster. One common trait of all these experiences is a clear intent to move away from inherited notions of taxonomic or chronological framings of design history and discourse predominantly canonized around styles, materials, objects, and buildings, and a search for narrative methodologies that are inquisitive, impactful, and inclusive.

Their interwoven juxtapositions are organized into six thematic chapters and together aim to reflect on the emergent conditions and ideas that shape design culture and its institutions in the 21st century.

The establishment of institutions or departmental divisions specifically dedicated to design and architecture is still a relatively recent phenomenon, considering their legacy dates back to the birth of the public museum in 19th-century Europe. For example, the Victoria and Albert Museum, which was first established as the Museum of Manufactures in 1852 and inspired the establishment of decorative and applied arts institutions in other cities like Vienna, Berlin, and Hamburg, founded its Department of Contemporary Design, Architecture, and Digital in 2013 (which was disbanded and reabsorbed after the pandemic outbreak of 2020). The National Gallery of Victoria, Australia's largest art museum, founded in 1861, inaugurated its Department of Contemporary Design and Architecture in 2015. MoMA in New York, founded in 1929, launched the world's first curatorial department devoted to architecture and design in 1932, and the Cooper-Hewitt, originally established in 1897 as the Museum for the Arts of Decoration, was renamed The Smithsonian National Museum of Design in 1976. Throughout the following decades, various dedicated archives, organizations, and research outlets for public access were created, such as the Canadian Centre for Architecture and the International Confederation of Architecture Museums—ICAM (both 1979), the first edition of the Venice Architecture Biennale (1980), the Deutsches Architekturmuseum in Frankfurt (1984), the Netherlands Architecture Institute (today Nieuwe Instituut) in Rotterdam (1988), and the Design Museum in London (1989). Many other millennial endeavors have followed, from the likes of the Triennale Design Museum in Milan (2007) and 21_21 Design Sight in Tokyo (2007) to M+ in Hong Kong (2021), just to name a few.

These sparse instances, to which many more can and continue to be added, sport different origin stories cast within specific national histories and the political strategies of their times. Yet, design and the museum have long endured a somewhat fraught relationship. Never quite emancipated from its lesser position in the hierarchies of heritage institutions of visual and applied arts, design and architecture have more prominently entered the precincts of the 20th-century museum as modern tools for civic education and industrial promotion, whose mundane status was opportunistically elevated through their staged equivalence to works of art, and collected, archived, and presented following these canons.[1] This shifty condition persists in contemporary discussions around design's exact remit of practice and discourse, the strategies for its display and proper contextualization, and its debated disciplinary autonomy across cultures and global histories.

1   Mary Anne Staniszewski, *The Power of Display: A History of Exhibition Installations at the Museum of Modern Art*, MIT Press, 1998; Zoe Ryan (ed.), *As Seen: Exhibitions that Made Architecture and Design History*, Art Institute of Chicago, 2017.

Many of today's encyclopedic museums were birthed from the vestiges of 19th-century world fairs and international exhibitions, which by the end of that century dotted cities around Europe and the USA. As physical displays that celebrated empires' scientific and industrial prowess, they were nation-building laboratories that aimed to project civilizational and racial hierarchies by offering views of natural, technological, and human wonders, which included exhibits of manufacturing equipment, technological innovations, raw materials, arts and crafts, as well as the "exotic" attractions of non-white people presented in lived-in dioramas reproducing the ways of life in the colonies.[2] Once the peripatetic spectacle of the fairs closed their doors, many of their goods and artifact holdings made their way into the collections of what are some of today's largest institutions of culture.

The public museum and its progeny, the international exhibition, were scripted embodiments of a specific form of categorization of knowledge based on societies' material and technological production and positioned themselves as proponents of a highly conceptualized order of reality that heralded the modern world as an ideologically Western project. Their disciplinary function as "passionless reformers," wrote George Brown Goode in his "Principles of Museum Administration"[3] in 1895, was paramount in shaping the self-regulating, moral individuals that modern political institutions expected citizens to become. The "exhibitionary complex"[4] of early public cultural institutions celebrated an idea

2   See, among others, Paul Greenhalgh, *Fair World: A History of World's Fairs and Expositions, from London to Shanghai, 1851–2010*, Papadakis, 2011; Peter Hoffenberg, *An Empire on Display: English, Indian, and Australian Exhibitions from the Crystal Palace to the Great War*, University of California Press, 2001; Penelope Harvey, *Hybrids of Modernity: Anthropology, the Nation State and the Universal Exhibition*, Routledge, 1996.

3   George Brown Goode, *The Principles of Museum Administration—Annual Report of the Museums Association*, originally published by Coultas & Volans, 1895 (accessible through Internet Archive—last accessed August 2024).

of progress with man, or a certain kind of man—white, liberal, industrious—as the master narrator within an evolutionary construct literally spatialized through exhibits' linear narratives and the design of galleries where the crowd itself surged to spectacle. Straddling the line between public and private, individual and collective, institutions remain powerful and essential dispositifs of mediated experience today.

The impermanent nature of the "object" of design as a transcalar practice—the Ernesto Rogers' maxim "from spoon to city" making a vivid point in case—and its fluid disciplinary autonomy that claims territories across the humanities, arts, science, and technology, have long posed challenges to its framing within collections and the modalities of its presentation. The materiality of design, shifting from the tangibility of industrial products to the invisibility of its outcomes as experience, interaction, and computation, constantly interrogates traditional museological practices of archiving, exhibiting, and documentation. Among the long-debated issues are the despoliation of functionality of its objects or systems once extruded from their original context of use and secluded into the "white cube," an issue further problematized by digital, data-driven, and open-source contents, and the future of AI's and machine learning's emergent authoriality;[5]

4   The *exhibitionary* complex is a concept first developed by Tony Bennet in relation to museological practice and institutional articulations of power across the late 18th and 19th century. Tony Bennet, "The Exhibitionary Complex," *New Formations*, 4, Spring 1988. "[...] a number of characteristics set the museum, international exhibitions and modern fairs apart as a distinctive grouping. Each of these institutions is involved in the practice of 'showing and telling': that is of exhibiting artifacts and/or persons in a manner calculated to embody and communicate specific cultural meanings." in Tony Bennet, *The Birth of the Museum*, Routledge, 1995, p. 6.

5   See on the concept of "artificial naturalism" Alexander Campolo and Katia Schwerzmann, "From rules to examples: Machine learning's type of authority," *Big Data & Society*, 10:2, 2023.

the absence of physical originals that can only be mediated by the proxy of drawings, models, and photos in the case of architecture and automotive design; and the processual character of social, critical, and speculative projects. Ultimately, and regardless of its formal manifestation, design is inextricable from the politics and discourse of its material, social, and economic production—territorial conditions, financial markets, industrial and innovation policies, scientific and technological discoveries, labor laws, land rights, vernacular and intangible knowledge—which must be summoned for its proper understanding as both a systemic and synthetic practice.

Not unlike their counterparts in other creative fields, institutions tending to design culture are today confronted with the urgent tasks of revisiting the restrictive narratives enshrined in their holdings, including challenging the canons of imperial histories, colonization, modern capitalist expansion, and industrial extractivism, as much as incorporating in their research and actions the demands for diversity and pluralism vocalized by contemporary societies. Growing literature in critical anthropology, design history, and philosophy has deservedly brought to light the intersectional reality of the discipline and its imbrication with social justice, as related

6   Among more recent ones: Claudia Mareis and Nina Paim (eds.), *Design Struggles: Intersecting Histories, Pedagogies, and Perspectives*, Valiz, 2021; Kaleena Sales, *Centered: People and Ideas Diversifying Design*, Princeton Architectural Press, 2023; Dori Tunstall, *Decolonizing Design: A Cultural Justice Guidebook*, The MIT Press, 2023; Anne H. Berry, Kareem Collie, Penina Acayo Laker, Lesley-Ann Noel, Jennifer Rittner and Kelly Walters (eds.), *The Black Experience in Design: Identity, Expression & Reflection*, Allworth Press, 2022; Alison Place, *Feminist Designer: On the Personal and the Political in Design*, The MIT Press, 2023; Sasha Costanza-Chock, *Design Justice: Community-Led Practices to Build the Worlds We Need*, The MIT Press, 2020; Ellen Lupton, Farah Kafei, Jennifer Tobias, Josh A. Halstead, Kaleena Sales, Leslie Xia and Valentina Vergara (eds.), *Extra Bold: A Feminist, Inclusive, Anti-racist, Nonbinary Field Guide for Graphic Designers*, Princeton Architecture Press, 2021.

to feminist practice, Black history, Indigenous, and non-Western traditions.[6]

From its canonization as a solutional praxis of benign improvement with the "good design" and "design thinking" of the 1900s, 21st-century design has experienced a pronounced transmutation into a form of ethical and cultural tooling that derives from its combined existence as practice, discourse, and activism.

Twentieth-century plastics, steel, concrete, and all the palpable ethos of progress, speed, and efficiency distributed through the global supply chains of industrial manufacturing are today replaced by soft strategies of attunement with the organic materiality of soil, seeds, algae, fungi, microbes, and plants in the connective rehabilitation of bio-systems, by way of collaborative methodologies honoring communal work, social care, and productive mutuality. From reconfiguring molecular structures and cellular interactions to produce textiles and food, to deploying earth and clay as building materials, biofabrication and bioconstruction are gaining traction as principled alternatives that help curb energy consumption, work with nature, and harness its power.

As the modern dichotomy of world centers and peripheries dissolves into a more profound penetration of its divisive politics across transnational and interregional networks, design increasingly becomes invested in situated practices of commoning and place-making, based on the adoption of manufacturing techniques harbored in traditional ecological knowledge, artisanal and grassroots intelligence, and the use of locally available materials, labor, and resources, by advocating for a reconfiguration of stakeholders' relations among natural, social, and technological systems.[7]

7   See Brittany Utting (ed.), *Architectures of Care. From the Intimate to the Common*, Routledge, 2024; Marcelo López-Dinardi (ed.), *Architecture from Public to Commons*, Routledge 2024; Beatrice Galilee, *Radical Architecture*, Phaidon, 2022; Julia Watson, *Lo-TEK: Design by Radical Indigenism*, Taschen, 2019.

As "ecological," "reparatory," and "regenerative" are attributes found more and more attached to any scale or domain of design's interventions, social and environmental impact increasingly define the discursive and practical ambit of contemporary design. One that profoundly interrogates its own dependencies on the material chains of production that have shaped the modern world, and consequently the geopolitical and geological engineering of its structural asymmetries. For attendant reasons, the critical inquiries and militant agency of design are moving into the geographies of interest to the profit-hungry industries of extraction that are forests, water basins, earth inner space, and the deep seas. The eco-social calamities that continue unabated in the resource-rich territories of the Global South and the vulnerability of their populations demand a shift toward planetary agendas where climate and social justice are coterminous, and in recognition that hegemonic narratives of discrimination and segregation persist in the conceptualization, design, and production of our contemporary environments, policies, and pedagogies.

The planetary paradigm disturbs the binary epistemology of Western anthropocentrism (i.e., a man-made world) with the transcalar politics of entangled systems animated by interactions of more-than-human nature, among and "with other media, other infrastructures, other creatures and things."[8] It acknowledges value systems of ancestral cultures that supplant concepts of land ownership and occupation with communitarian belonging and collective existence predicated on rituals of knowledge transmission embracing natural, social, and spiritual dimensions.

As previously observed, the scientific and philosophical theories that redistribute agency across objects, microbiota, living species, and machines confound dominant material and social histories of linearity and can lead us to excavate

[8]   Shannon Mattern, *Code + Clay, Data + Dirt.*
        Five Thousand Years of Urban Media, University
        of Minnesota Press, 2017, Introduction,
        p. XXX.

novel interpretations of how pasts, presents, and futures, in the plural, enter dialogue in the physical environments of our buildings, neighborhoods, cities, and regions. More broadly, they call for a reorganization of the systems of production, education, research, and development in which design is embedded, and therefore a reassessment of the role institutions play in nurturing and empowering this transforming culture.

The horizontal methodologies that subtend the production of planetary knowledge have formulated a new design syntax which has followed its critical and speculative turn around the start of the millennium and could be termed an investigative aesthetics. Inhabiting simultaneously various scales and domains of distribution—commercial, cultural, pedagogical—a distinctive act of design is an aggregate of collective knowledge that finds expression in a summa of findings and formal choices resulting from study and fieldwork produced by a cross-disciplinary team effort. Its research-centered narratives are brought to life in a forensic constellation of products, built and ephemeral gestures, multimedia and generative contents, parceled into books, websites, pieces unique, material assemblages, photographs, films, and performative activations. This is also the result of a necessary balancing act between the practical constraints of time and resources involved in the development of market-viable products and services, and the articulation of principled approaches that require iterative testing and extended research, which are often incompatible with corporate logics of fast returns on investment in today's economic environment.

For museums, this interrogates not only the methodologies of representation or narration of design's formal developments (materials, shapes, manufacturing, and building techniques) but also the ways in which its ethical intentions and implications, its conceptual strategies, and the localized complexities of its implementation can be brought to fruition. The outcomes and, often, the temporal arch necessary for this type of design to make itself manifest are not something a 200-word caption, a building model, or a prototype under glass could suffice to elucidate. The durational nature of design as a process and method that does not find expression in a singular finished item presents questions of various nature for traditional institutions. For example: technical issues of conservation when dealing with living or bio-materials, problems of integrity of representation when a project is not reducible to a discrete object but encompasses the development of material solutions, tools, and often new subjects of research that bridge disciplinary categories, or ethical and practical implications involved with documenting forms of design knowledge that are traditionally transmitted through oral history or preserved by regimes of cultural secrecy and of non-representational nature.

This ultimately begs the question of how to re-position commissioning and collecting as part of a larger portfolio of practices institutions could and should perform to serve the discipline and public interest at their best, and whether new approaches and strategies that normally motivate investment into institutions (public or private they might be) should instead be put forth.

If institutions are required to be active conveyors of the ideas mobilizing design and of designers' fundamental role in the practice of everyday life, it increasingly appears crucial to augment their traditional functions as awareness-builders with strategies that support the professional recognition and active participation of practitioners across the industries that today need them the most for prototyping the common future. This includes fighting the precarity of a sector in which financial self-sufficiency is not left to volatile exercises for marketing and branding industries or drained by meager project-focused grant seeking but reinforced through better elaborated policies, forms of funding, and revenue awarded for the structural transformations designers can implement if we are to repair and nurture the biosystems that support life on Earth: food production, transportation, construction, healthcare, housing, energy, public infrastructure, and any of the productive engines that move as much as divide societies. It is at these crossroads—supporting novel areas of cross-sectoral research and enabling practical application of ideas that can foster and inspire public participation in urgent debates—that new horizons of transformative agency can be created for institutions of design culture to keep performing their essential role as platforms of collective engagement.

Reflecting once again on the visions and missions of institutions is a matter of concern also for the practical reality of their financial sustainability, which has drastically deteriorated in the aftermath of the Covid-19 pandemic outbreak. While funding mechanisms differ greatly from country to country, the resulting life-or-death imperative of regaining publics exposed the vulnerability of homogenized business models across museums globally, many of which never recovered.[9]

If the signification of "making things public" invigorated the "exhibitionary complex" of the reforming politics in the 1800s, which shaped museums as spaces of mass education and, by extension, social distinction, today's *engagement complex* plunges specialized institutions, regardless of their size, funding, and operational structures, into the highly competitive arena of edutainment and its fast-paced mechanisms of content creation based on performance metrics ruling over the same attention economy of streaming and the celebrity culture of social media. This might have fast-tracked a welcome digital transition for the few that could afford it but also opened up the programming capacity of others to the dangers of consumption-driven dictates based on market research and a relentless search for the "new." The general overreliance on exhibition ticketing and tourism as revenue and investment generators has also intensified polarizing scenarios by affecting more strongly those dependent on public

9   See *Museums around the World in the Face of Covid-19*, United Nations Educational, Scientific and Cultural Organization (UNESCO), 2021; *Assessment of the Impact of COVID-19 on Cultural and Creative Industries*, published by the United Nations Educational, Scientific and Cultural Organization (UNESCO), 2022.

funding and the small- and medium-scale institutions that exist to primarily serve local communities, as cumbersome budget cuts and diminishing public subsidies become the norm. Furthermore, mounting social and environmental protests have forced many to apply corrective strategies, from ensuring diversity across staff to reducing carbon footprints in their operations and accounting for the origins of their corporate sponsorships and private philanthropy.

Museums sit on political grounds; they always have. The ostensible contemporary agitations that have taken place in their lobbies or the attacks on their curatorial choices and exhibited works are performative actualizations both against their symbolic charge as multipliers of exclusionary narratives of power and in support of their enduring importance as public stages. These demands for just representation challenge the authoritative voice of the institution, i.e., who has the right to tell what stories, by shifting its functional definition from that of a repository of specialized connoisseurship to a broadened remit of civic agency capable of engaging the pressing emergencies of our era while mediating and facilitating, with both academic rigor and moral integrity, a connection with its underlying complexities and therefore accommodating the polyvocality of the constituencies it serves.

The engagement complex conjures various phenomena attendant to an identity crisis that revolves around recasting the central role of culture and its institutions in a radically and rapidly transforming world, thus eliciting new conceptions for their internal and external operations. All this adds to a variety of contextual phenomena in which design, as practice and discourse, confronts its own disciplinary expansion, repositioning, or instrumentalization within academia, as part of larger institutional constructs, city planning strategies, and national agendas. The voices collected here speak to this wide diversity of experiences, contexts, and communities, and it is in the recognition and strategic empowerment of this diversity that the future of institutions resides. It suggests that by embracing design as both a resourceful and forceful practice of societal impact and intellectual enlightenment, the mediating agency of institutions can be differently configured and distributed across research programmes, forms of curatorial practice, editorial work, partnerships, alliances, and collaborative frameworks, with online, offline, and off-site agency not solely confined to exhibition making.

If we adopt the vantage point of Sylvia Wynter's *homo narrans*—the idea that we create stories about life and how we live within those stories—as essentially a praxis of design,[10] then the trope of storytelling emerges as central in thinking through institutional trajectories of transformation. In a historical moment when a systemic reconfiguration of the world and our place in it is ever more necessary, we need places where the processual performances of meeting in and with ideas can unfold and be sheltered from the confounding agonies of risk-averse solutionism, political short-termism, competition- and profit-driven economies of innovation, and ideological manipulation. The cultural infrastructure of design and its multidisciplinary, cross-sectoral networks of knowledge can become home to these productive rituals of civic encounters for the origination of purpose-driven ambitions and values that could inform emancipatory educational blueprints, professional training, progressive and anti-hegemonic urban and social policies, and regenerative investments in various productive sectors, in ways that would be otherwise hardly achievable in the hyper-privatized sectors of today's education, R&D departments, and corporatized think tanks.

The incumbency of chronically rapturous events characterizing our times—armed conflicts, climate collapse, and socio-political instability—requires a capacity for fast reaction, flexibility, and self-organization that institutions have traditionally seldom cultivated. The development of strategies of diversification across temporal and formal scales of production becomes, therefore, essential to maintain a congruous

10   I am borrowing Sylvia Wynter's perspective as elucidated in the first chapter of the book *Relationality* (op.cit.), 2024.

balance between intellectual integrity and institutional identities that are confronted with the task of speaking to a highly segmented demographic pool of general and professional audiences. More importantly, diversification demands both pace and direction, a capacity to discern and choose exactly how many things an institution can be for how many people.

The temporality of institutional practice that can no longer solely anchor itself to exhibition making is distributed across durational experiences that are required to be interactive, dialogical, and based on knowledge exchange. In her study of the historical evolution of institutional displays and interiors from the 1800s until 2000, Charlotte Klonk observes that "experience is, in itself, a category subject to social and historical forces."[11] A wide prism of contingent factors—like scientific research (think of physiological studies on visual illusion, light, and colors, for example), philosophical notions of individuality and personhood, technological progress (telescopes, augmented reality, the metaverse), or market conditions (discretionary spending, inflation)—all contribute to defining changing notions of spectatorship and social performance. She reminds us that the Latin root of the word experience means trial, proof, experiment—and it is in this sense that institutional spaces have long constituted a hybrid border between subjective and collective spheres, as spatial moderators and important markers of their times.

What emerges across the present is that whether applied to the use of collections, off-site projects, or public programs, traditional strategies of a purely presentational nature are counterweighed by those generating more "embodied experiences of intimacy" and meaningful social encounters that celebrate the "power of small gestures," mutual care, and the building of "communities of interest" and "solidarity."

By seeking engagement with publics in ways that endow cultural experiences with a sense of fulfillment in sharing and co-producing knowledge, here the institution becomes a

11   Charlotte Klonk, *Spaces of Experience—Art Gallery Interiors from 1800 to 2000*, Yale University Press, 2009, p. 8.

"site of discovery," a "site of production," and a "place of imaginative freedom." The siloed hierarchies once embedded in disciplinary and departmental knowledge make way for programmatic and research agendas occupying the hybrid in-betweens of the "trans-", "cross-", and "inter-", as explorative domains more attuned to the planetary paradigm and the systemic challenges imbricated in the remit of contemporary design at large.

The static spatiality of the front- and back-of-house experience, which has traditionally designated zones of competence by separating the public areas of exhibitions from the technical precinct of storages and conservation laboratories, is also progressively abandoned in favor of more dynamic strategies of intervention, ranging from opening up collection warehouses and archives to project-driven galleries and varied forms of temporary presentations that break up the prototypically fixed blueprints of viewing galleries.

This "generative" disposition starts permeating various levels of institutional action, whether informing acquisition policies, thematic exhibitions, public programs, or, tout court, redefining the institution as a "system demonstrator," a prototyping platform of "enacted speculations," and a conduit to fund research around uncharted territories of critical production to test ideas that could benefit "public life" and ultimately engender true societal impact.

As the object lessons of design move away from mere physical instantiation into the realm of ideas, process, and method, as discussed above, the nature of institutional practice, as much as its methodologies, necessarily must endeavor to create a context for their appreciation and discernment. This requires a reshuffling of internal and external dependencies among stakeholders—public funders, companies, citizens, professionals, educators, researchers, policymakers, and producers of all kinds.

Certainly, this repositions the eternally shape-shifting figure of the curator once more. As Fleur Watson states in her book around the subject in the context of contemporary design and architecture, "here, the curatorial intent is not simply to create spectacle or to activate benign participation. Nor does it perform expertise in the museological tradition. Rather, the intent and position are situated in an emergent form of curatorial advocacy and activism."[12]

While this would sound familiar to those who have long run on independent tracks, the notion of the curator as a co-conspirator, co-writer, and active participant in the ideation and development of a project appeals more and more to institutions' need to tread carefully around the narratives they choose to champion and the ways in which those arguments are put to public fruition for open debate and confrontation. Not least, it ensures that they remain relevant players in gauging the future of specialized fields of practice by sheltering nascent forms of expression, research, and production from the corrective forces of rapacious commercialization and trends consumption.

Debates around the values of design, pervasive as they should be for their relevance in subjects that range from city regeneration to reproductive rights, and as elusive in their comprehension when decoupled from their more popular figuration as products or crafts, have also progressively disappeared from the culture of public discourse across mainstream information unless subsumed to sections about style or interior decoration. With specialized media left competing in the aggressive arena of digital publishing and advertising, this zone of intellectual cross-pollination and critical interactions is one that institutions have the responsibility to rescue and cultivate with novel platforms.

The participatory ethos that underlies many of the institutional propositions here presented is notoriously one that animates bottom-up initiatives and experimental alliances—movements that attempt "trojan-horsing" the systems they intervene in by way of parasitic, tactical, productively disturbing actions. This is an expression that appears often in these conversations as a modus operandi fertilizing visions of structural impermanence and adaptability that institutions

12   Fleur Watson, *The New Curator: Exhibiting Architecture and Design,* Routledge, 2021, p. 13.

increasingly must learn to embed in their planning. It suggests that infrastructures of convergence allowing for more porous interactions across communities of affinity and institutional collaborations predicated on shared challenges rather than solely circulating exhibitions and collections are essential to co-create and prototype imaginaries of long-term futures.

As often happens, it is from the front lines of independent practice that inspiring examples come to the fore. The initiatives here selected bear testimony to the enduring and resilient power that comes from collective action and self-organization, which characterize connective enterprises built on peer-to-peer support, learning, and scrutiny. The collaborative ethos of the 21st century is tethered to a globally distributed territory of intertwined networks: these are communities of intent that self-assemble around systemic defaults and urgencies that manifest similarly across far-removed geographical contexts; theirs is the hyperlocal vantage point that Ezio Manzini describes as situated and simultaneously boundless.[13] Hyperlocalism is the remedial alternative to the unilateral hegemony of globalization, its disattended promise of a borderless world, and its perpetuation of socioeconomic protocols of market expansion continuous with the regional imperialism of the past.

These collective strategies of interaction are characteristically transnational, transscalar, and transmaterial. They are hybrid, rhizomatic, digitally connected, and physically intermittent. They are often less invested in the delivery of brief-oriented or problem-solving outcomes and instead focused on supporting novel knowledge-making methodologies, producing resource and archival platforms,[14] shaping

13 Ezio Manzini, *The Politics of the Everyday*, Bloomsbury, 2019.
14 Archival and resource platforms created by independent organizations, collectives, and individuals are numerous and might deserve dedicated analysis on their own. Some are represented by the case studies featured here, but many others exist, particularly devoted to supporting minority groups, decolonial

alternative pedagogical curricula, and building capacity programs that can enrich and sustain the professional and intellectual vocations of their evolving members. They do so by celebrating positions of liminality that operate on their own terms, infiltrating the cracks of depleting or dysfunctional systems (productive, educational, social, territorial) by crafting new ones, as opposed to antagonistically reinforcing peripheral perspectives that engage confrontationally with pre-established hierarchical orders. And it is in this sense that they become generative dispositives of planetary articulation, allowing the diversification of localized voices and ensuring that these experiences are not only preserved but also continuously created.[15]

Their strategies of adaptive growth are also predicated on paced mechanisms of sensitive and intimate dialogues among

studies, and design traditions or repositories of knowledge that would otherwise be completely lost. For example, the Brazilian *Design e Opressao* (Design and Oppression), https://www.designeopressao.org/home/; *Futuress.org* (on design and feminism), https://futuress.org/; *Office Hours* by Ester Choi, https://www.instagram.com/office_hours.nyc/; *Singapore Graphic Archives* by Justin Zhuang, https://graphic.sg/; *Malaysia Design Archive,* https://search.malaysiadesignarchive.org/; the online platform and community *Alphabettes*, https://www.alphabettes.org/. On alternative education see Beatriz Colomina, Ignacio G. Galán, Evangelos Kotsioris and Anna-Maria Meister (eds.), *Radical Pedagogies*, The MIT Press, 2022; *Urgent Pedagogies*, the digital platform and editorial resource led by Magnus Ericson and Pelin Tan, https://urgentpedagogies.iaspis.se/.

15 I borrow this reflection from the philosopher Yuk Hui: "Planetary thinking is not about the preservation of diversity, which posits itself against external destruction, but rather the creation of diversity. This diversification is creation grounded in the recognition of locality—not simply to preserve its traditions (though they remain essential), but also to innovate in the service of locality." Yuk Hui, "For a Planetary Thinking," *e-flux journal*, December 2020.

individuals, communities, or collaborating entities, devoted to sheltering research-intensive processes from the "discourse extraction" that increasingly permeates institutional approaches in search of the new and latest. The critical agendas-embedded in the programs and projects selected therefore highlight theoretical and practical fields of exploration that address the fragile yet fertile arenas of eco-social imaginations, convivial reparation, and collective renewal. They address phenomena that are evidently constitutive or byproducts of the planetary condition, such as the decolonization of architecture, design practice and education, participatory forms of territorial regeneration, and civic innovation, as well as the social and economic challenges of forced migration and climate mitigation, thus cultivating reciprocation and care as tools that can support underserved and marginalized communities, remedying racial, gender, or cultural biases. The fundamental value of the networked response capacity these initiatives embody was certainly brought into stark relief by the sudden outbreak of Covid-19, and it was in its aftermath that the use of digital/online resources intensified. While this expanded tremendously the possibilities of collective agency, it also exposed the precarity of its normalization, which funding policies should consider through structural investments rather than project-based subsidies.

A reflection around institutional practices would also have to consider recurrent temporary events like fairs, biennales, and festivals, which have increasingly grown in number across the global cultural calendar. While the subject might deserve further space than it can be given here, it is undeniable that they, too, need a reassessment of how the economic, cultural, and social capital they mobilize can be repurposed to reflect the post-global state of affairs we are living through. As aggregators of collective intelligence that can impact cities and countries, if not entire regions, it is ultimately a question of what role they can continue playing as incentive providers within a vital sector like design at large.

In her seminal work on governing the economics of the common good, Mariana Mazzucato reminds us that innovation has both a rate and a direction aimed at "turning challenges into concrete problems"[16] that can be tackled with inspirational missions. A purpose-driven innovation labors with the creation of the common good as a collective objective, achieved via co-creation, participation in debate and consensus-building, collective learning, and knowledge-sharing, which can galvanize systemic transformations around shared goals, like the green transition, social justice, or sustainable development.

Funding mechanisms for cultural institutions play a central part here, especially in defining the terms of accountability —private and corporate philanthropy dominate the American landscape, while public subsidies are the main source of sustainment in Europe, for example. The best course would sit in the middle, across public-private partnerships that recognize the value of institutions of design culture as conduits of contextualized delivery for shared ambitions made possible by the situated knowledge of their communities, the productive assets of the various industries the discipline is imbricated with, and the know-how embedded in its professional constituencies. In the context of the EU and particularly in the post-Covid period, the importance of culture in society has been the subject of ongoing campaigns like the Cultural Deal for Europe[17] and reports bringing evidence to the "clear and positive correlation between rates of citizens' participation in cultural activities and indicators of civic engagement, democracy, and social cohesion."[18] But

16   Mariana Mazzucato, "Mission-oriented innovation policies: challenges and opportunities," *Industrial and Corporate Change*, 27:5, 2018.

17   https://culturaldeal.eu/

18   European Commission, Directorate-General for Education, Youth, Sport and Culture, W. Hammonds, *Culture and Democracy, the Evidence—How Citizens' Participation in Cultural Activities Enhances Civic Engagement, Democracy and Social Cohesion—Lessons from International Research*, Publications Office of the European Union, 2023. See also Christos Carras (ed.), *The Handbook of Cultural Work*, Bloomsbury, 2024.

the journey is still long ahead of us, as the policy landscape around cultural funding remains highly fragmented, poorly designed in terms of its strategic direction and allocation, and weak in the recognition of institutions' crucial function as generators of socioeconomic value.[19]

This editorial project, while not exhaustive in representing the bold and intellectually courageous work done by practitioners in different parts of the world, is motivated by the desire to bring forward case studies that already approach institutional practice as exactly this process of civic rehearsing through which we shape the culture in which democracy can survive. It is an invitation to continue the conversation and take action in the long term.

19   European Commission: Directorate-General for Education, Youth, Sport and Culture, *Stormy Times—Nature and Humans—Cultural Courage for Change—11 Messages for and from Europe*, Publications Office of the European Union, 2022, https://data.europa.eu/doi/10.2766/90729.

Legacy, Heritage, and Storytelling

I

Commissioning Design: From **Indigenous** Initiatives to Investigative **Research**

Senior curator for contemporary art, design, and architecture
Ewan McEoin

The design and architecture department at the NGV is of recent establishment (2015) compared to the history of the institution itself. Can you explain the context of its creation, what the challenge was back then, and where you are now after ten years? The NGV was founded in 1861 in Melbourne, a colonial city with a predominantly European settler population enriched through the gold rush of the time. It was resourced by very strong philanthropy and the wealth of Melbourne as a city.

Today, the gallery holds the most significant collection of art in the region, with more than 76,000 works that span thousands of years and a wide breadth of ideas, disciplines, and styles. Within that trajectory, there was a strong history of collecting decorative arts and crafts.

I joined the NGV in 2012 to work on an exhibition called *Melbourne Now.* Our new director at the time, Tony Ellwood, felt that the institution had degraded its contact with the contemporary art and design community, and through that, our engagement with contemporary issues and modes of practice. I was invited as a guest curator of design and architecture, along with Simone Le Amon and Fleur Watson, to address this.

Melbourne Now was a massive show; it was, at the time, the largest and most ambitious project to be undertaken by the gallery, celebrating the latest art, architecture, design, fashion, and dance produced in this city. It brought together over 130 artists and 30 curators to activate the spaces across both of our buildings.

Seeking to engage directly with the design and architecture community, we quickly went into commissioning new projects. We wanted the exhibition to feel collaborative and energetic, reflecting the DNA of Melbourne as a city of design and architecture. It wasn't about only borrowing work, but rather engaging in making something new. We commissioned performance spaces, pavilions, data visualization, graphic design, objects, and architectural spaces.

Reflecting on this time from today, it was through this highly collaborative, entrepreneurial headspace that we defined a fundamental part of our DNA as a team in terms of how we think. It became a model of sorts.

The show had 750,000 visitors; it was very popular, and it helped the whole institution understand that design and architecture were relevant and interesting topics for a broad public. After that show in 2014, I worked with our directors to develop the strategy for the opening of the Department of Contemporary Design and Architecture, which was the first new department at the NGV since Photography was opened in 1979.

Ten years in, we have built a team and a strong program. We have run three NGV Triennials, which have enabled the collection of hundreds of works. We have delivered ten NGV Architecture Commissions, three MECCA Women in Design Commissions, and multiple solo and group exhibitions, alongside eight Melbourne Design Week programs. All of this activity—while hugely rewarding—is leading us toward the opening of a new major building dedicated to 21st-century art and design, The Fox: NGV Contemporary, which will open in 2028.   **You've developed over time a series of recurrent events, some of which you have just mentioned, like the NGV Architecture Commissions, Melbourne Design Week, and the NGV Triennial, that act like big satellites to your activities. So, what is their positioning within the program and their function in relation to your wider strategy?**   The Contemporary Design and Architecture department here seeks to present the most relevant and resonant examples of design and architecture today, with a focus on exploring design and its role in enriching culture and society.

We focus strongly on critically regarded projects by leading international and Australian practitioners to understand the shifting motivations and technical capabilities of design studios and the industry, as well as designers working on the periphery of the commercial sector, which represent excellence in technical production, craftsmanship, and conveying contemporary issues.

Representing the increasing global role of design that is research-driven and experimental, as opposed to commercially available, we have been active in commissioning or investigating leading local and international examples of research-driven and experimental or critical design.

To provide a structure for this activity, we have developed a series of recurring programs. This is in part a collection-building strategy. As was proven by *Melbourne Now*, ambitious, free exhibitions draw stunning audience figures. Through this, a virtuous cycle is created. Anything we commission or collect as an institution is enabled through philanthropic support. We work hard to generate recurring projects that offer frameworks that drive collection outcomes and simultaneously grow the community of support around them.

The first of these properties, as we call them, was launched in 2015. The annual NGV Architecture Commission is delivered through an open competition process. This year, we will have completed 10 of these commissions. The longevity builds engagement on many levels and has meant we have really consolidated our relationship with the Australian architecture sector. Since the outset, the program has been partnered with RMIT University. We also run a triennial exhibition program called The Rigg Design Prize, which is the richest design prize in Australia, offering $30,000 to a winner selected from the group exhibition every three years. Every edition, we adjust the brief—focusing on furniture practice, interior design, advertising design, and this year we look at emerging practice.

Perhaps our most important recurring project, the NGV Triennial, was inspired by that first show, *Melbourne Now*. It is a vast show, with over 100 artists and designers in each edition; it is diverse across the disciplines and global in scope. It is free to the public, with the 2023 edition receiving over 1 million visitors. It is an amazing engine for growing the collection.   **So, back in the beginning, becoming part of Australia's longest-standing institution with a power of outreach and reputational heft, what role did you see yourself playing for the local community, and how have these "properties" helped you shape audiences? Who are your publics?**   In 2015 an opportunity to bid to run a design week for Melbourne came up from the state government. With the backing of our director, we successfully bid to host this. Today, Melbourne Design Week is an annual 11-day program that celebrates and interrogates design through its varied disciplines. The festival has grown from just under 100 programs in 2017 to over 350 in 2024, making it Australia's largest international design event.

Melbourne Design Week has been important in the building of the NGV collection of Australian design. Leveraging this opportunity every year, we support exhibitions across the city, at times working curatorially with independent designers and collectives. Our objective has been to bring the sector together to establish some common values, but also to create a sense of community and collaboration. One outcome of this is that we've seen an annual improvement in quality, scale, ambition, and sophistication in terms of what people are achieving. I see this as part of our role in helping nurture the local sector.

In terms of the architecture commission, the brief is extremely open; we specify that we do not want it to be a pavilion nor a venue for talks. It is much more about criticality and opening new conversations. Over the 10 editions, this program has helped the architecture sector and us as curators to understand how architecture can tell a story and how it can engage the public in that.

With the NGV Triennale, we started on the first edition in 2015. We had amazing support from our directors to engage with international designers in commissioning new work. Our approach was to be actively involved in the development of briefs around what those projects were to explore. We've really found that to be one of the most important parts of what we do; we are committed to being part of changing the way design practice thinks—about the types of projects people can make and exhibit within institutions. On that basis, our audiences are both the sector and the public.

We are not working much in the commercial sphere of design. We are not prioritizing doing retrospective shows about "successful" designers because we don't see these kinds of exhibitions as being generative. We are much more interested in looking outwards and being driven by socioeconomic and geopolitical contexts rather than looking inwards at design practice itself. I have a fundamental belief that most design and architecture are still trapped in just doing what they've always done; it's a business model. It's a mode of practice. People are earning incomes; that's fine. But I don't know that that deserves to be recorded in the history of a museum for years into the future. What I'm probably trying to think about is how the world is changing around us, but also participate a little bit in changing that as well.   I said elsewhere that I see many new practices becoming a "program," meaning both producing design and contributing to the development of its critical discourse as part of their output in being involved with a transforming world. In this sense, how much is this dialogue between local and global, or "local versus the rest," part of your research agendas or conversations with practitioners and your colleagues at the museum?   We are equally interested in global practice and local practice. We are not trying to define what it means to be an Australian designer; however, we do look at some of the characteristics that might help us communicate how our values and beliefs are reflected through design practice. For example, in Australia, there is an ongoing reappraisal of how design and architecture could relate to or reflect the philosophies and knowledges of our First People. There has been an increasing movement within the design spheres here, and we see this internationally, to understand how to design with and on Country, which is what we call the active and passive systems of nature and ecology that we live with and within. So how to tell that story? How does that come through projects?

Not having a strong collection of contemporary design or architecture to work with in the beginning was an important factor. We had the freedom to think: what should a design collection of the 21st century be and do? Do we want to do what other institutions are doing?

Drawing from these questions, within our collection strategy today we have classic disciplinary areas—but we resist the role of simply recording what has happened in the design industry. Instead, we are looking at how what we collect can articulate the issues shaping the world around us. As a team, we have decided to prioritize the future rather than record the past and present.

We are also very clear that design curation needs to be understood and articulated as something generative, not simply reflective. Design curation today should be propositional, offering outcomes and solutions that are relevant to the world. Not all curators agree, and I often am disappointed that more institutions are not seeing their role as facilitators sitting between the industry, researchers, the public, government, and design practice.

This might mean that in some eyes we are irreverent about curatorial traditions. But we like to think of ourselves as narrators of sorts—we are heavily audience-focused, and we want to create exhibitions that change people's minds and shape behavior.   Certainly, this approach of working with practitioners, entering into a sort of partnership in the development of ideas, research briefs, and outcomes is unique and pushes the institution into a more active role when it comes to bringing to the forefront urgent issues. You have often advocated for a kind of design ethics where the practice cannot be decoupled from its motivations and its contribution to the civic or societal dimension. What do you see happening nowadays in design? What are the novel horizons of criticality?   Design and architecture are industries. Let's be realistic that 90% of the activity in both of those industries is probably of no great interest to a design museum or to the public. I'm interested in the 10% that communicate design evolution, in terms of how ideas and practices evolve through objects, buildings, cities, or systems. I'm interested in the conditions that create any situation in time. Design is heavily implicated in the problems that unpack hyper-consumerism, extraction, and the associated ills of today. At some point, there needs to be a catharsis around the complex and at times conflicted role design has and does play in a changing value system. If design is based on the act of making or building something, are we always caught in a trap in relation to labor, extraction, waste, etc.? How do we move through that?

If we know that everything is interconnected and things correlate with each other, we ask ourselves what we are curious about as a museum in Australia, on Indigenous land. What stories should we be telling?

What is interesting is to look at where design is catching up. That is where we get involved in commissioning; sometimes we're interested in how you create the time with resources for design studios to explore new thinking or new adjacencies.   Well, that is the core of your job description: opening up that question from both sides of the dialogue. What you do, you don't do just for the sake of preservation; you're doing it to set up a conversation with the public, essentially providing them with an opportunity to speak back.   Exactly. I don't see our primary role as being the custodians of a collection. I see us as the creators of a collection. I wonder, as we move through what we are doing—in creating situations for people to encounter things—can a collection radiate an energy field? Could we create environments for people to change their minds about things? That seems like a worthwhile pursuit to me. Let's speak about this massive new project that will open in 2028, which is a 30,000-square-meter building, part of a huge public investment in what is the largest cultural infrastructure project in Australia since the Sydney Opera House.

How do you feel about the fact that you will be working within yet another huge temple of culture built on somewhat past institutional models—a big building, ecologically, financially, and operationally resource-heavy? It sounds like a dream scenario compared to the cultural landscape in Europe, which is being intensely defunded.   It may be a very simplistic way of viewing it, but the more we do, the more people come.

And if we think ahead of us, we definitely need more people to be pursuing design as part of their lives. It's interesting when you talk about it as a temple of culture because we also live in a society where there are fewer and fewer places to go to believe in things. Where do we find solace? Where do we find inspiration? Where do we connect with the stories of other people from other places? How do we truly understand what's going on in the world?

In the "negative everything" of the media environment that we operate in, I think it's very relevant to ask for more places that allow us to do things and reach people in ways that we can't do right now. There is something quite symbolic about that scale of the investment, that scale of ambition in this place at this time. It is a very significant project for Australia's cultural sector—and a direct outcome of the trajectory the institution has been on: growing audiences, growing the collection, being relevant and engaged.

I think these things mean something in societies. Now we need to invest in culture more. Culture and creativity are literally direct solutions to the complexities of the world because they build empathy, they build understanding, they give a sense of agency in the future, and they provide us with a critical perspective on the world around us.

So yes, we're going in the opposite direction than some places—our trajectory is to do more, be more ambitious. That sense of generative energy is exciting. It makes a difference. **What encounters do you wish to create for publics once the new building is open, across the work you'll do with the collection as well as the expanded arena of design and contemporaneity?** More than ever before, art and design shape the way we experience the world around us. We believe this influence is growing—almost everywhere we turn, art and design are reaching into uncharted terrains and diversifying in exciting new ways. Our vision for NGV Contemporary (NGVC) is of a place that reveals this potential.

This gallery will be a place where we freely explore new possibilities for the presentation and interpretation of art and design that reflect our unique position in the world but also our deep engagement with it.

In our globalized world, we believe that contemporary designers are breaking free of historical constraints, developing sophisticated connections to the past while also forging new possibilities for the future. We see that traditional disciplines and their boundaries are rapidly eroding, becoming porous. Silos are turning into networks.

We believe that the design gallery of the 21st century should reveal and amplify the connections, commonalities, and interrelationships across design practices rather than their historical differences. NGVC will be a gallery that realizes this ethos in physical form. It will be one of the largest purpose-built design galleries in the southern hemisphere. It will be free to enter, reflecting our belief—and ambition—that this potential in design is a potential for us all.

We are at a point in time where the complex problems of the world are so dynamic and multivalent that creativity is understood as a future pathway to some kind of better world. NGVC will be a gallery that takes its lead from contemporary practitioners—generative, dynamic, and alive, rich with collaboration, encouraging conversations to flow across boundaries. The gallery will work in dialogue not only with artists and designers but also with researchers, educators, students, government and industry bodies, and our community as we respond to the world around us. **In this course of action and preparation, how has the pandemic outbreak affected your work, your strategies, or your thinking through the department?** What was most important about the pandemic for me was the deep sense of our responsibility to offer support to the community. I was reminded that people come to museums to learn, but they also come for emotional relief, connection, and inspiration. The NGV pivoted quickly when we had to close to become a broadcast platform. The level of output was amazing—it underscored our civic responsibility. We worked throughout the pandemic and opened the 2020 Triennial in December that year—during a lucky gap in the lockdowns. I was proud of the fact that we committed to opening the show even if it was only possible virtually. I realized through that time that we were seeing the downside and upside of globalization simultaneously. We were adversely affected by a rapidly traveling disease while also being in conversation and collaboration with fabricators, artists, designers, and colleagues in over 35 countries. We were all sharing the same complex experience. I will value what I learned at that time for many years to come. **Can you speak a bit about what initiatives you have at the museum that tackle these entangled issues with colonization and restitution, given you are one of the major encyclopedic institutions in the world?** Truth-telling, I suppose, is part of what the process of reconciliation is, and accepting that Australia wasn't discovered by European people. There are many different international relationships that existed between our First Peoples and other countries before that. We also opened a permanent major display of Australian Indigenous art on the ground floor of our Australian building. We have a focus on Australian and global First Nations in the NGV Triennial, with major commissions underway that look at the synergies between Australian Indigenous people and other First Peoples, both through an art and design lens.

A good example is with our collection of Australian art curated by the Department of Australian and First Nations. Recently, that team has rehung the Australian art collection to address the reality that Australian art does not start in 1788, which is when the English arrived. Instead, it represents a 60,000+ year history, with other stories of contact between Indigenous people and other cultures facilitated through trade and earlier colonial exploration. This reality needs to be respected and understood as a fact, not a perspective.

Another good example is the project called *In Absence*, a collaboration between contemporary artist and Kokatha and Nukunu woman Yhonnie Scarce and Melbourne architecture studio Edition Office. *In Absence* was an architectural installation that invited audiences to better understand the fallacy of the British colonial premise of Terra Nullius, which declared Australia as an emptiness awaiting ownership, by revealing and celebrating over 3,000 generations of Indigenous design, industry, and agriculture. This project resonated nationally and even internationally as proof that contemporary architecture can ignite important moral and culturally significant conversations.

Considering this particular approach you have built with commissioning, how do you go about picking the stories you want to champion? How does your internal research process work? What interests me the most is whether a project embodies the elements of a story that a broad audience can engage with. That's not easy to do. We live in a complex world, so there are many different trajectories we could follow. We are looking for the stories that we might tell today and that will still resonate years into the future. We are trying, in our small way, to help the design sector and the public to make sense of the world and what is taking place within the common systems that we live with, but we're very careful that the research has to be able to translate into something very tangible and accessible for a broad audience.

I was talking yesterday with author and researcher Kate Crawford about the imminent ecological implications of accelerating AI. I asked her what was the most effective way she found to communicate with the public. Her response was that, frankly, when we get down to it, it's films and museums, where you get the big audiences, which are trusted places. In the world today, especially when the media environment is so polluted and unreliable, where will people spend time? If you can get someone to read a book or visit an exhibition, maybe that will change their mind. We feel a sense of responsibility to look into the emerging situations in the world that are driven by design but are often misunderstood by the design sector itself. So many of the complex situations that have emerged from the 20th century were the unintended consequences of the status quo. We need to learn from this.

What relevance do you think the big commercial events have in terms of public engagement with the reality of design nowadays? Clearly, if we look at major platforms like Milan Design Week, the overwhelming influence of marketing and the PR industry has completely pushed out diversity, given the unaffordability of everything connected to showcasing. The anarchy driven by the promotion of endless consumption and unmitigated growth is devastating for the city itself and certainly not healthy for the sector and its future players. I have a problem with the idea of pure growth as the fundamental mechanism for the improvement of the quality of life. Many large international design events are a mixtape of design, luxury, lifestyle, and social media. Those elements are often in tension with what we need to do within the design industry and society at large—reducing consumption, reducing pollution, etc. Design events should embrace an ethical charter around what is presented, the content, and how people are accepted into any program. Fundamental principles need to exist around sustainability, or some kind of ethical code needs to be established. Design and its industry events are poorly guided by national or international policy; it's all a bit of a free-for-all in terms of what people want to do. There is room for improvement here.

The design week we run in Melbourne is predominantly ideas and small exhibitions of people who are small producers making their own work. I think that creates a culture, an ecology of opportunity, for small independent studios. Other "alternative" or emerging design events in the world have a sense of criticality and curatorship and a sense of relevance. I think there could be a problem with scale and the sense of this being an engine that needs to be perpetually accelerating for society to work because it's not sustainable from many different perspectives. The reality is that you're seeing this right now in some of the major fairs, but what's the outcome? It's just a lot of moving things around. It's like uploading and downloading content constantly, but I'm not sure what we are achieving as a sector. That's a very good way of describing it because the original nature of that transaction is completely neutralized; it is no longer about innovative products because the cycles of production are shortened year on year, and it's not about ideas either in terms of future scenarios in which innovation can play out because marketing trumps meaning with aspirational expedients. Yes, being offered things we already have and solutions to problems that have been solved. The only way you could have a massive shift in something like a big furniture fair is if you just had way more rigor around ecology—where things are manufactured, what type of labor is involved, and if people actually had to go through some kind of assessment process. I think if you're going to be accepted into exhibiting in a trade fair for medical instruments, you probably would have to go through some kind of process, the same with cars. Something that needs to be reformed really across the international design scene. In other conversations for this book, we have discussed the issue of the temporality of an institution—the idea that its actions, programming, and planning need to be geared to different paces. The long haul of projects like exhibitions must be balanced with the fact that, for institutions to remain valuable resources in our societies, there is a demand for more responsiveness to current topics. So, what are the horizons you are currently looking into? I'm actually very interested in thinking much further ahead than we have done traditionally as curators. For example, as someone trained as an environmental scientist, I'm interested in the fact that we saw the signals of where we are now 50 years ago. If I reflect on that, if I were a curator in the 1950s or 1960s and had championed speculation on fossil fuel use, accelerating resource extraction, or interrogated the proliferation of plastics—what would the result have been? If we had been more actively engaged in researching and interpreting those possible futures—rather than celebrating form and function, free from externalities—then we may have put things into the world that were more helpful and necessary, even transformational.

Looking much further ahead allows us to bring together the threads of things that are emerging. Today we are seeing the emerging rights of natural systems, the acceptance of a multi-species worldview, the rise of quantum computing, and, of course, accelerating AI with all its cascading implications—these are some of the things we need to focus our minds on.

It is not all a shit show. We need more positive content in the world, and we need to see design as active, creative, and optimistic. I really respect practices that are using more forensic tools to understand what is taking place. I believe that we need to use these methodologies to build a new language of design geared around transparency—seeing what is happening behind the scenes within any system. We are still perpetually partially informed.

It is certainly a new kind of long-termism we need to put in place, not to disjoin it from the present but to articulate and project outcomes of possibility without feeling overwhelmed by the now. Culture plays a huge role in rewiring connections among different forms of reading and living in the world to create new ambitions. Absolutely, museums are fascinating places. Where else can you bring scientific research, journalism, cultural discourse, and opinion into active dialogue? In these places, there is flexibility to draw from many different aspects of life and recombine things. It's a unique space. People seem primed on arrival. They offer special dispensation because they walk in expecting to think about something differently. It's a unique environment that exists in the world. Where else do people come with an expectation that they might change their minds about something? There are not many places where that happens anymore.

Regenerative spatial practices that take an interest in learning from the land implicitly understand that "building otherwise" has both a material and spiritual connotation, one that demands resetting human interactions with the totality of relations that inhabit a given environment. This foundational principle is at the heart of the *Manifesto Cuerpo, Tejido y Territorio* (body, fabric, and territory) of the Fundación Organizmo, whose establishment began in 2008 when its founder, Ana María Gutiérrez, returned to her native Colombia after studies in the United States. Organizmo has literally built itself on a 30-acre plot of land Gutiérrez inherited on the outskirts of Bogotá, where, for the first ten years, she has endeavored to reconnect with and learn from local Indigenous communities and turn the edification of the foundation into a testing process for a mode of living on and with the land inspired by ancestral ecological knowledge and a cosmovision predicated on an ethics of respect between human and non-human communities.

Gutiérrez's passion for bioconstruction combined with her frustration with the standards of Western education, which she felt did not prepare her to actually build architecture, gradually ripened into the development of a living laboratory for ecological restoration. Starting with the regeneration of the ancient forest and the richly biodiverse habitat in which it is situated, the foundation's headquarters are a physical repository of knowledge in fields like biodynamic agriculture, permaculture, artisanal crafts, and nature-based construction methods employed to erect its various facilities. All of this has become the subject of pedagogical programs aimed at nurturing an idea of "architecture as a portal to connect ancestral and hybrid (i.e., contemporary) cultures" to promote co-creation processes that can strengthen local territorial management and entrepreneurship, and therefore reinforce emancipatory practices for local communities. A dedicated department (Departamento De Asentamientos Sostenibles) focuses on transgenerational and intercultural know-how transfers, supporting self-sufficiency through recycling and reuse and the adoption of "intuitive technologies" inherited from traditional wisdoms. The ongoing laboratories, courses, and workshops have been a sustained source of income for the foundation, which has collaborated with a variety of organizations, including the Colombian Ministry of Culture, to support artistic residencies in the region. The pulsating heart of the site is the Casa de Pensamiento (House of Thought), a collectively built toroid structure inspired by Indigenous ceremonial houses, where collective learning, dialogical encounters, and intercultural activities happen to reawaken connective rituals centered on the idea that the body is the first territory we inhabit and through which we weave ties with the wider cosmic forces and elements that constitute the fabric of reality.

Organizmo's current activities, which are benefiting from funding support from the Danish re:arc institute, are divided between the ongoing research and laboratories hosted on its site and operations carried out in other communities across Colombia.

All quotes are from a conversation between the author and Ana María Gutiérrez (September 2, 2024).

Amelie Klein and Vera Sacchetti started the research platform Design & Democracy in 2019, but long before this joint venture, they both had explored the generative potential of curatorial practice to elicit conversations around the broader social and political implications of design by 'disturbing' its traditional sites and formats of action—be these museums, schools, biennales, symposia, or exhibitions. In the same year, they joined the OECD's International Innovative Citizen Participation Network as members upon the invitation of Claudia Chwalisz from Democracy NEXT,[1] who has been working on innovative systems of participatory governance for over a decade and is now a regular partner.

Klein and Sacchetti are bringing much attention not only to the practical, historical imbrications of design work in political action (from ballots to campaigns or posters) but also to the idea that democratic politics is a feat of social collaboration whose methodologies and processes need continued rehearsing, and in which design has a part to play. These thought ramifications have been unpacked through various projects, for example, *All in! Redesigning democracy* (2024–25), developed with the Bundeskunsthalle (Art and Exhibition Hall of the Federal Republic of Germany) in Bonn and the Kunstgewerbemuseum, Staatliche Kunstsammlungen Dresden (SKD, Museum of Decorative Arts and Design), where the titular exhibition is accompanied by the organization of Citizens' Assemblies aimed at suggesting ameliorative strategies of openness and inclusivity, which the museums have committed to implement. This exercise of self-reflection, which could scale out across other vectors of societal interaction through the civic space of the museum, is a powerful lesson in how institutions of culture can mitigate the extreme polarizations and flailing trust in political institutions that clearly abate our times. In an advisory paper written by Sacchetti for the Kulturstiftung des Bundes (German Federal Cultural

Foundation) in 2024 around the future of design museums, she points out how a "change of focus" toward "mediation, education, and public programming"[2] and the deployment of novel participatory formats is needed to actively and regularly converse with the public if we are not to dangerously sidestep museums' representational power.

Initiatives like Design & Democracy perform an essential function as both network builders and stimulators of practice and discourse that can rewire the connective infrastructures of society—in culture, education, and the service sectors—through principles inspired by a 21st-century design ethos of transformative openness, as found in notions that range from more-than-human governance to participatory urban planning.

1 See https://demnext.org/.
2 Unpublished paper written by Vera Sacchetti, January 2024.

The design studio PINWU, founded by Zhang Lei, Jovana Bogdanovic, and Christoph John, is part of a generation of practices that emerged in China around the 2010s when homegrown talents became synonymous with a transformative and personable innovation culture that countered former dominant narratives associated with anonymous and cheap manufacturing.

With distinctive entrepreneurial flair and an aesthetic sensibility borrowing from traditional crafts and know-hows, PINWU established itself as a unique collaborative venture that aimed at championing artisanal heritage and safeguarding the fragile landscape of its communities. What started as an explorative application of techniques and materials to contemporary lines of products in bamboo, ceramics, enamel, and paper labeled "Future Tradition" steadily evolved into an ecosystem of research and development intertwining studio practice, cultural programming, and territorial regeneration.

In 2015 they established the Róng Design Library (róng means to fuse or melt in Chinese) in a repurposed industrial space in Yuhang, an urban district on the outskirts of Hangzhou city—a platform for the study, preservation, and knowledge transfer of various forms of craftsmanship endangered by mass production and rapid deskilling. Its seminars, exhibitions, and hands-on workshops with cohorts of local and international designers have nurtured a collaborative culture of respect and mutuality across generations. Multi-year research agendas aim at mapping crafts by analyzing and illustrating methodologies, tools, and processes to build a repository of actionable knowledge around materials such as bamboo, textiles, lacquer, ceramics, glass, and leather.

The studio currently operates from the rural village of Qingshan, close to Hangzhou, an area replete with scenic natural vistas near the Longwu water reservoir, where they relocated upon invitation by The Nature Conservancy to join a preservation project aimed at mitigating the polluting hazards caused by intensive farming. A regenerative and participatory planning process began by moving the library into a decaying mud building from the 1960s. Restored by the studio with traditional building techniques in 2018, it is now home to 14 years of investigations across 32 Chinese provinces, which involved the realization of 500 craft workshops and the assembly of more than 8,000 materials and artifacts for their cataloging and public display. The largest of its kind in the country, it continues its activities as both a pedagogical outlet and an active research and production laboratory that manages a residency program for practitioners (over 200 to date) interested in giving new life to these centenarian traditions, working with woodblock engraving, sunmao (wood joinery), mineral color painting, metal casting, among many others.

Ongoing cooperation with local authorities, residents, and like-minded practitioners led to the development of a visual identity for application across public areas and infrastructures, and the repurposing of abandoned mud buildings, which have been converted into an information center, three schools, and bicycle and bus stations. A separate Weaving Pavilion dedicated to textile crafts and weaving techniques was created in collaboration with the JNBY Foundation of the eponymous famed Chinese brand. The amelioration of public facilities and a focus on an education-centered economy revolving around traditional crafts and handmade production provides a virtuous cycle of communal sustainment for residents and local producers alike.

New functional pavilions to restore the architectural heritage of the village's earthen buildings are planned for the coming years, while residencies, courses, and exhibitions of applied research continue.

Design History Through Other-Than Western Perspectives

M+ built itself around the idea of taking Hong Kong's unique features and its surrounding regionalisms as a prism to look at global history. Speaking about your vast and diverse collection, you once stated that "while Western museums are worried about filling in the gaps of their collections, we're extending and augmenting the canonical story by showing the connections to Asia. We're not trying to make a comprehensive survey like other encyclopedic museums in the world, but to tell stories about people's lives through design products." So how and where does the story start?   Our story mainly starts from the second half of the 20th century. As a museum of visual culture dedicated to Asia, we largely look at the condition of the postwar, postcolonial, postindependence. Asia went through various "posts," so it's from there that we look. And sometimes, of course, we look at earlier moments too, like the beginning of the 20th century, but because what we are trying to cover is so vast, we need to apply a lens to provide focus, and those "posts" are a useful set of conditions to make visible the idea of this transcultural, trans-Asian, transnational inference, which appears particularly in the second half of the 20th century.

Other colleagues of yours have spoken about the idea of the museum re-centering the perspective from an Asian vantage point, but are these constructs (center/periphery), which are very much a product of an old global order, still useful or valuable nowadays to build a narrative?   The idea of decentralising is, in itself, from a Western perspective, so we don't even consider this center. Re-centering does not necessarily mean shifting the center to Asia. As a museum established in the 21st century, it is inevitable that we will examine the history of existing design and architecture from a non-traditional center. Of course, we refer to established artistic canons and design histories, but we don't emphasize them as we are trying to make them more inclusive; we are augmenting existing or recognized histories with others, we are saying there is more than what has already been written.

I was never really a fan of using this idea of decentralization because I myself come from Asia. When I was growing up, our textbooks on design were all about the

Wiener Werkstätte, Bauhaus, Black Mountain College, and largely Western-centric history. We never really read any design history or art history about India or Thailand and so forth, so what we learnt about design history in Asia was the same as the rest of the world, written with a Western perspective. We are building the chapters, so to say, that were missing in that history.

You are located in Hong Kong, and the city is your lens because of its cross-border transnational ethos emerging from that specific situatedness. For example, the value of informal approaches to design, the collective intelligence of certain models of self-building, etc., which you have investigated, among others, in your programs. Tell me more about how Hong Kong is a central node of your narratives. Yes, Hong Kong is very important in this sense. It is a very small city, but Hong Kong has been an important part of international history because it has long been a trading hub—of things and ideas. Many countries have a historical relationship with Hong Kong, whether consciously or unconsciously. For instance, in the 1960s most Japanese electronic appliances were shipped worldwide from Hong Kong, and many American jeans and cotton T-shirts were produced there. This means that whether you are a consumer or involved in trade, you have likely encountered Hong Kong's influence and experienced how cultures infiltrate daily life. This phenomenon showcases a local specificity alongside similarities with numerous other Asian countries and beyond. I look for the center of the ripples and recognize that there are multiple centers of influence across Asia, both large and small. This diversity creates echoes and commonalities that weave together a transnational and global design history.

It's not just a physical place. Hong Kong's 20th century was already internationalized at a higher level. As a crossroads of trade and colonization for over a hundred years, the city has been in constant dialogue with the rest of the world, which made the city ideologically multicultural. This mindset allows us to think through and of Asia beyond a nationalistic perspective.

So why is the second half of the 20th century important? Because that is the time when these countries were working to reclaim their identity and pride through nation-building in response to various postwar and colonial periods. During this time, design and architecture played a significant role in reshaping both economic and living conditions. However, these nations were already highly diverse and hybrid, leading to inherently transcultural outcomes, which often believed in distinctly nationalistic identities.   If you had to enuclate some characteristics of the way in which design and architecture play a role in unpacking these intersections, in building countries, economies, identities, could you give me some examples of how you believe design with an Asian perspective—its notions, values—truly counterbalances those coming from a Western one?   I don't think in terms of binaries between an Asian and Western perspective or that an Asian perspective counterbalances a Western one. Let me give you an example—the Thai Silk Company, known today as Jim Thompson. Jim Thompson initially served in high military positions, which brought him to Thailand in the 1940s. However, from the late 1940s until his mysterious disappearance in 1967, he devoted his life to rejuvenating the Thai silkweaving cottage industries for export during the Cold War, helping local artisans earn foreign currency. Local weavers traditionally used natural dyes, but these colors were often unstable and unpredictable. To stabilize production, Thompson introduced Swiss and German chemical dyes, resulting in the vibrant and vivid tones of silk now considered typical of Thai silk. His stylish and bright silk products quickly became popular among the local société, helping to solidify them as the quintessential Thai identity.

Another interesting case is the export of the Japanese Daihatsu Midget MP5 (1962) in countries across South and Southeast Asia. This three-wheeled mini-truck was initially launched in the USA and received a positive response. Following its success in the USA, it gained popularity in Japan and was subsequently exported to Pakistan and Thailand in the early 1960s. Its nimbleness made it well suited for the narrow and busy unpaved streets, significantly transforming local mobility. While Japan eventually shifted to four-wheeled vehicles and discontinued the Midget, South and Southeast Asian countries began developing their own versions, which were smaller and more open. These vehicles became known as tuk-tuks and became distinctive of South and Southeast Asia. Today, Thailand and India are the leading manufacturers of tuk-tuks, exporting them further to Africa and Latin America.   **You have worked across continents, you have been involved with education, independent practice as a curator, and you were often asked to bring forward voices and stories from the East. So now that you are embedded back in that context, what are the key stories that you believe are important to tell?**   While I was living in Sweden (for over twenty years), the stories I would share through my work were somewhat simplified. I believe this was partly a response to that binary vision of East and West. However, I also recognize that I was not aware enough of the transnational influences originating from the East at that time. It is really about embracing a different mindset and experiencing new perspectives. Today, the culture we consume has become increasingly homogenized globally, influenced by capitalistic forces and the rise of right-wing populism. An essential narrative to unpack is that, throughout history, the world has always been transcultural, interregional, and inclusive—especially in design and architecture—demonstrating the impracticality of nationalistic isolation.   **Given the wealth of stories you can and need to cover under this Asian framework, the diversities and interconnections, how do you balance personal histories of individual figures, practitioners at large who have their own, perhaps sometimes even conflictual, relationship with their own identity and provenance, and the logic of larger group shows that are about casting a wider net to contextualize those very stories?**

What are your priorities for architecture and design within the institution?   We don't aim to be comprehensive or encyclopedic as a museum started in the 21st century. With the wealth of documented histories and available technology, our observation platform is elevated, giving us a bird's-eye view of history. At the same time, it allows us to focus on specific points and then zoom back out again.

Today's technology enables us to visualize data traffic easily, so, in a way, I feel what we collect and exhibit manually visualizes the geo-locations and their networks and influences.

At M+, we use the lens of visual culture, which enhances the connectivity between disciplines, people, and places. There are no individual and personal stories that do not lead to others; there are always relationships and contexts to explore. The curator's role is to investigate these connections and provide context for the audience.

Particularly in the design and architecture collection, including the context is inevitable, as I'm interested in design as a social object. The original context of the objects is often removed when we bring such projects to the gallery. I constantly contemplate how we can preserve and even elevate their original significance and what value the objects might lose when they are removed from their native settings. **And that begs the question: how do you fill those gaps? How do you mend those moments when you might lose something? Prototypically, the problem of design institutions is decontextualization, so the losses endured once design is extracted from its environment of use—be it an object, a service, or an application. Are there specific strategies in terms of programming that you are putting in place to fill those gaps?** Yes, the most significant challenge in collecting and exhibiting design and architecture is understanding and crafting a balance in including the context of the objects. Fortunately, we collect process materials, which is one type of contextual documentation. I always take into account the social environment of use and consumption surrounding the objects, as this helps determine how much contextual information we should include. This context can take the form of written documentation or references to historical events, both of which are valuable for future research. I think of the museum collection as a "toolbox," so it's essential to consider how other curators might use it over time. Including context is similar to adding multiple "tags" in the information data, which enhances the potential for future interpretation.

Sometimes, it can be a more physical manifestation. One good example (unfortunately, I haven't succeeded yet) is that I'm still looking for an old vending machine of Fujicolor Utsurundesu (often called a disposable camera) from 1986. It manifests the ethos—handiness, the boom of travels, and people's urge to document their own lives—which clearly contributed to the integration of cameras in mobile phones. Sometimes, those stories of long-lasting impact are far more interesting than the object's visual aesthetics or technical significance (although the Fujicolor Utsurundesu has a super interesting story of innovation).

So considering you have been open for a relatively short time (three years), would it be accurate to say that you're still reckoning with how you can bring further evidence to the stories that you want to tell and how that constellation helps you tell new stories, more than going and experimenting with ways of using the collection? I think our collection is already experimental in itself, in that it deploys a visual culture lens across disciplinary environments. We actively considered this while building the collection and started experiments with display at M+ Pavilion (2016–20), a temporary space we had before the official museum opening.

We have recently presented a new hanging of the design and architecture collection with the exhibition *Making It Matters* (2024–ongoing). Here we have tried to provide context by unpacking and highlighting the processes involved in making. The thematic sections trace the evolution of crafting and creating objects.

This exhibition was informed by my reflections on the inaugural collection show titled *Things, Spaces, Interactions* (2021–ongoing). During our tour of the exhibition, the audience was captivated by the stories behind the objects, particularly how these items have influenced society and our daily behavior—something many had never considered before. It became evident that our usual approach of writing label texts and providing a few contextual videos was insufficient. Tell me more about *Making It Matters.* The exhibition is organized into four sections: *Ceramics: A Story of Shifting Values*, *Material Potential*, *The Hand and Machine*, and *Actions and Consequences*. In the first section, we explore the evolution of our relationship with objects and how the process of making influences their value and environmental impact. To illustrate this concept clearly, we decided to focus on one medium—blue-and-white ceramics—with a question, "how can one material shift so much in value, circulation, and reception over time?" This associative material allows viewers to easily recognize the contrast between the values—from simple noodle bowls to expensive antiques.

This is presented in one long display case with 15 works that include pieces like a 1500s Ming dynasty imperial vase in a highly popular style from the East India Company trade period (1600–1874), Julie & Jesse's design work that critically addresses mass manufacturing in Jingdezhen, China, and it ends with a conceptual piece by Ni Haifen, an artist who casts discarded everyday objects in blue-and-white ceramics. The presentation makes the story very consequential. Instead of adding individual descriptions of the objects, the display is accompanied by a long-scroll-format video illustrating their evolution. Also, this section serves as a prelude to the three facets of making that the exhibition explores—material experimentation, the evolution of tools, and the impacts on our environment.

I really wanted to try to explain that socially you are part of this whole chain. I wanted to narrow the distance not between the audience and the museum, but between the audience and the world. And this is the power of exhibitions. **You mentioned earlier that your collecting and working method is already rather different than that of similar heritage institutions in the world because you don't work with disciplinary silos, and you have instead a more fluid way of looking through visual culture. Can you make an example of how you deliberate on the value or the significance of an item entering the collection?** The simple way to say this is that we can no longer isolate design and architecture, and they cannot be looked at as something separate from their historical context and the conditions of their production as much as other artefacts. So, what we're doing is adding a wider reading and understanding of a piece of work by using a visual culture lens.

For example, a neon sign. If you look at it from a design and architecture perspective, it's craftsmanship, typography, and sign design. But if you look at it from the perspective of visual art, it can be examined within the history of neon art, while the moving image reading is about light and props in the city, creating a distinct vibe depicted in cinema.   **How do you approach things from the point of view of historical narrative, meaning how do you deliberate around the relevance of an item in a specific intersection or period of time? Do you work also with these types of chronological or temporal frameworks?**   Not really. We look more at certain phenomena. For example, Tokyo's 1980s. We examined various aspects of postmodern culture, including airbrush illustrations, to understand how Japanese artists adapted American nudie pop to their own. This adaptation often depicted empowered women or cyborgs, as seen in the works of Yamaguchi Harumi and Sorayama Hajime. The glossy aesthetics of these works have been reflected in popular culture, particularly in fashion and music scenes. The scene and aesthetics became significant influences in Hong Kong and subsequently spread to Southeast Asia.

So we look at how these movements influence each other, the speed of information, their global impact, and what drives that difference of speed—technology, culture, etc. We target certain decades and movements, and how those have the potential to become transdisciplinary.   **If it's true you are the only museum dedicated to transnational Asian culture in the region, there's really not a wealth of institutions dedicated to design and architecture in Asia, perhaps with the exception of Tokyo to a certain extent. Why is that?**   It's partly a social issue because, again connected to our interest in the second half of the 20th century, countries were busy rebuilding their own nations. So with Japan, it is the same question; the postwar period was its design pinnacle, but the country was busy with developing, selling, and using, not archiving.

There is also a financial reason, but more pragmatically, design and architecture were seen as functional. It's also that in Asia, there had been a longer tradition of craft and decorative objects, and partly this is related to different phases of modernization. So-called modern design things have a shorter history of use; for example, in Japan, they were still sitting on tatami mats, and it was only about 70 years ago that they commonly started using chairs at home.

This is not about "not having design"—it just took longer to recognize what design is. The concept of copyrights and intellectual property has been misunderstood or ignored for a long time in Asia. After various recriminations from the West, Asians have learned to recognize design. However, when I started to reflect on the accusations made against Japan and China about copying, even this very idea appeared very Western-centric. As you know well too, because you lived in China for a long time, in Asian countries you master a skill by repeatedly copying the master. Look at calligraphy, ceramics—you have to remake a ceramic vase hundreds or even thousands of times before perfecting your craft. Asia has been through different phases, each country at its own time, in terms of formulating an idea of what design is.

As for museum development, many Asian countries are likely to follow our lead; Hong Kong was able to start earlier due to strong governmental commitment and generous funding. In 2024 we hosted the International Conference of Architecture Museums (ICAM) at M+, and amongst many Western institutions, we also welcomed delegations from Indonesia, India, Sri Lanka, Taiwan, Korea, China, Singapore, and Japan. All of these countries have begun building architectural archives. While design may still be lagging behind in this area, architecture archives are experiencing a new boom. Additionally, there are several discussions and plans in progress regarding design.

Why do you think there has been this surging interest, particularly in architecture? We're probably a bit part of the reason, as we may have shaken this discourse a bit about ten years ago when we initiated our efforts. We acquired some important collections from Taiwan, Japan, Singapore, and India. But it's not only us; museums like the Museum of Modern Art (New York) and Centre Pompidou (Paris), in the course of their decolonizing spree, started to look at architecture archives in Asia. For example, recently, Toyo

Ito donated his archive to the Canadian Centre for Architecture (Montréal), and in 2011 Kenzo Tange's archive went to Harvard University. So there is a sense of threat, that other major museums would come and take hold of their cultural heritage, and so they have started to realize the value of architecture archives.   I know you are also interested in curatorial archives, in terms of audio notes, writings, and informal memories that one generates as part of the research process. Can you tell me more about this?   For a collection, it is important to understand context, and curators produce a lot of informal content as they research, interview designers and architects, etc., and none of this material is systematically archived or taken into account as an official record. Surely once an object comes in, there are protocols to record it. But I would be interested in more informal, unprocessed research material in addition to the information that is effectively archived with acquisitions.

We do try to keep some of these, but they are not publicly accessible because, as a public museum, we are confronted with issues of copyright, fact-checking, and trust of the source, etc. Therefore, this material is not often shared, even among other colleagues. I think this unedited information is an interesting category.

What about the changing context of Hong Kong? I'd like to address if and how the transforming politics of the past few years have affected your work as an institution. This is not just related to the most recent political events, China's encroachment onto the island and the social unrest that has surrounded it, but also the idea that there was a lot of hype around the making of M+ as a moniker of the coming of an Asian century, which has manifested itself differently than we imagined due to world events we are still living through.

Has this affected in any way either the politics of the museum or the way you think through the museum?   There has been no significant impact on programming and the collections. I also want to emphasize that this shifting political wind is occurring worldwide.

When we opened the museum, there were considerable tensions in Hong Kong, especially highlighted by international media. Issues such as social unrest, Covid-19, and the debate surrounding the national security law contributed to this atmosphere. Like any other place, Hong Kong has its political sensitivities, but we navigate through—as human beings, as an institution, we navigate through times.

The museum is a long-term endeavor; it's not just about what we show or say at the moment. As a keeper of the future, we aim to offer various possibilities and scenarios based on the prevailing circumstances.

Additionally, it's worth noting that around 40% of our visitors come from the mainland. This figure may suggest that Hong Kong provides unique value or a different perspective that draw people in. After all, visitors no longer come to Hong Kong primarily for shopping; they seek something more meaningful.   **What about conversations with your peers internationally? Are you already entering into collaboration with others, or are you still more focused on consolidating your position as an institution?**   We have a lot of ongoing collaborations already, from exhibition co-productions to co-commissions, collection sharing, and co-programming.

Only mentioning officially announced projects, we are working with the Canadian Centre for Architecture in Montréal on socialist modernity in China, and with the National Art Centre in Tokyo on a particular period of Japanese art between 1989–2010, as the subjects are beneficial for our research, but the outcome at M+ may not be an exhibition in a classic sense. It's a shared effort but with different outputs. The logic also applies to the fact that different countries have different audiences, so it's not like a one-solution-fits-all. Collaborative projects are a more efficient form of investment in labor and financial resources, as well as augmenting outputs and being more sustainable.

Public(s)
Display

Reconfiguring
Design **Narratives**

I would like to start with the first project you developed at the V&A for its partnership with Design Society, the then newly established museum in the city of Shenzhen.

If you could give a bit of context to that endeavor, which happened at a pivotal historical moment when China had clearly emerged as a global political and economic power, wherein the making of a "culture of design" was deeply connected to shaping a national narrative no longer centered around its manufacturing capacity but on the qualitative innovation of its creative communities.   I was hired in October 2014 specifically for that job as lead curator on the Shenzhen partnership for what would then become Design Society, and I had just been in Shenzhen the year prior at the UABB (Shenzhen-HK Bicity Biennale of Urbanism and Architecture) because I was working as an editor at *Volume* magazine, and we had been hired by the UABB to do a catalog for that edition. So, I had come fresh from that experience of being in China.

On the one hand, I was incredibly curious about Shenzhen in particular and its manufacturing landscape and how that fed into a wider global system. But also, I felt that the strength of a museum—versus that of editorial practice—was its wider public reach and the added benefit of engaging in a discourse with a more diverse audience of museumgoers.

What we were asked to do was to produce a gallery for a new design museum, which was being touted as China's first. It was designed by Fumihiko Maki, featuring several large temporary exhibition spaces and an 800-square-meter gallery space devoted to the V&A. We were asked to make a design gallery consisting of objects from our permanent collection and to think about how that would fit within its wider framework. It seemed a relatively straightforward task, but still, my colleague Luisa Mengoni and I would have regular discussions around the challenges and limitations of the original brief, particularly thinking about audiences and expectations.

We wanted to come up with a gallery that would require no previous knowledge of design. Your first question when you walk into a museum, when you're confronted with something, is "why did they choose that? Who was the person thinking about when putting this in the museum, and what was the reasoning behind it?" So, the structure of the proposed gallery, which eventually was called *Values of Design* (opened 2017), was putting that up front and center in the narrative, so that each of the groupings was basically saying, "here is a framework for understanding why somebody would value this object and therefore why a curator might be interested in collecting it." It was based on trying to come up with as low a barrier as possible to enter the world of design. Because everyone, every day, has their own personal version of this internal conversation about what they value and what they don't.

The other limitation with that initial brief was that it was drawing from our permanent collection, which contains some objects from East Asia but is primarily a Western collection, and so we wanted to create throughout the gallery some touchpoints that would draw closer links to the lived experience of people in Shenzhen.

Can you talk a bit more about the context of Shenzhen back then, its encapsulation within a wider global movement of makers and grassroots culture, and therefore if and how it affected your curatorial choices and approach in your subsequent work at the museum? Because we didn't have many objects from Shenzhen in the collection, we applied for a grant from Design Trust in Hong Kong, and Luisa and I embarked on a pilot project that would show at the UABB the following year (parts of which ended up eventually in the V&A Gallery) called *Unidentified Acts of Design* (2015), which was a way to really focus on the incredibly interesting kinds of design phenomena taking place in Shenzhen that might not necessarily be labeled as design.

I was interested in how one goes about measuring the quality of a design scene. Shenzhen doesn't compare to the bigger design capitals, and the actual proportion of working designers compared to the city's population is minuscule. Nevertheless, it applied to UNESCO to be designated a "design city." I was really interested in this idea of "what does a 'design city' look like with the absence of designers?" In the end, I truly believed Shenzhen was a design city; you simply had to shift your definition of design from the traditional codified professions of design to include the vast amount of making and production happening in the city that might not naturally self-identify as design.

Unidentified Acts of Design was trying to point out all the instances where there were really interesting kinds of design outcomes, but not necessarily produced by named designers. This approach opened opportunities to expand the conversation about design in the city while pursuing acquisitions for the museum that would enrich the public experience of the gallery. So, my experience with Design Society taught me to look for spaces and opportunities within an institutional brief to push things a little bit further.   This is a pivotal issue, I think: how can long-standing institutional structures, like the V&A, be transformed not just from a program perspective but from a methodological one? I think it's interesting here the advisory role the V&A played in Shenzhen, which was not one of franchising the museum per se in China. It was also particularly momentous because this was a time when China represented this potential to rethink so-called global discourse in design, as a political system of enlightened pragmatism was moving away from the 'made in China' framework to the "created in China" narrative.   You're right that during that period there were several forces at play within the Chinese production landscape that posed and continue to pose a major challenge to Western structures of design production. When we were doing *Unidentified Acts of Design*, the division between the entrepreneur and the designer was blurred massively. Often it was an entrepreneur who had some engineering background and some affiliations with and connections to manufacturing who was able to launch a product.

That's DJI with drones, for example, which came from a guy who was just really interested in toying around with remote-controlled helicopters and cobbling together and making refinements to a product that would become the world's largest commercial drone manufacturer. Another engineer was obsessed with robots but also education and wanted to come up with a way of teaching how to both do software and hardware engineering through robots, which became Makeblock.

In the West, a designer is a service provider to a company, but in China, you become the company. You cannot divorce the market from production. The second thing that is so pervasive in China is this kind of bricolage form of creation, which comes from having all the materials and parts available at your disposal. In an electronics market like Huaqiangbei in Shenzhen, design really becomes not a way of conceiving a perfect form. With electronics, often that comes last. You kind of come up with a shape to embody all the moving parts within it at the very end.

Which is something we don't do in the West because we don't have access to those parts. So, it goes the other way. Somebody produces a sketch, and then you figure out if you can make it.

And then production and design in China are informed by a rapid feedback loop online, often driven by digital images. What's really interesting is that when a certain design gains a lot of currency online, primarily as an image, it can then rapidly be realized by many different producers as a physical object within weeks in China—a virtual to physical cycle. It's a major challenge to international IP rules but shows the elasticity of the Chinese production system. All of these factors, I think, are shaping the global design landscape, and Western design needs to catch up to that reality.   **This was almost ten years ago— where do you see a sort of comparable shift happening nowadays? What areas of research or phenomena are emerging that you believe are similarly posing questions around established definitions of design?**   In terms of design dialogue and discourse, it's fascinating that in the 1950s and 60s, with shows like MoMA's Good Design series, a designer was meant to give unique shape to something, and we were meant to applaud the interesting shapes, forms, and aesthetics of those things. Within the museum sector, it was all about a lineage of evolving aesthetics and aesthetic expressions produced by singular authors, and I think what has disrupted that is what happened in China, which challenged copyright and production and made it very hard to control the authorship and provenance of things. You have fashion and design brands now that, to reassert their authority, deploy "culture" to show superiority because the physical things they produce don't really matter anymore and can be copied a million times over. So the last ten years have seen an enormous amount of design commissions and design works led by traditional manufacturing and design companies to show that they support young designers, that they're pushing aesthetics forward, and have a certain critical cultural cachet. And the museum also buys into that.

But museums, in general, are increasingly moving away from collecting straightforward furniture and product design because there's a wider sea change. Let me go on a slight detour here.

When the V&A was founded, "design" as a term was used quite differently than it is today, more to connote the drawings used to make something rather than as a broad field of practice. Instead, "applied arts" was used to describe the wide array of things we might call design today, but it also included, to a certain degree, sculpture and painting when they were literally "applied" to things like buildings and public space design.

If you go back to the original idea of applied arts, it was a lens for understanding art that's contextual, situational, and relational, which is the opposite of what the contemporary "white cube" practice of showing art and design does today. Prior to the 20th century, you could argue that all art was understood as conditional on its surroundings and its context. Slowly, though, art practice took on a notion of autonomy, for which the "white cube" was the ideal setting. You needed a place devoid of distraction to concentrate on the work of art itself, and context was purposefully erased. Because the fine arts lead all debates around museological thinking, eventually places that traditionally showed "applied arts" started behaving like white cubes, showing objects highly dependent on context in abstracted spaces.

The point of this diversion is that there's actually some magic to the old term "applied arts." I think rather than using the term "design" to describe the V&A, it's quite interesting if we return to the applied arts and start modeling that for new practices in the 21st century. There is a major shift among many practitioners today who are also thinking that a singular product is not enough, that no art or design is autonomous and can be divorced from its context. And so you get a lot of practitioners who are working on long-term projects that are heavily participatory, relational, and in highly context-driven situations. It's a new model for all kinds of creative practice going forward, and we can't really call it design or art. Perhaps it's a mutation of the 19th-century notion of applied arts.

Practices like Forensic Architecture, Assemble, or Cooking Sections—all Turner Prize nominees—fall into this category and are really blurring the line of what kind of work is finding currency in gallery spaces. We're shifting to new kinds of practices where the white cube model is no longer sufficient (and perhaps never was).

How are these shifts affecting the internal work and conversations within an institution like yours, where disciplinary definitions and departments' names have also changed a lot over decades? Even the Department of Contemporary Design, Architecture, and Digital (DAD) was founded only in 2013. How do they challenge the practice of collecting for an institution like the V&A? Because the V&A was born in the 19th century with collecting divisions of those times, it has always struggled to take into account emerging forms of design. We're really this historic beast, constantly trying to catch up. Contemporary design, if you look at the history of the museum, has always kind of existed in the margins.

Some such margins include the Circulation Department, which was established not around collecting but around the notion of bringing the V&A's collections to different parts of the country. It had this very egalitarian stance and very socialist ideals around museum collections, education, and equality. Because of that political stance, it started actually collecting more everyday design objects, which were being ignored by other departments. So, that's where you get a lot of the mid-century design objects that we have in the museum. Then the 1980s rolled around, and you get *Blueprint* magazine and the likes of Steven Bailey and Terence Conran, owner of Habitat, who started a space in the basement of the V&A called the Boiler House, which planted the seeds for the birth of the London Design

Museum. Fast forward to 2012/2013, when we again started talking about the lack of a contemporary design department at the V&A, and so the Design Architecture Digital (DAD) department was formed, with Kieran Long as department head.

It's always these fits and bursts at the museum. To round out that story, following the pandemic, we went through a series of restructures, and the collecting departments got redefined again, leading to the disappearance of DAD. DAD curators were absorbed into the other collecting departments with the notion that a lot of the things that DAD was collecting could also easily go into other departments. For example, the DAD department was collecting protest posters, but we have another division that looks specifically at works on paper, where occasionally other curators were collecting similar items, alongside more historic works. It would be an unfair characterization to say that this one department was the only one connecting contemporary things. In fact, one of the strengths of the museum is the sheer diversity of curators and their interests, even while they are embedded in collecting departments defined by 19th-century terms.

This is to say you have several different voices within the museum. I think what people get wrong about institutions is that they think they are these monolithic entities. But these collections are incredibly heterogeneous, and there is no consensus whatsoever within the museum that the things we're collecting are universally right. We're always arguing over that every day.

One of the things that is happening as a direct result of this expanded field of design practice, which we're seeing now, is that a certain object could easily fit into many different collections. **Can you give me some examples of projects that speak to this?** Sure, for the 2016 Venice Biennale I did a show for which I commissioned Forensic Architecture to make 3D-printed bomb clouds, stemming from research they were conducting around using user-generated images to understand attacks in the Middle East. Originally, I thought that would be a great acquisition for our DAD department because there are architectural principles behind it, but then our photography curator said, "Well, these bomb clouds are just really 3D photographs; they're literally constructed from photography," and so they can fit into the photography collection. This creates a situation where an object can either fit into multiple collections vaguely or fall through the cracks completely and fit into nobody's collection. You have, again, the problem of traditional collecting remits and new kinds of practices and outputs, which are very heterogeneous because they come from complex projects that are situational, contextual, durational, and often do not consist of a singular physical thing. We started discussing this specifically with digital objects, but I think it's now pertinent to all projects where, in order to capture the essence of a project, you have to start thinking in terms of a constellation of objects. When you acquire something, there's no singular way to tell the story, so you have to patch it together with several different outputs from that project. It's one of the challenges of this kind of practice that there's no one singular way of showing it.

So, if we can no longer encapsulate the significance of design in one singular output, how is this challenging the ways you build narratives through the institution?

I find that nowadays you cannot really divorce the formal outcome from conceptual underpinnings and motivations. In a way, the practice itself becomes a program. Forensic Architecture is one very potent case, but many other younger practices that are closer to topics around environmental and social justice present similar modalities of work. How are you addressing this in terms of programming? I'm thinking, for example, of the *Pandemic Objects* project, which you have explained was also an exercise in trying to write about certain objects in a way that removes them from that traditional encapsulation into material histories or the evolution of styles and techniques.   That project came about when the pandemic started. The museum closed, and there were all these different discussions about how to become an online museum—VR tours and the like—but that would have taken years to get off the ground. None of it was very manageable, so I just decided to use a piece of digital infrastructure that we already had, which was our blog, and build around it to talk about the pandemic through the lens of things. I've always been interested in thinking about objects at scale; that is, not thinking about the impact of a single spoon, but a million spoons. I have an urbanism background, so I'm used to thinking about systems and have always wanted to apply that to objects. The pandemic brought the question of scale to the forefront. And so the blog became a really good space to write about the pandemic, and then prompt my colleagues to write about objects at scale, and how the pandemic had changed the meaning of that object or revealed hidden truths about it.

People would write relatively short pieces, 500 to 1,000 words, about toilet roll, door handles—about anything—because the pandemic was so pervasive. And what was really interesting was the public reaction. It was well received, but immediately people would ask: when am I going to see the exhibition? And I was like, what exhibition? What do you want me to do? Put some toilet roll on a plinth and have you read an 800-word essay about it? *Pandemic Objects* was always simply meant as an editorial project, but the museum model is weighted so heavily toward exhibition-making that people just assumed it was a precursor to an exhibition.

In general, we have a problem of representation in museums, where the exhibition and display format is woefully inadequate for talking about more complex ideas.

Give me an example. Going back to Forensic Architecture, the main output of their work is evidence, ultimately intended for the courts. But they know that to gain currency and public awareness, the art world is a good vehicle and therefore they need to build products that can sit within the framework of an art space. The result is their film work, maps, installations, or 3D-printed bomb clouds.

The representation question is nothing new. Architecture has presented a museological problem since it began to be shown in gallery spaces. To show architecture in a museum is to almost always show a representation of the thing itself—models, photography, etc. And increasingly, more and more projects are difficult to convey in a singular neat and tidy object. So, on one side, we can continue in this direction, and the museum becomes a purely representational space, showing representations of things happening out in the world. But I think on another side, a lot of people are starting to think about how the institution itself becomes the site of the production or becomes an active player in the production, and there's a whole kind of public experience built around participation in that project. So do you think in this sense that the terms are being reversed? In that the role of the institution is no longer about drawing the perimeter of discourse and bringing it to public fruition but about being a conduit, or one of the different contexts, through which practices can express or transfer their goals and ambitions? I think that if museums want to have the ambition of moving beyond the representation of projects, they have to become the projects. They have to become active agents in that project.

Not all the time, and it's certainly difficult, but I think this has to do also with how we inspire new generations of practitioners. How do we introduce people and give them the tools and a sense of closeness to certain kinds of participatory, engaged, and situational projects? I am thinking of Cooking Sections, which has been working out in Skye for the last five or six years around mussel and waste and coming up with prototypes to improve the circular economy in the region. It's fascinating. It's nowhere near a mass public to see, so then it becomes a museum's job to be able to bring audiences to that. I believe many large-scale museums are going through a very similar crisis, one that can be taken as an opportunity to really rethink their portfolio of activities. In this sense, you have been since last year in charge of the V&A East and Storehouse, the world's largest endeavor of its kind, which brings the museum's massive holdings to public fruition. Tell me more about how this changes your internal and external work and what some of the key ideas are to mobilize this vast repository through programs and initiatives. We were kicked out of our old offsite storage space, which was in a former 19th-century postal sorting building in West London called Blythe House and was shared with the Science Museum and several other institutions. Eight or nine years ago, the government that owned it asked us all to leave as it was going to convert it into luxury housing. All the other institutions quite sensibly moved their facilities out of town to places where rent would be cheaper. At the same time, there has been a growing discourse around the question of storage and the fact that national collections can only show 1% of everything they own at any given time. It's a statistic that often elicits outrage, particularly if it's around contentious objects that were taken during the empire and are now in inaccessible storage spaces.

One response has been to digitize collections and make them accessible online, which most museums have been doing for the last 20 years. With this, there have been really interesting and productive conversations around Creative Commons, licensing, and releasing imagery for free online. And now there is this new wave of interest in the physical spaces of storehouses and how to open them up.

Depot Boijmans van Beuningen, designed by MVRDV, is the first building in a new wave of projects thinking about how storage can be a public experience. At the V&A, we had already experimented with public access to storage through our Clothworkers' Centre at Blythe House, where, if you wanted to study any garments in the fashion and textiles collections, you could write us an email requesting a certain object to be put out for you, and someone would reply, arranging a time for you to view the object in, say, five weeks' time. We have a similar system with our prints and drawings in South Kensington. So, there were already mechanisms in place, but the question then became how we could radically expand that access because the process for making a request up until now has been in a relatively out-of-the-way place on our website. In essence, you have to have a certain kind of base knowledge in order to access it. Fast-forward to now; we've had to move our collection, and instead of going out of town, we decided to stay in town and use the opportunity to experiment with this radical public access to the collection. **How will this work practically? Can you describe it briefly?** When you come to the storehouse, there's a public route that walks you through the building with displays that also double as storage—

curated storage—which will tell you about the nature of collections and museum work. Throughout your experience, you are treated to sight lines of an active storage facility, with forklifts moving around and curators, conservators, and technicians retrieving and sorting objects. You'll be able to look down into the new Clothworkers' Centre and see people researching objects or look into the conservation studios. There is also a suite of rooms called Order an Object, where you can walk in and a receptionist will help you through the process of requesting objects to see.

This is already a fundamental step toward access, but it's still not enough in my mind because of the question of knowledge barriers and the idea of search mode versus discover mode. Researchers will be adept at search mode; they know exactly what they want to see and will simply ask for it. But for a more general public, we need to build in a "discover mode" that gives them a similar experience of closeness to objects without needing prior knowledge of the collection.

On top of refining a system by which you can call up anything that you like, if we really want to give people more meaningful, deeper access to the collection, we have to come up with ways to facilitate that experience. That is being managed through a whole host of different programs and ideas that we're trying to get off the ground.

My concern is about how we create as many meaningful experiences and new narratives from the collection as possible. How do we bring in not just general visitors to engage with objects, but how do we turn regular audiences into researchers, empowering people to have a closer stake in our national collections?

An example could be a mini-residency program in which we could invite 25 young people or people working in different local communities, targeting specific demographics. We want you to come in and spend five days in our Storehouse. You'll have someone to aid in your exploration. You can look at whatever you like. If you have any questions, we'll follow up with answers, and at the end of that residency, you will have one day of public presentation, where you are out in the public realm to have conversations with others about what you've been looking at. This enables a really easy two-way conversation. It becomes a public-to-public dialogue rather than the typical curator-to-audience model, which also radically opens up the number of objects that can be discussed at any given time in that space, and I think that's really essential.

This is so important—for me, the issue of institutional transformation is really about how to build a new relationship with your audience, and all the internal mechanisms are secondary to that question. **With such a massive operation, and the vast amount of intersecting histories, stories, and publics you can and need to attract, would you say such a novel approach renders obsolete other practices that have been historically central to museums' identity—i.e., exhibition making?** It rearranges priorities slightly. I'm interested in questions of who has the right to interpret an object and who has the right to write the label. One of the things that we're trying to do in Storehouse is also to radically open that up. We have about 70 different displays, and every label gets authored and dated, working against this notion that the museum is a singular voice. This is already at odds with many of our modes of working, where we try to unify a "tone of voice" in label writing for consistency. I would really like to move against that so that anybody can use whatever tone of voice they like as long as it's understood and their point is being made. **This is so crucial because, due also to immense financial pressures, we are trapped in this paradigm of the museum regimented by entertainment metrics that demand constant audience engagement and content production. And I think what is going to happen with the V&A Storehouse can ideally change everything; you can reshape or rearrange the roles of those that are, or become involved, with the museum.** Yes. I'm really interested, in that sense, in how to change the hierarchy of communication from curator to public to more public-to-public conversations, where the curator becomes a facilitator. I can imagine if we nail the operationality of the Storehouse right, there would be a community group like, for example, Flock Together, which is a really interesting group that organizes ecological walks around East London. They have their own networks, and they can just come to the Storehouse and stage things for their community, and we exist as kind of facilitators. One has to really start to think about the role of curatorial and museum practice moving away from being the loudest voice in the room.

But on the other hand, there's also an additional component, which is that our job is to inspire, to introduce people to new things, and to advocate for why we think they're important. Nowadays, we are tending toward the complete abdication of that responsibility, but we almost need to be motivational speakers because, otherwise, people just won't care about culture. That is the danger. And I do think that in these new conversations around polyvocality, the rightful naming and shaming of our past practices around collecting, and broader efforts to decolonize the museum, all this kind of runs the risk of driving curators away from making bold statements and taking positions about culture. So, it has to be balanced.

The point being, how you transform that polyvocality into the new terms and conditions for cultural production, and with the Storehouse, you have this opportunity.

Remaining on this subject of methodology and audience engagement, how do you see the role of the V&A transforming in the context of London and its institutional landscape? What new alliances or partnerships do you think could emerge? And then secondly, what do you think smaller institutions than yours can take away from this new bold adventure the V&A is embarking upon, particularly in consideration of the stark financial challenges many face? The V&A, like other big national museums, has seen, over the last 20 years, a massive withdrawal of public funds under the mandate from the government to become more financially independent. It's something I consider problematic, and yet at the same time, undeniably, there have been some benefits to this process, which is to say that the pressure to bring in more people to pay for culture has undeniably made the V&A more successful in reaching more audiences.

The V&A is more popular now than it has ever been, which means, at a very baseline, we're fulfilling our mandate of engaging people and culture. The risk, however, and it's also what I face with V&A East, is we have a museum with a temporary exhibition space that, through our business plan, requires us to have lots of people come through the door in order to remain financially stable.

The challenge behind that is it starts to drastically limit in scope what kind of exhibitions you can do and the framing of those exhibitions. So, from the outset, we need to choose topics that have mass public appeal; they have to be something that everybody has at least some kind of prior knowledge of and interest in. This means we can't do a monographic show about an artist nobody has heard of or on a topic that will be completely new to people. If you want to have any ambition of saying something new, bringing a new twist to something, or pushing discourse forward, it almost always has to be through a kind of Trojan horse methodology, which is to say, to come up with a big topic that everybody has broad interest in and then, through the discussion of that topic, veer people onto unexpected paths.

I was once asked to do a major exhibition about cars. People love cars. Cars are extremely interestingly designed objects. There are several ways you might go about curating such an exhibit. One way you could spin it is just a purely celebratory show that looks at a lot of beautiful cars, and people come out happy. But you don't have to do it that way. You can use the premise of the car to open up questions about identity politics, sustainability, manufacturing, and inequality—all through the lens of a car.

Luckily, if you can nail the big topics right, you can actually bring in lots of discussion. The more successful you can be in that regard, the more it frees you up in other spaces to do more experimental things through commission programs, live events, and durational work. But it is not a perfect system. The good thing that's come out of it is forcing museums to think really long and hard about audiences and audience engagement because of financial metrics. If you go to institutions that are more financially free, they move towards programming that I might find really interesting, but it's reaching very few people, and it becomes hard to kind of judge the relative merits. I would argue both are good, but it's also about who the people in the room are.   Absolutely, this is really valuable—to share the challenges that come with keeping institutions alive and to make people understand the crucial importance of their existence in our societies, and alert them to the perils consequent to their potential demise.   We see a trajectory across museums moving along very similar paths, which comes out of the pressure to bring in audiences, and it means you start to engage in a lot of market research around what people like. The risk is you get this very reductive way of producing programming based on a one-way feedback loop about popularity.

That is problematic because, as I said earlier, one of our fundamental roles is to introduce new things to people. You're meant to come to our museum and see things that you've never seen before, to see artists that you've never heard of before, and to learn about topics you've never considered before.

If you let the pendulum swing too much into this popularity contest, you actually move away from design and architecture, because, in the grand scheme of things, they are not so popular. You may shift to things like using celebrities to attract people, or film, which is much more popular, as in let's look at a famous film director through a design lens.

These are all things I've put forward myself, but at some point, I wonder how much you can—to contradict what I just said—"Trojan horse" things. At some point, you should just be saying, "We really believe in this," and then concentrate all your efforts on getting people through the door to experience something new.

Cultures of Assembly names a programmatic agenda of research-in-action devised by the architect Markus Miessen and his collaborators in the Department of Geography and Spatial Planning at the University of Luxembourg, where he holds the position of Chair of the City of Esch. Over the past 20 years, Miessen's work has consistently interrogated the agonistic relations embedded in both spatial and political practice as performative constructs of participation. This ongoing research trajectory has found form in cultural and advisory programs, as well as various editorial ventures,[1] which uniquely seek to bring the empowering agentivity of collaboration and the deliberative informality of community-making into processes of social and urban formation. His latest anthology, *Agonistic Assemblies: On the Spatial Politics of Horizontality*,[2] gathers perspectives from a populous cohort of fellow critical practitioners from a wide geographical expanse that testify to the power of situated knowledge and the responsive precision of its scaled agency.

Cultures of Assembly ultimately actualizes Miessen's past cultural and academic speculations in the real-life context of the city of Esch-sur-Alzette and the Minett region of southern Luxembourg, a once-rich territory of mineral extraction that is currently divesting its mining tradition in favor of the service sector as part of a socioeconomic transition toward carbon neutrality and sustainable growth. The urban research project incubated at the university is channeled through a series of non-partisan, public think tanks named Esch Clinics, housed in a physical space in the city centre named Brill 24, from the street where it is located. Launched in July 2024 for the following three years, the initiatives that will take the shape of investigative formats (workshops, public discussions, assemblies, research residencies) will engage various civic, professional, and political stakeholders in the practical goal of informing policy-making affecting the future development of the region at local, regional, and national levels. Operating in a hybrid configuration that connects theory and practice under the aegis of political and civic constituencies, Cultures of Assembly produces methodologies for the edification of novel "urban commons"[3] by embedding forms of critical spatial practice within deliberative social processes. Collaborations with international cities confronted with similar challenges are planned for the forthcoming years.

Cultures of Assembly intends to transform its research practice into a permanent independent agency that can survive political change by shaping urban management protocols that support just representation and active participation across all the social strata that nurture the cultural and economic life of a city. Its namesake website is a virtual repository of documentation and tools produced along the process.

1   Markus Miessen and Shumon Basar (eds.), *Did Someone Say Participate?*, The MIT Press, 2006; Markus Miessen, *The Nightmare of Participation (Crossbench Praxis as a Mode of Criticality)*, Sternberg Press, 2010; Nina Valerie Kolowratnik and Markus Miessen (eds.), *Waking Up from The Nightmare of Participation*, Expodium, 2011, among others.
2   Markus Miessen, *Agonistic Assemblies. On the Spatial Politics of Horizontality*, Sternberg Press, 2024.
3   From a conversation between the author and Markus Miessen, (July 9, 2024).

Logroño is a medieval city in the autonomous community of La Rioja in the north of Spain and the hometown of Javier Peña Ibáñez, the founder of Concéntrico, its festival of architecture and design. Ibáñez, an architect himself, ideated the initiative in 2015 as a remedial exploration of "urban disconnection," as he felt citizens had grown disaffected with the built and social heritage of their city. A thorough mapping of its neighborhoods, the frictions, porosities, and adjacencies that characterize it, cemented an interventionist methodology that has now become a signature of the festival, through which acupuncture-like activations engage residents and visitors in a rediscovery of the endless potential of collaborative interactions in public space. The first editions focused on bringing attention to underserved areas and communities with site-responsive installations carefully crafted to elicit communal encounters and civic dialogue, an approach that the original team of the festival still retains. "There is no pdf of locations," says Ibáñez, as the festival, now reaching its 10th anniversary, hasn't lost its ambition to enable meaningful connections with its naturally transforming environment, which are mediated through contextual dialogues responding to emerging needs and conditions. Installations, numbering over 150 since the first edition, are commissioned through a curatorial selection and by way of an open-call process that, in 2024, attracted 600 applications from 50 countries, out of which 20 were realized. The projects are paired with local producers, companies, and cultural and educational counterparts that secure sustainable management of processes, resources, and materials, as well as long-lasting impact.

Although the festival is organized in collaboration with Logroño City Council and the Government of La Rioja, only 30% of its budget comes from public subsidies, with a clear intent to make itself independent from the whims of political orientations and rather root itself in a horizontal network of like-minded collaborators near and far. In 2025 Concéntrico enters a new phase of development by strengthening its ties with the city and other locations in Spain through educational activities and kits that will be distributed through schools to divulge design methodologies founded on communal work and collaborative approaches. It also launches the development of a permanent public facility with an open call (2024/25) for the creation of an Urban Climate Island, a mitigation solution to face extreme weather events and rising heat waves to which the southern European city will be increasingly exposed. A new open call for alliances with local and international entities and municipalities further reflects and rewards its unwavering determination to consolidate a network of collective know-how that takes an interest in participatory urban regeneration, nurturing methodologies that can channel civic and creative cooperation into public policies of true social and environmental impact.

All quotes are from a conversation between the author and Javier Peña Ibáñez (September 3, 2024).

Although operatively situated in Palermo, the Fondazione Studio Rizoma actualizes its presence by way of capacity and knowledge-building programmes extended throughout the island of Sicily, engaging its putative liminality as a productive observatory for eco-social renaissance. It officially started activities in 2020 after some of its members met at BAM – Biennale Archipelago Mediterraneo, an initiative aimed at exploring the cultural and political ecosystems of water cities through themes of hospitality, diversity, and social care.

Rizoma is a multidisciplinary collective that looks at the challenged situatedness of a city like Palermo to address critical phenomena central to contemporary debates around material scarcity, natural resource depletion, precarity, and social exclusion, of which Sicily has historically been a crucible and increasingly an example of failing political determination.

The foundation focuses on decentralized activities that aim to support network-building among individuals with residencies and fellowships dedicated to creative practitioners, activists, and thinkers, as well as with other local small-scale entities, which collectively compose a constellation of research-focused, situated programmes tasked with entering into dialogue with different territories and local and transient communities. 'Nodes' define mid- to long-term research areas that are regularly and collectively revisited with members and collaborators, informing a variety of cultural and social activities that range from mentorships to festivals. *Between Land and Sea* focuses on marine ecosystems and liquid territories, critically looking, for example, at fishing and agricultural practices and their imbrication with phenomena of water shortage and migratory fluxes across the North and the Global South. *Room to Bloom* further tackles migration through an ecofeminist perspective to offer artists and cultural operators tools to navigate discrimination and racism within their professional fields and wave counter-narratives of emancipation. Izabela Ana Moren, Rizoma's creative director, is adamant about refuting the model of a "project factory." While the foundation supports and organizes temporary or one-off experiences, its goal is always tied to multi-annual programs that can impact both social and political groups, "embedding the production process in existing sites of struggle and political imagination."

Rizoma is also part of the European Cultural Hubs Network of Allianz Foundations, which has consolidated a transnational outreach with other initiatives and locations (Istanbul, Brussels, Kosovo) that operate with similar ambitions to join social innovation and eco-critical practice by building alternative knowledge-sharing infrastructures for civic engagement. Rizoma is behind the organization of *:AFTER* (2023), the first festival of architecture in Sicily, which, through a series of curated expeditions, took audiences to rediscover the forgotten architectural and spatial history of the island over the past 100 years.

All quotes are from a conversation between the author and Izabela Ana Moren (September 17, 2024).

The Museum as
Social Hub

Tell me about your relationship with the city of Barcelona, how your professional practice evolved prior to your appointment as director of the Design Museum at DHub (Disseny Hub Barcelona), having been involved in the development of many independent initiatives and ending up in what is a major governmental project. The reason why I moved to Barcelona from my native town of Seville was that in the late 1990s and early 2000s, after having majored in English Literature, I kind of bumped into this thing called "curation," and I was fascinated by this specific methodology for intervening in the world. Here was a form of practice related to knowledge production where you also had to create an experience, produce communities, design space, and materiality. The kind of work I was interested in didn't really have many institutional points of reference yet, except for a few festivals.

I had been very involved with online digital culture, which at that moment was an exciting, emerging community of practice. I started my career working in journalism precisely during the emergence of the Web, writing on the internet about culture and about the cultures of the internet. This put me in contact with the space of new media festivals, this emerging hybrid territory that was not the tech world, was not the art world, nor the music or design world, but overlapped with all of these communities. "Art and technology" was a no-man's-land that was very conscious of its interdisciplinarity and was very much defined by it.

Also, in the late 1990s many new European arts organizations were born in the aftermath of the explosion of club culture. It was the moment of "the rave as an institution" but also of the rave entering into the cultural institution, and the possibility of an intermediate space between the rave and the museum.

My first curatorial experience was for the oldest festival of art and technology in Spain, Art Futura, which was founded there in 1990. **There is also a big watershed in the history of the city, the pre- and post-Olympic moments. What was the most significant impact for the cultural and creative industries?** That was a very interesting transformational moment, incredibly full of energy, in spite of grassroots cultural communities being reasonably skeptical and hostile to what the Olympic project was going to do to the city. Still, as part of that project, new institutions were produced, spaces that allowed for new methodologies, formats, and practices.

One of them was what I would consider my alma mater, which is CCCB (Centre de Cultura Contemporània de Barcelona), founded in 1994. It took certain elements of the Pompidou or Barbican model and projected them forward, questioning what an institution that has no collection and is not defined by any discipline could be, and how to thrive in the spaces in between.

The other institution that was deeply influential for me was actually built on top of CCCB. That is Sónar, undoubtedly the most successful cultural institution of the city in the 1990s and throughout the next two decades.

In spite of being understood by many as essentially a music festival for the electronic scene, Sónar has been a space of freedom that allowed for the superposition of the experimental with the popular, of the commercial with the niche, and the obscure. It was making possible a superfluid space in which many different communities and audiences could mingle and coexist.

Today we have become very critical of the ideological project of Olympic Barcelona, but it's hard to deny it was a turning point in which suddenly the city became the center of many new things.

Post-Olympics Barcelona became a brand city, selling the promise of a fun, playful place, of Mediterranean values and cultural sophistication. It was, of course, a marketing strategy, but it's also true that this is a city with a very long tradition of artistic experimentation, with a taste for the new that, for instance, Madrid has never had.

So this uncharted, unplanned, and, in a way, spontaneous bottom-up agency clearly is where you're coming from. We live in a moment when many cities like Barcelona, London, and Paris are somehow living in the vestiges of what "global" culture manufactured them to be. Today you are operating from a rather different position. Can you briefly explain the history of the place where you are now—DHub, which has been very much a product of a top-down municipal planning strategy of the new millennium? What was the context of its creation?   I need to mention two different things here. One is Barcelona's long relationship with design and what it represents for the city. The other is the complex process of production of this institution and the circumstances of its creation.

Barcelona is historically the center of the system, the ground zero of design culture in Spain, with only maybe another truly relevant spot in the country, which is Valencia. It is one of the cities in Europe with the highest number of design schools, close to 20. Particularly in the 1980s, Barcelona very much used design as a flag to reinvent itself and project a new vision for the city. While Europe has produced very specific design cultures in Italy, Scandinavia, and Germany, in the Spanish context, only Barcelona believed in design as a value, an important creative community, and an industry.

I remember that in the early 2000s, I had the perception that design had given the city much more than the city had given back to design. Of course, there were institutions like FAD (Fostering Arts and Design), which is the association of designers, architects, and artisans now hosted in DHub, but there was no major public institution to speak of that would represent, especially after the big success of the Olympics, where design in all dimensions—from Mariscal's work for the visual identity to the regeneration of public space—played a big role.

There is a strong political project around the creation of this museum; I find these details important to understand the crafting of an institutional storytelling that is cognizant of its own history as well as the future conditions of its becoming. Can you give me a sense of Dhub's prehistory?   It's not until 2007 that a certain consensus emerged around the need for a new institution devoted to design in the city. It was founded in a smaller location in the Born district by the director of the previously existing Decorative Arts Museum, Marta Montmany, and Ramon Prat, a very important figure in the local community as the founder of the architecture publishing house Actar.

After the success of the Guggenheim in Bilbao as an agent for urban regeneration, we see a huge wave of investment in big cultural institutions throughout Spain. The success of Bilbao started producing copycats like Laboral in Gijón, the Niemeyer Center in Avilés, and the City of Culture in Galicia, designed by Peter Eisenman. All of these institutions start with a huge emphasis on big infrastructure and grandiose architecture, with little social demand for it.

In the culture sector, these political choices feel, in the best case, well-intentioned but a bad strategy for resource management and, in the worst case, a dishonest manipulation of the social mission of cultural institutions. All of this happens during the peak "star architecture" age, when big museums become political instruments. In Barcelona, the moment of the megamuseum has DHUb as its main product.

The building was designed by Oriol Bohigas, architect, urbanist, and master planner of the 1992 Olympics' reinvention of the city, undoubtedly the most influential designer of Barcelona's urban fabric since (Ildefons) Cerdà. A champion of public space, he was also a very influential politician who had been head of culture in the city council and a believer in the need for a design and decorative arts museum that could represent the importance of this legacy in Barcelona.

A very symbolic location is chosen to locate the building: Plaça de les Glòries, where the three big avenues of the city intersect. The Cerdà plan imagines Glòries as the actual center of the city, but for decades, this urban spot was problematic and unresolved. The building itself is a monumental 30,000 sqm construction, one of the largest in Barcelona.

By the time the building opens in 2014, the local political context has changed, and what started as a small, agile contemporary design center is now envisioned as a major design and decorative arts museum, absorbing the collections of small, older local institutions like the Ceramics and Decorative Arts Museum, as well as municipal collections in graphic and industrial design. The museum is funded exclusively by the municipality, with a modest team. To make things more complex, in 2020, the building becomes attached to the creative industries section in the city government, absorbing other extra functions and obligations, such as programs promoting talent development in sectors like film and TV, video games, fashion, and others.

Today, this huge building sits in the center of a square that, after 15 years of renovation, is about to open and has to balance a constellation of stakeholders and functions that include the communities of decorative arts, design history, contemporary design, and the broader creative industries.

It is a lot of arbitration. It's a lot of imagining how it can operate as a platform to activate many ecosystems and a meeting space that also recognizes that it sits in a city where one out of four local residents was born outside of Spain. **What motivated you to apply for this position, what were the expectations of the public entities for this role, and what was your central pitch, which eventually landed you the job?** I have told you before that I am a convinced curator and a reluctant director—because I love curation as a methodology. I have operated in many languages, from the exhibition at consolidated cultural institutions to the citizen lab in emerging institutions to the festival as a huge temporary autonomous zone. I was very interested in the possibility of an institution that did not have to identify itself just with one very focused disciplinary space. I believe in the possibility of operating in fluid dynamic spaces.

Culture today has the capacity to become the social laboratory of our time. It's this place where we rehearse and imagine other ways of living. And design sits at the center of all the main conflicts in our society, from the ecological to the material to the tensions in identity politics.

In 2014, I did a project at CCCB, the exhibition *Big Bang Data*, which was very important for me. We looked at the emergence of data as raw material in political, cultural, artistic, and social terms. Another important project was *After the End of the World* (2017), a show on post-climate change scenarios that was more of a theatrical essay than an overtly didactic exhibition.

These two projects taught me how to produce these intermediate spaces where the scientific, the technical, the social, and the political can talk to each other and produce design prototypes. And how the prototype acts as a cultural device to open up spaces of debate, exploring how we are going to live.

If we look at the evolution of culture over the past 150 years, we can see this trajectory from culture as identity and memory to culture as a social right, to culture as an exploitable resource. I think today we are trying to sketch an additional mission for culture and the arts as an experimental space to discuss, imagine, and test the futures of our societies. In this, design is in a privileged position because it can be useful both for hypothesizing, critiquing, and dismantling, and also for rehearsing and proposing. Design can operate easily in the space of the what-if, of the hypothetical.

I firmly believe in this notion that we're going to need artists, designers, architects, and creative technologists to help solve problems that today we are only addressing through policy, business, and academia. Europe has been incredibly committed to building a rich, extensive network of museums, festivals, and citizen labs that it has been funding with public money for decades. This is now a key base infrastructure for creating a Euro-vision for some model of innovation policy that is going to have to be different from the American and Chinese ones.

How are you reconciling your vision of this productive, experimental spatiality you want to attribute to the museum and the context of the city of Barcelona and its history of design? Can you give me some examples? I love the idea of the curatorial project as a temporal institution. You can produce an exhibition or an experimental laboratory whose goal is to locate one field of inquiry or one public concern in the public sphere for the duration of the project. So the aim is to activate the communities of practice that can potentially engage with it in multiple ways.

We opened a show in October 2024 called *The Ocean Speaks: New Ecologies and New Economies of the Sea.* It starts from the premise that this city, like all cities by the sea, has a specific relationship with the body of water on its horizon that is going to change in the coming decades. It is already changing. Our proposal, which we are presenting through the show, is that we stop considering the line of water as the border with an alien planet and instead start naturalizing the idea that the body of water close to us is also the city; it's also an urban ecosystem. The exhibition explores how to reimagine our relationship with the sea in urban coastal communities in the context of radically changing conditions. I'm particularly excited that the show happened at the same time and in dialogue with two big events that have opposing narratives. One is the America's Cup, the biggest sailing competition in the world, representing the model of the brand city, the city of public events, and Manifesta, representing one specific take on the art biennale. So that, for me, is an example of this mode of intervention that you are mentioning. **When I saw you in Barcelona not long ago, you had just come back from Sweden, visiting IKEA. What about that project?** Yes, that is a project that reconciles the local histories of Barcelona with the future of design and the distances between the local and the global. It is a show we opened in October 2024 *(100 IKEA objects we would have liked to have at VINÇON)* that looks at the most important design institution in the city before this one was created, which was a store, Vinçon.

Vinçon has legendary status for anyone in Barcelona. It introduced the notion that there was such a thing as 'design' in the 1950s. It was also a shop that was an experiment in how much you could stretch the concept of a store. You had a gallery inside, storefronts that were used for installations, and it would commission paper bags to designers in the city as a creative platform, etc.

When it closed in 2015, it gave us its archives. This show is a comparative analysis of Vinçon versus IKEA. It includes a large installation curated by Fernando Amat, the founder and soul of Vinçon, presenting the "100 IKEA products that we would have liked to have at Vinçon." In the city's perception, it was the rise of IKEA that killed Vinçon, so the exhibition becomes not only a comparative analysis and anatomy of Mediterranean design versus Scandinavian design but also of the tension between the local and the global: what does it mean to operate on the scale of the local versus IKEA'S planetary scale as a corporation? If you could imagine a parallel universe in which Vinçon would have become a global brand instead of IKEA, and if Vinçon's story ended in 2015, what could one day be the end of IKEA's historical cycle.

How do you see the positioning of design within the wider construct of cultural infrastructures evolving, both as part of your conversation with publics, its academic and productive systems and institutions, as well as other disciplines? My personal position here is very particular because I am not wedded to preserving hard borders or rigid limits to defend any historically constructed notion of design. I come from a no-man's-land, and that has a lot of advantages.

I always speak of discipline as a vector and industries as context, and I am not very tied to the idea of things being built on top of the historical definitions of art, design, or architecture, or treating these as sacred. These spaces can today be seen mostly as contexts of power. In a way, today there are no disciplines, but only institutions. Institutions produce power, and they are interested in disciplines because they reinforce and recognize those forms of power.

One thing that art, though, has done very well, and I think that we should totally be doing more in design, is revising and rewriting our own history. One project that we're working on currently for our collection is called *Design: The First 100 Years*, because you can say that, in Spain, 1928 is really the starting point of design. Since this is the only museum that has a Spanish design collection, we have a certain responsibility for that and to write what has been the story of design in Spain. **Do you think that institutions nowadays really need to define their publics, considering those dedicated to design are playing in a very competitive field of cultural offerings?** I love the idea of engineering spaces of possibility and this mission of fostering the social imagination. I always use this example that has fascinated me for a long time: the idea that sleeping eight hours straight all night is a historical invention. That it is something that you think is biological, and it is not. Until not long ago, people would sleep around four hours and then they would wake up, and they would stay in bed; they would pray or eat or have sex and then sleep for a little more.

So the production of sleep is one configuration of the everyday that was just made in a set of conditions. If we can redesign the role that sleep has in our lives and its temporality, imagine the number of things that we can actually twist around and reshape and reimagine.

I am constantly reminded that opening up hypotheses of the possible is the main challenge that we have today; that there's an opportunity for saying about almost any aspect of reality, "it could be done differently, it could be a different thing, it could have a different shape."

This is extremely powerful because it produces livable one-to-one prototypes extended to the scale of human lives. The main force pressing in the opposite direction is the market and the manufacturing of desire, the market that produces a colonization of the mind. And against this, design sits at the center of conflicts today. We are designing policies, designing institutions, designing communities, designing systems, designing life. We are redesigning climate. When Bruno Latour said, "I think design is one of the terms that have replaced the word revolution," he was clearly being sarcastic, but I still think we have to hold onto a certain kind of utopianism.

These transformations around what we understand design and its role to be really affect curatorial practice. You mentioned to me before that you are working on a book about this. And I loved this expression you used, that you are producing "dramaturgies of the Anthropocene."

Can you explain how this is conveying your idea of what a curator's role is, which you have described as a sort of co-conspirator more than just a producer?   In the last eight or nine years, I have found myself working very closely with designers, architects, and artists, building these devices that, in different forms or shapes, are telling the stories of some of the nonhuman actors, landscapes, and spaces of the planetary crisis. What we ended up producing were, to a certain extent, theatrical narrative devices.

One, developed with light designer Antoni Arola (*Oasi. Sky Archive*, 2023), is a light projection dome, a device used to talk about the evolution of the color of the sky after the anthropogenic intervention into the chemical composition of the atmosphere.

Another is this experiment that sits between the immersive environment and the exhibition called *Atmospheric Memory* (2023), realized with Rafael Lozano-Hemmer, which is about the intertwined history of carbonization and computation, how the beginnings of computation happen in the same place and moment as the carbonization of the atmosphere, and what this says about memory and the imprint of our actions in the world.

Or another project with TAKK that talks about the colonization of Low Earth Orbit today, and about who has the right to put a light in the sky (*Satellite Chandelier*, 2023), for which we have not set a cultural conversation or a political framework to decide.

In all of these cases, we were producing artifacts—some were exhibitions, others were objects or experiences, and others were even frameworks for a debate.

The most extreme of them maybe was with the philosopher Timothy Morton for the show *After the End of the World* (2017). We built a series of waiting rooms because we had the idea that the experience, the phenomenology of climate change, was that of waiting. Those waiting rooms were dramatizations of ideas that Timothy wanted to explore in his work as a philosopher and were staged in three dimensions by designer and architect Guillermo Santoma.

In those waiting rooms, we gave Timothy the title of Minister of the Future, as a hypothetical political figure representing the interests of the more-than-humans of today and the humans of tomorrow who have no say in the political process. This piece, in a very surprising set of events, ended up directly inspiring Kim Stanley Robinson's influential book *The Ministry for the Future* (2020).

My book is going to be a collection of essays that, on one level, tell the stories of these nonhuman actors and nonvisible spaces in which the planetary crisis is manifesting. It is also a curatorial journal because it really is a tracing of the production of these projects, and in a way, it is a distributed catalog including projects that have been made over the last 10 years.   By way of a conclusion, I think this conversation is presenting the counter-idea to the preconception that institutions are something unmovable, and that it is important to create an arena of discourse and exchange to transform the public's perception of what institutions can do. For both general audiences and the stakeholders that sustain them, we live in times when cultural infrastructures are being gravely underfunded, if not defunded altogether.   Yes, I agree, and I would like to say, because I don't want to sound incredibly naive, that there is a very complex framing in which all of this happens when it's a public institution, and a public institution in the south of Europe. We both know of many cases of great professionals in public institutions being very conditioned by political pressure and interference.

Public cultural institutions have been historically subjected to these forces. But lately, I think more so because the pendulum is swinging back again to positions where we think of an institution as a device designed to fulfill a series of social needs and functions, when in many cases, it's just an aggregation of political needs and checkboxes. And those two things are not the same.

Big questions remain about whether, in these conditions, the public museum is the perfect vehicle to achieve the kind of goals that we want to achieve. We know that institutions are slow-moving. We know that public institutions are ingrained in cultures that, in many cases, make things very difficult, and also we know they are political instruments, and those realities remain.

I think it is crucial to remind ourselves and be very transparent about the fact that all sorts of institutions exist, in small and large urban centers, in radically different contexts, with specific complexities that they need to contend with, regardless of size or reputation. There is no ideal nor winning model to speak of—and these stories of struggle, of producing thinking, methodologies, and strategies to cope with those complexities, are very important to bring to light, to be shared so that they might find their way to inspire or support others in similar conditions.

Eco-
criticality

Building
Actionable Environmental
Knowledge

Director, Emilio Ambasz Institute
for the Joint Study of the Built and Natural Environment
→ Carson Chan

In a review you wrote back in 2016 around the Venice Architecture Biennale curated by Alejandro Aravena titled "Reporting from the Front," which for the first time featured an approach where the context of architecture ruled over its contents (i.e., buildings), you made this statement which I find interesting to revisit now: "The problem here is the architecture discipline's age-old inability to discern between learning from a condition and intervening in it— between its intelligence as an analytic tool and its separate role as an agent of design." Are we still in this condition today? I definitely think the distinction between "learning from" and "intervening in" is something that still needs to be maintained in the field. The article was a response to Aravena's prompt to exhibitors at the Architecture Biennale to "widen the range of issues to which architecture is expected to respond." I just found that to be kind of an error. An architect's training requires them to think holistically, and that creates an illusion that they should or could have a solution to all types of problems. My point is that our training allows us to analyze all types of problems through an architectural lens, not solve them. I think the best thing architects can do in the face of all sorts of issues—including the climate polycrisis—is to learn what the limits of our capabilities are and try to operate fully within those limits. Sometimes the best thing an architect can do is nothing. Sometimes the solution to an architectural question is not to build, but to abstain from building. We can't always build our way to an answer. If we stay for a moment with this idea of how we speak about architecture today and how we engage publics with the urgencies and systems that it's embedded in (economic, political, intersectional, etc.)—you have worked with this arena of discourse for a long time, since your curatorial work in Berlin with Program: Initiative for Art and Architecture Collaborations, the space you co-founded with Fotini Lazaridou-Hatzigoga. Can you comment on what has changed now, almost ten years later, when you have shifted from an independent position to one within a major institution like MoMA? In the early 2000s, when Fotini and I started Program in Berlin, the idea was to think about architecture not as buildings or objects, but as a kind of process or method—a question that arose from asking how we exhibit architecture. When we go to an art exhibition, we see the actual artworks. When we go to architecture exhibitions, we see mostly representations: drawings, photos, models. We asked, can architecture be exhibited in a gallery without representation? At Program, we asked: if we can't put an actual building into a gallery, what can we show while still having it be architecture? How do we expand the definition of architecture to allow for this? This is a question that I've explored in many different ways since those early days in Berlin.

This was when architecture became a way of thinking for me, a way of seeing rather than just building. We tested the disciplinary boundaries of architecture by engaging non-architects like artists, dancers, musicians, and writers to create "architecture exhibitions."

The question of "how to make an architecture exhibition" has stayed with me, but it has mutated—it has evolved. Until quite recently, the tradition of thinking about architecture at MoMA was really predicated on architecture as buildings, as objects, and this kind of definition privileges design in terms of how a building looks and its formal attributes. One of the key aims of the Ambasz Institute is to expand, if not redefine, architecture as a process. Everything from material extraction, the labor involved in that extraction, the social, economic, climatic, political, and racial context of a site, to the afterlife of buildings—what happens when we're done with them?—all of this is architecture, and the building is just one moment within that entire process.   Given your interest in forms of experimentalism with displaying and narrating architecture, what made you choose to move into an institution like MoMA? What were in a way your expectations, and what was your pitch when you were conversing with the museum about the position of director for the then newly established Ambasz Institute?   Even when I was interviewing for the position, I already mentioned that part of my mission with the Institute would be to undo MoMA's assumptions regarding architecture in the way that I just described. Emilio Ambasz, I might add, has always prided himself on doing things his own way, so my stance, if anything, was on brand! My doctoral research looks at the intersection between "the environment" and exhibition-making. I was writing about the history of public aquariums in post-war USA and tracking their development during the rise of environmentalism as a social and political movement, so thinking about how nature was defined and how that was interpreted through building-sized exhibitions was what I spent almost a decade doing. When the opportunity to work at MoMA came, I saw it as a continuation of that research.

In terms of expectation, I knew that the Ambasz Institute was a completely new initiative and that there was an opportunity to take it in whatever direction was needed. MoMA has, historically, had an outsized influence on how architecture is framed and defined in the West, and I was keen to use that platform to promote architecture in a way that would be more amenable to a sustainable future. I was coming into the job fully aware that architecture and the building sector more broadly are the most polluting things we do on the planet. Thirty-nine percent of global early greenhouse gas emissions come from the building sector. The hope was, and still is, to contribute to a cultural transformation where architecture would become less destructive.   Tell me more about how the Ambasz Institute sits within the megastructure of MoMA, as what seems to be a research platform more than a departmental division.

From its public description, we read that the Institute "promote(s) the exploration and study of creative approaches to design at all scales of the built environment—buildings, cities, landscapes, and objects—with an emphasis on understanding their joint relationship to the natural environment." This is quite a big remit of observation. So how does this entity operate within the knowledge system of MoMA?   The description of the Institute was there before I took the position. It sounds grandiose, but I read in it the freedom to interpret what the study of "design at all scales of the built environment" means.

The dynamic between the Ambasz Institute and the rest of MoMA was also something to be defined, and three years after the Institute's founding, that relationship continues to be defined. There are two institutes in the museum formed from gift endowments. The Cisneros Institute, founded in 2016, deals with Latin American art, and the Ambasz Institute deals specifically with the intersection of architecture and environment.

The urgency of the climate polycrisis and the role of architecture within it compelled me to expand what a research institute could be. Supporting scholars, students, and architects in their work to engage with environmental issues is definitely important to our mission, for which we've organized discussions for professionals, scholarly conferences, and workshops for PhD students. Being at MoMA, the Ambasz Institute's audience automatically includes the many other publics that visit the museum. One early realization was that if we're going to be communicating and supporting the latest thinking on climate, then we should really be engaging with children and young students who, of course, are the next generation of policymakers and people who will be defining future culture. So, helping the youngest generation frame the world we live in through the urgencies of the climate crisis is something that I'm taking quite seriously now within this research institute.   By now, you have built quite a wide spectrum of activities, but more generally, if we stay with this issue of building audiences—a true imperative of survival for most museums since the pandemic outbreak—can you tell me about any specific strategy you have put in place to target the variety of publics that MoMA already attracts? They range from students and residents to tourists; these floating audiences pass through the door not necessarily knowing about the existence of the Ambasz Institute. Who is your audience?   I think you're right that the question of audienceship post-pandemic has made museums question the way that they've been operating in the past. There's a lot of discussion about what the 21st-century museum could be, but we should really talk about the post-pandemic museum. If we understand the Covid-19 pandemic as a climate issue—it was caused by human encroachment on the habitat of an organism we previously had no contact with—then the post-pandemic museum is a climatically aware or literate place. It's not just about reducing carbon or reducing shipping; it's about imagining our cultural institutions as part of larger, biotic ecosystems.

In terms of strategy for dealing with the museum's various audiences, one thing we understood early on is that there is no one thing suitable for all audiences. Even those who visit our exhibitions at MoMA are a subset of society at large who choose to pay admission to see exhibitions. What I've been trying to do is create a number of programs that would address the different publics beyond the museum walls. For example, we have a video series called *Built Ecologies* on YouTube, which is freely available to anyone in the world, allowing us to reach new audiences beyond the geographical and physical limits of the museum.

I mentioned younger audiences, and I've been trying to address them in several different ways. One is to transform our research into activities for children. For *Emerging Ecologies: Architecture and the Rise of Environmentalism*—the exhibition I opened in September 2023 on the history of environmental architecture in the USA—we transformed a number of the projects in that show into activities for children. For example, we transformed architects Phyllis Birkby and Leslie Kane Weisman's Women's Environmental Fantasy workshops from the 1970s into a drawing activity for children, in which they could project their own fantasy environments. Our learning and engagement colleagues at the museum have distributed these activities to more than 5,000 schools in the New York area. We made an exhibition with the children's work that was sent back to the museum. We've also organized field trips for teachers, bringing them to revitalized landscapes and visits to the offices of sustainability-conscious architects. Instead of addressing each individual child, we try to give ecological literacy to K-12 teachers. By exposing them to culturally transformative people and places, the hope is that they can bring this back to the classroom and instill that sense of ecological literacy in their students.

So your activities are parasiting the existing structure of the museum, if I can say so, in the sense that there isn't a physical Institute inside the building, so you have to interact or interface with your colleagues or whatever else happens on-site within the museum.   I like the biological metaphor, but I would call the relationship between the Ambasz Institute and MoMA mutualism, not parasitism! At the same time, sometimes parasites have a positive effect on the host. Some tapeworms or roundworms give their host's immune system a boost. Perhaps we can imagine the Ambasz Institute as a positive parasite.

In any case, I find working with MoMA's existing structure incredibly exciting. After *Emerging Ecologies*, we acquired a number of works in the exhibition to grow the museum's environmental architecture holdings. At the same time, I've been seeing an increasing number of colleagues gravitate toward environmental and ecology issues in their curating, programming, and acquisitions. It would be amazing if the Architecture and Design department, or even the whole museum, sees all aspects of their work through an environmental lens, in a way negating the need for a separate Ambasz Institute. Maybe finding overlaps between my work and that of other colleagues creates the condition for this.

In the summer of 2024, during artist Joan Jonas's retrospective at MoMA, we took advantage of the fact that Jonas's work for the past 15 years or so has focused on marine animals and the ocean as both an ecosystem and a source of narratives, and made an event that drew out the same theme in our work at the Institute. In *Emerging Ecologies*, we featured the work of architects like Carolyn Dry, Wolf Hilbertz, and Ant Farm, who all designed architectural structures in the ocean. We also invited a marine biologist, an anthropologist, and a historian of marine science, among others, to convene about the spatial, architectural, scientific, and aesthetic aspects of the water world.

For Earth Day 2023, I wrote some alternate wall labels for works displayed at MoMA, interpreting them through an environmental lens. For Lee Bontecou's untitled wall work from 1961, I highlighted the fact that, because she often made art out of the used, greasy canvas conveyor belts thrown out by the laundromat below her East Village apartment, she was anticipating our current conversations about upcycling or the circular economy. To re-narrate works within the museum, to carry out this parasitical kind of work, is to actuate the dream of transforming the entire museum into one that puts environmental sustainability and ecological issues at its forefront.   Let's go back to the exhibition *Emerging Ecologies*. It focused on the American context, advancing this idea of "environmental architecture" countering the "modern architecture" movement of which MoMA had been a conveyor in terms of its conceptual and material stances. Also, MoMA is the institution that essentially canonized a way of exhibiting architecture relying on objects and drawings—the presentation of architecture by proxy—which you have long tried to undo in your past career. Considering that you have set for yourself the goal of speaking of architecture as method and process, how have you dealt with this sort of internal conflict in light of the exhibition?   The exhibition itself doesn't deal with the questioning of architecture exhibitions in the way that I did in my earlier work. But what I did try to do with it is to challenge the canon of Western architecture, as you say, by including what people might not assume to be architectural to hopefully expand the definition of architecture.

At the center of the exhibition are two protest movements. One is the documentation from the so-called Orme Dam protest. By the middle of the last century, the US federal government had planned to build a dam northeast of Phoenix, Arizona, at the confluence of the Verde River and Salt River. The dam would have facilitated the irrigation of farmland around Phoenix and helped prevent the intermittent flooding of the city, but it also would have flooded two-thirds of the Yavapai Nation's land. They were not a large community, but they protested, spoke to the papers, appeared on television, recreated the so-called Trail of Tears, and eventually got the dam canceled in 1981.

By exhibiting this history, I wanted to recognize Indigenous primacy in all environmental issues, especially in the US. By including the Orme Dam protest in the show, I wanted to insist on the fact that preventing a structure from being built is as architectural as building something. Preventing something from being built affects the built environment as much as building something. It was key that this project was at the center of the show.

Nearby the Orme Dam documents, we exhibited another protest movement, the Warren County protest, which occurred around the same time in the early 1980s. This protest was a response to the dumping and spraying of PCBs in Warren County, North Carolina. The dumping of toxic chemicals was essentially instituted by the government to take place in majority Brown and Black neighborhoods. The residents of Warren County joined forces with the Civil Rights Movement and protested, as they saw the dumping of toxic chemicals in their communities as a civil rights issue. What was interesting about these protests is that they didn't succeed per se, in that the government continued to dump toxic chemicals in marginalized communities, but they did galvanize everyone and started the environmental justice movement, which has since its inception changed the legislation regarding where you can dump toxic chemicals, zoning laws, and has thus profoundly changed the built environment.

We're seeing these two instances in which the built environment was radically transformed not by one person designing something in an office but through other means—through community organizing, legislative action, and protest movements. By expanding the definition of architecture, or at least what gets included in an architecture exhibition, the aim is to include many more people—many more stories—in architectural history than we have in the past.   **How are you addressing such relevant topics at the museum through your specific lens— topics on indigeneity, land dispossession, etc.? Is that an active line of research?**   One thing that I started to do early on at the Institute is research the question of Indigenous architecture. What is it? How is it defined? Should we define it? That research has yielded many fruitful conversations with Indigenous architects and historians. Early on, we had thought about making a reader about indigeneity and architecture, but soon it became a question of MoMA's positionality regarding these issues. Should MoMA be the one doing this work, or should we be the ones assisting Indigenous folks to do the work? An argument that I've really taken to heart is literary theorist Walter Mignolo's idea that you can't decolonize the museum or the university in the West, but you can do decolonial work within them. What does this mean? Are land acknowledgments, for example, purely performative, or do they serve as a constant reminder of our settler colonial legacy? Part of the joy or the value of a research institute is that all of these questions can be kept in suspension—they can be examined and reexamined. Our minds can always be shifted through more engagement with scholars, research, and the audiences that we work with.   Particularly in the aftermath of the pandemic, there has been increased engagement with all kinds of platforms and media by museums, pushing the production of content that is not purely exhibited in galleries. Therefore, digital, durational, participatory formats have majorly become conduits to engage more publics. I wonder whether through the type of research you endeavor to do, for example, with Indigenous forms of knowledge that resist archival methods, given they are often based on relational, oral forms of transfer, there are novel niches or areas of experimentation that have opened up in terms of changing or challenging the way a collecting institution like MoMA operates.   A discussion series that I've been running with the art and environment advocacy group Art2030 called *Circular Museum* asks what it means to collect art in perpetuity in a world of change, where we see the idea of permanence with much more suspicion. The climate crisis compels our rethinking of the museum and its processes and methods at large.

One thing that I've dreamed of doing at MoMA is starting a farm. On the museum's Hamlin site in Pennsylvania, I've been dreaming of starting a sustainable, experimental, regenerative farm on that land where we could produce food for the museum staff and restaurants. There we could establish an artist, architect, ecologist, or farmer-in-residence program, connecting intellectual and aesthetic production with primary production. The idea to start a MoMA farm came to me for two main reasons. One, the land was there already, and secondly, the carbon footprint of each MoMA staff member is mainly from food, not electricity or travel.

Running a farm also allows for a radical shift in the kind of discourse we could have on art and architecture. By producing our own food, we can introduce issues related to food security into the museum's work. Many of the artists in MoMA's collection, whose work is on the walls, faced food security issues when they were alive. Many people that we work with today have food security issues. So, having something like a farm allows for this kind of expansive conversation about how we discuss art beyond what we've traditionally done.   The environmental agenda is central to contemporary global politics. How do you see yourself and the mission that you have with the Institute in the context of New York, a major urban center where the topics you choose to give voice to can truly resonate, as you operate from a very visible platform?

How much do you see the museum becoming more engaged with the civic, policy-adjacent aspect of everything that concerns the climate? Is there a position or role for a cultural institution to play in that context?   Museums are already part of the political world—of course, we don't exist outside of it. Some museums participate in policy writing, but I think focusing solely on that would overlook the cultural potential of museums to operate outside of governmental structures. Simply put, the museum and the cultural sector can do things that government cannot. If governments can change how we do things, they don't always change why those things were done in the first place. Museums can change the conversation in a more lasting way. If we can shift the culture in which politics occurs, we can change the premise of the questions about the policies to begin with. This is not an overnight thing, and in terms of climate, we probably don't even have the luxury of time, but I still think a fundamental cultural shift is where the power of cultural making lies.

So, for example, instead of advocating for changing policies on single-stream material usage or waste management and promoting the circular economy, what if I organized programming or created books for children in which the word "garbage" or "waste" was never used? In which there was no such thing as waste, but everything that we consider garbage is, in fact, raw material for something else? In a generation or two, the children who grew up with that book will think it's completely ridiculous that we use a plastic cup for five minutes and bury it underground for 500 years. I'm not discounting the power of policy; I'm making a case for the unique work of the museum as an institution of public education.

Across the conversations I had for this book, it's clearly emerged that there is a shift toward the idea of the institution as a site of practice and production, rather than purely a representational kind of medium.

In this sense, what do you see in the state of architectural practice and, more specifically, within younger practitioners? I find that in design at large, there is a growing disinterest in the idea of working on large scales and instead a move into site-bound, localized interventions that are capable of addressing systemic transformation.

What have you encountered in your conversations with practitioners? And do you think new, younger practices challenge the way institutions can represent or narrate architecture?   The shift that you're describing is really happening right now. In the last three years of taking a deep look into the field of architecture, I've seen a shift in thinking toward the concern that architecture needs to change its ways if humanity is going to survive for another 100 years. How the architecture discipline needs to change is definitely going to be a challenge, and we've been engaging practitioners and students in that pursuit. For example, we've worked several times with architect Charlotte Malterre-Barthes, whose work endorses the idea of making architecture without building—an incredibly urgent and central provocation for all young architects today. Questions like this make me think about my work at the Ambasz Institute. If architecture isn't defined through building, how do we define architecture? What can be exhibited? What is the role of the museum in this redefinition of the field? These rather basic questions are, in fact, the most difficult ones because they gesture to what you said, which is a whole-scale change in what we do. Should museums really be focused on exhibition? What should the museum of the 21st century look like? As I mentioned earlier, for me, the museum is fundamentally a place of public education. We can debate the definition of public; we can debate the definition of education; but by and large, in the West, the museum is a unique place in which many different publics can come together and collectively inscribe meaning onto objects that we care about as a culture. How this inscribing of meaning happens, how public education happens, is an open question. There are ways to do it beyond exhibitions. One thing the pandemic has shown is that we can definitely think about reaching audiences on line in far more creative ways.   I found this is something on everyone's mind, which is an issue partly connected to how to remain financially afloat, but also, in the long term, institutions seem to be veering away from the exhibition as a main site of action, working differently with collections, etc. So now, after three years since the Ambasz Institute started operations, what is urgent? What's the next important step for you?   Finding new and engaging ways to bring the issues around the built and natural environment to MoMA's various publics that wouldn't naturally navigate themselves toward that topic is important to me. It may be my "architect's syndrome" that makes me think that the architectural purview is, in fact, everything, that the work of the architect touches on everything, but I can't think of anything that doesn't fall under the realm of the built and natural environment. I personally don't make a differentiation between the two. They're both just "the environment," and humans are as natural as other animals—the structures we build are just as natural as beehives or birds' nests. Humanity is part of "the environment," and the challenge of the Ambasz Institute is to instill in our audiences the fact that when we say that the human-made climate polycrisis is damaging the environment, we're really saying that we're scripting our own extinction. Methodologically, the climate crisis erases historic boundaries between disciplines and institutions. In that way, the work of the Ambasz Institute goes beyond educating people about sustainable construction or even the building sector's role in the climate crisis. Rather, it asks how can MoMA be used as a platform beyond its four walls to address as wide a public as possible about humanity's trajectory on this planet. It sounds a bit grand, but I think it's true. Concern for the planet and humanity's relationship to it should be embedded into everyone's pursuits. **If museums should try to change themselves from within by different means in empowering and supporting the critical importance of design by abandoning or adapting their strategies, what of other long-standing platforms, like perennial events, design weeks, etc.—do they remain useful? For you, as a curator, as a researcher, what do you make of them? What do they offer?** I've always tried to understand biennials and triennials as kind of urban institutions; they exist in cities, and although they're not always activated, they're basically permanent institutions that don't realize that they're permanent institutions. They often see themselves as temporary events, but in fact, some of them have been around for several decades.

When I was working on both the Marrakech Biennale in 2012 and the Biennial of the Americas in Denver a year later, my immediate questions were how do these exhibitions interact and engage with local audiences? This was a time when it was common for artists, curators, and other art professionals to travel around the world to go to biennials, and the organizers of these events planned them for this international crowd. I think biennials are more aware that there is also a local population that needs to be addressed.

In both Marrakech and Denver, I really wanted to create something that the locals would enjoy. It was important for me to spend time living in these places to understand what the city itself demanded from the biennial. This question is further expanded when we think about environmental and ecological issues and how these exhibitions contribute to harm or continue or perpetuate issues that need to be addressed. Shipping and air travel come at a high environmental cost.

One model to learn from is the Echigo-Tsumari Art Triennale, in which all the works are public, and they become permanent installations in rural Japan after the show. The other extreme is the Venice Biennale, where works are shipped in and out and staged almost as if meant specifically for the opening when the art world elites are in town. One thing that I thought about in Denver is how we can transform the city itself into an exhibition. It was kind of a shift in focus, but what we did was put museum labels on buildings, which made people see the buildings not just as something to walk past but as objects of scrutiny. By seeing these museum labels around town and transforming a city into an exhibition, perhaps we can see it and care for it in a way that we do for things in museum collections.   Do you work with that notion? I mean, how much of that dichotomy between serving mass tourism and your local community enters your day-to-day operation with MoMA?

I'm also interested in understanding, in the context of New York, how your Institute enters that relationship with the city, the local scene, its residents, and its needs.   New York City is a particular context because it is so connected to global infrastructures. Part of the local experience includes tourism, international students, and living amongst people who moved there from all over the world. This is all the more reason not to neglect those who make New York City their home. During *Emerging Ecologies*, we worked with a public engagement colleague to engage the Lower East Side Girls Club of NY to interpret some of the ideas in the exhibition and to create a kind of activity space in the museum where people can see the work that they're doing in the Lower East Side and how that resonates with some of the historic ideas we have in the exhibition. In fact, working with MoMA's learning and engagement staff is one of the key ways the Ambasz Institute addresses the needs of locals. On Election Day in 2024, for example, schools in NYC were closed and used as voting places, so we helped organize environmental literacy workshops at MoMA for local teachers. They went through *The City May Now Scatter*, a collections exhibit curated by the Ambasz Institute featuring Frank Lloyd Wright's Broadacre City model (1934–35), with prompts that trained their attention on the ecological dimensions of the displayed works. We gave them a presentation of the history of utopian city planning ideas, and we gave them all a chance to design their "ideal cities." The hope is that by training teachers to see exhibits through an environmental lens, they'll be able to bring this perspective into their classroom.

For the 2025 Venice Architecture Biennale, its curator

Carlo Ratti has proposed the idea that the Biennale enters dialogue with the city of Venice and its ecosystemic features, and how a form of collective or hybrid intelligence, forged by natural, human, and machine systems, could preserve, repair, and therefore generate environments of life. Are these kinds of conversations around mixed forms of spatial production part of your own research at the moment? I don't know too much about Carlo's framing for the biennial, but I often think of humanity's collective intelligence. What is it about humans as a population, as a collective, that gives us the predilection for destruction—the destruction of our surroundings and ultimately ourselves? I'm fascinated by AI and its political potentials. As Asimov has wondered, could an AI differential calculator make better, less flawed, or less biased decisions than human governments? The collective intelligence we need is one that includes the intelligence of plants, animals, fungi, and even viruses. We need to think with the other life forms if we are to stand a chance to live amongst them.

As a curatorial dimension, the digital realm has galvanized the growth of self-publishing practices and content creation, bypassing the arbitrage of academic thresholds and specialized discourse that was once the purview of magazines, conferences, and exhibitions. While foraging the multiplication of perspectives and the availability of materials and documentation, the internet remains an unmediated informational space–unless we see it, in the words of journalist Joshua Rothman, as "a social nexus capable of putting people into formation." The World Around operates in this productive breach between publics and institutions by anchoring its peripatetic convenings to an archival effort aiming at capturing "architecture's now, near, and next" into an online repository of lived stories from the contemporary front made available to all. Beatrice Galilee founded the global platform after the success of the conference series, *In Our Time: A Year of Architecture in a Day*, which she curated at the Metropolitan Museum of Art during her tenure there as curator of contemporary architecture. The contingent nature of the curatorial effort bracketed in a yearly hiatus foregrounds the processes, people, and ideas–instead of the outcomes–that animate design and spatial practice, profiling them as crucial conversationalists that "speak to the times we are living in."

The World Around has developed into a global series of gatherings with and for an interdisciplinary cohort of design and architecture professionals, devoting their efforts to the urgencies of social and ecological justice, with the aim of championing "real projects with real impacts, and practitioners who have dedicated their lives and careers to a form of practice that is civic and for the world." As a registered charity in the United States that supports itself through donations and corporate sponsorships, the project does not operate as a franchising model. Its convivial spirit of itinerant encounters seeks instead to nurture a culture of community, mutual support, and encouragement among transgenerational professional groups, building upon alliances of affinity with institutions of various kinds and scales. This tactical temporality of urgency and peer-to-peer scrutiny, which produces "time capsules of contemporary thought" in global conversation, casts the agency of The World Around in methodological resonance with the pervasive reality of environmental and social emergencies. In this spirit, it has initiated the Young Climate Prize, a mentorship program for young visionaries under the age of 25 to enable practical change at scale.

All quotes are from a conversation between the author and Beatrice Galilee (May 7, 2024).

Incubating Ecological Innovation

Director
Justin McGuirk

You came to the Design Museum from independent practice, from writing and journalism. In 2015, at the time of your appointment as chief curator, you also started as founding director of the Design Curating and Writing course at the Design Academy Eindhoven and made this statement: "design has emerged as a kind of meta-discipline of the early 21st century capable of addressing complex issues at multiple scales. We need the critics and curators that are able to do justice to that role." So, almost 10 years later, can you elaborate on that definition and what progress or changes have come about since then? I can't believe it's been nearly 10 years, but I still believe that very much, and I think that all the work we're doing now at Future Observatory is the logical continuation of that statement. I've never been more conscious of what a meta-discipline design is because I just look at the portfolio of things we are funding, which spans from circular fashion to architecture and construction, not to mention system design and technology. On the one hand, they're unified under this word "design," and on the other hand, those practices have perhaps no direct connection except a methodology.

What I mean is that design has a role to play beyond the object. I still think the object is critical, don't get me wrong, but as the thing that sits at the center of a series of concentric circles that are systems. Increasingly, the object is like the center of an onion with many skins that are all of the externalities or the second-order effects of that object. And I think that where designers can be supremely effective is in using an object to change a system or to identify problems within the system. And that's why we talk a lot about system demonstrators at Future Observatory because a thing is a very useful and tangible artifact for identifying all of the intangibles around it. And the designer is a synthesizer of the various forms of expertise required to produce an object. So why would a museum be a more apt place to disentangle those complex stories rather than, say, journalism, which you practiced for a long time before switching to institutional work? I think there is relevance to how these stories are told and how the systems have changed—in terms of outreach, in terms of capacity to impact public discourse. So, can an institution do this job, and if so, does it do it better than other means of communication?   The question is, what is it about the institution that makes it an effective narrative creator or shifter of discourse? I think museums have always played this role—obviously, the canonical case would be, say, MoMA in the 1950s or even earlier. All of the work that people like Alfred H. Barr and Philip Johnson were doing was holding up a mirror—a highly selective mirror—to architecture and design in ways that shaped what modernism or the International Style became.

But I don't know if that's the thing that we're doing now. Museums are amazing gathering places where you can get ideas in front of an awful lot of people. The museum is a powerful tool to crystallize certain ideas. Exhibitions can be very good at that; they are cultural markers. And to be honest, there was definitely an institutional learning curve for me, but I think being an outsider and not having been trained within an institutional context was, in some ways, useful.

You're right that I came to it as a writer, and many of the exhibitions we did were based on ideas and concepts that were not necessarily always easy to turn into an exhibition. A more classic curator starts with the objects, thinking about how to frame, interpret, and present them. For me, it was always the other way around. It is very difficult to try to reflect a concept like waste, which was a show we did a few years ago, or our first show, which was called *Fear and Love* (2016). It was pretty abstract! And then you have to try and bring that concept to life and elucidate a story that is possibly much better as an essay!

But you had a very specific pitch in mind when taking up the job at the museum, which was that of making it "a forum of ideas that could make [the Design Museum] a centre of debate around global design," and that first show *Fear and Love* (which inaugurated the move to the new building in 2016) was really an embodiment of that sense of design being inextricably connected to reading through or wiring the world differently.

What was your expectation with starting off with an exhibition like that? What type of conversation did you want to start with your audiences, and how has the relationship evolved? I had two clear objectives in mind. The first was to try to reflect the global systemic discipline that design had become and, to some degree, had always been. But let's just say to reflect design in an expanded mode in the 21st century and to move on from the 20th-century definition of design as the interface between commerce and culture—governed by taste, efficiency, and standardization—and to reflect something much more complex, much more intangible. The other clear aim was to try to reposition the museum. When I joined the Design Museum, it was a very classic design museum with monographic shows about designers and architects, not very thematically inclined, possibly slightly anti-intellectual in the British tradition—not anti-intellectual in spirit (the then director, Deyan Sudjic, was a writer) but wary of high concepts because they put off larger audiences.

So the aim was to suggest that it wasn't just the old museum in a new building, but a new museum.

Can you mention any specific strategy that you put in place to shape your publics, in terms of whom you wanted or needed to talk to? It's a crucial question. And there's no way to talk about a strategy without understanding the context of the Design Museum, which is that it's not publicly funded. Or rather, less than 2 percent of its operating budget is.

I would say there was a honeymoon period for me in the first year or two when it felt like one could do anything. And then quickly, we had to adjust when we realized that actually, we might be in this grand new building with exciting curatorial projects, but ultimately we needed more people through the door. And so, to sustain this giant vessel required a balancing strategy. I broke it down into three levels of activity. One was "design for an expanding audience." The idea was that the most successful shows at the museum would be the ones that were not about a famous designer or design practice, but cultural topics with design at their core. So an exhibition on Stanley Kubrick used Kubrick as a Trojan horse to bring the biggest audience we've ever had into the museum. And that audience was able to see how important design was to a film director in his world-building. Shows like that enable us to get an audience to the museum that doesn't know it's interested in design.

Because one of the challenges of being a design museum, probably not just in the UK, is that a lot of people don't think design is for them. They might think there's something rarefied about it, that it's to do with taste and money. I think at some level even now that is a bit of an issue. Indeed, we took "design" out of our exhibition titles. There's a percentage of the audience that is simply alienated by the word; it's divisive.

On another level, there was a category of programming that was about reflecting a changing world, so about contemporary issues. And then there was a strand about design as a practice, focused on the work of practitioners themselves. But the way we worked with designers, with people like Hella Jongerius and David Adjaye, was not the classic retrospective. We said: we want you to come with a research project and build an exhibition about that idea. So Hella Jongerius did this show that was entirely her research about color. And the David Adjaye show was not really a retrospective; it was about monuments.

What I'm saying is that there were strategies for appealing to different audiences, and so we had to make sure we kept the design community engaged along with this newer, larger audience.   I'm a bit surprised that you say—and I don't know if this is the case in the UK— that there is a perception of design as some sort of elitist practice. Would you say that design is on the same playing field as, say, contemporary art in this sense?   I don't want to overestimate the elitism because the art world is much more elitist than the design world. But I think that design is seen as more of a specialist or niche interest. I think there's definitely a larger audience for art than there is for design. London is saturated with art museums and galleries.

You are right that the conversation we're having about audiences is, to some degree, common to all museums, and it's becoming even more the case with the reduction in public funding. They're having to plough a more populist furrow—and you could say that's a race to the bottom, or you could see it in positive terms and argue that the more people that come to museums, the better. But ultimately, it's a question of survival. And museums across the board are having to work harder to survive, especially after the pandemic reduced audiences and changed audience behavior.   **In an ideal world where clickbait and performance metrics, the way we know them today, don't count, what makes a good exhibition for the kind of stories you want to tell?**   It's funny; 10 years in, I still find that a tremendously difficult question to answer!

I guess as a curator, one has an intuition of what one tries to create for people. Having said everything we've said about objects on plinths, people still need to be moved to some degree or intrigued or challenged by experiences in a space. That might be through beauty and form or ugliness or craftsmanship, but ultimately you enjoy an exhibition that helps you understand a piece of the world. And that piece of the world might be a designer's point of view or the story of their life. The most classic show I ever did was a retrospective of Charlotte Perriand, and there you understand that, over a 60-something-year career, you can see how the world changed through one person's eyes, and that's a powerful experience.   **Let's talk about this new adventure that is Future Observatory and how it came about for the museum. What had the Design Museum achieved that made this large public funding, which feeds into Future Observatory, come to you and not, say, a V&A or the Science Museum?**   It is inextricably linked to the fact that we're a design museum. Because we had been making the case that a design museum has a role to play in helping deliver industrial strategy. So we were thinking about the government's five industrial strategy pillars, which were things like an aging society, urban mobility, data, and AI—these kinds of questions. The Design Museum was actually founded as a conduit between designers, industry, and the public—this trifecta. So we have natural links to industry and the economy. We were making the case for something we were calling Future Observatory as a way of thinking about and helping policymakers and industry think about the future of the country. We began that project in 2019, and it took a couple of years to percolate. We were talking to the Arts and Humanities Research Council (AHRC), which is part of UK Research and Innovation (UKRI). There are several research councils under that, and most of them are science-based. AHRC liked this idea, but they encouraged us to focus on net zero because that was a big concern in government at that moment. And that was absolutely the right thing to do. So they funded a pilot project in 2021, which we launched alongside our *Waste Age* exhibition, and then after six months, they recognized the kind of impact you can have through a museum in terms of profile and outreach, and then suddenly it was a £25 million program over three years.

This origin story lies in our perception of a museum as a place where you can think through issues that are relevant to the future of the economy. That would be the pitch to the government because, of course, the government is interested in things like "innovation" and "growth," and they see design as a kind of enabler of those things, but I am not interested in innovation and growth per se.

What are you interested in then? The question is innovation for what? And obviously, growth has its own problems. I'm less interested in what design can do for growth than what design can do to transform the economy to a green economy.

And likewise with innovation, I think in the UK we tend to fetishize it for its own sake. This logic applies more and more to everything I look at. We are desperately trying to think about how to expand our energy capacity. But energy for what? Energy to continue the sixth mass extinction? Why does everything we do seem to require more and more energy? I think innovation needs to be treated in a very critical way. However, we launched Future Observatory to look at what design can do to promote the transition to a net-zero economy. And we can all agree that the role that design plays there is critical in terms of materials, energy use, and infrastructure. Any issue you care to name, design will have a role to play in terms of behavior change.

But as soon as we got funded, I erased all mention of net zero, because I find it just too limiting a frame, so we're now the national design research program for the green transition. And even the green transition is a limited frame;

really, it's the transition that matters, both a just transition and a green transition.

We fund any research that can reduce carbon emissions, reduce waste, or promote regenerative approaches to landscape and biodiversity. And it's hard to overstate what a shift that is, not just for us but for any museum. Because to use the museum as a conduit to channel government research funding into research and innovation is really unusual. Most research funding goes to universities. And even with Future Observatory, that remains the case. But channeling the funding through a museum is a very interesting move. It redefines what a museum can be because suddenly it is not just a place for engaging in the continual process of interpreting and reinterpreting artifacts and telling the story of what the world has been or how the world is today.

Suddenly, the museum can be a place that is funding and driving the change it wants to see in a mission-oriented way. The museum is no longer just shaping understanding; it is helping shape the future.   **You have written a paper on these ideas titled** *The Museum as Catalyst*—**explain to me how it connects to Future Observatory's activities and strategic framework.**   The work we do falls into three categories: symptoms, strategies, and stories. The symptoms part is most of what we are dealing with, realistically, because we're funding design that can reduce carbon emissions or waste in practical ways. Strategy is much more about system change and influencing policy and regulations. And then, ultimately, there is the overarching story. This is the reason why we launched the *Future Observatory Journal*. It can be quite frustrating to see how constrained design practices are by the discourse, by phrases like "net zero." Design can feel like it is stuck in shaving mode—shaving off some carbon emissions, shaving off a little plastic, shaving off a little waste. But where is the structural change?

The climate crisis is partly a crisis of storytelling. As Arturo Escobar says in the Journal, we're transitioning from one story of the world to another. The problem with net zero discourse is that it's ultimately defuturing. There's no future in just counting carbon. One of the reasons why I think progress is so slow is that we have such a technocratic approach to the problem. Ultimately, we're operating in systems that don't want to be changed, and so there's this notion that we can just be efficient carbon calculators. It's like we're becoming accountants as opposed to having a new vision of the world, which means acting and thinking differently. Fundamentally, it's a shift in consciousness that we're aiming for. There's a sense that the prevailing narratives are just wrong; we need a return to a grand narrative about our relationship with the living world. Design has a role to play in shaping that narrative. Arturo talks about narratives as a designing force, and I find that very interesting. I don't think, by any means, that design has a monopoly on that—there are all kinds of disciplines with a case to make for shaping the story of civilization—but design is one of them.   **What is your vision, or what is the projection, in terms of how Future Observatory coexists with the regularity of the other museum activities? What do you think is and will be its impact in general?**   I think that the reason why it works well is that there's a virtuous cycle between the research and the communication of that research. A museum is a wonderful place to get new ideas in front of a large audience. The museum sets a research agenda, and the funding goes out through grants. It's a crucial point to say that I don't get to decide who gets the funding—I have to be impartial. The grants are managed by the research council, and the applications are selected by expert panels.

We use the museum to oxygenate the research, which could be through displaying it, or it could be through inviting people to come and talk about it at conferences, or it could be through publishing it in the journal. So the museum becomes a kind of amplifier. It's a way of getting that research out into the world. And all of our grants are framed as partnerships—it's explicit that all of our grantees have to partner with either a business, a local authority, or a charity. Whoever is the relevant partner to deliver impact in the real world. Because the object is not to inflate the research economy, it's to get the research out of academia and into the world as impact. Evaluating impact is difficult, of course, and can be a long game.

So, nearly three years into the project, what have you learned about the nature of that impact? If I could change anything in the next phase, I'd like to be able to channel more funding into practices themselves that are not based in universities. A lot of great work is happening in practice and in the delivery of real projects. And the question is who's going to fund that research? Because it's not the government necessarily, are we expecting private clients and businesses to fund experimental ways of doing things when there might not be a return on investment? For example, making a building out of low-carbon materials that don't come from the regular supply chains, that don't rely on the regular trade skills to build, that aren't guaranteed to be insured, and that may be harder to get planning approval for... As soon as you try to change something in the way you make a building, you rub up against all these systemic obstacles. And the tremendous labor of overcoming that friction needs to be covered by someone. Is it the client who's going to cover that? In some cases, yes. There are clients willing to experiment with these things, but the more we can fund system demonstrators in the real world, the better. Creating things that demonstrate how the system can behave differently and show the market that it can be done, *that* is impact.

How is the existence of Future Observatory playing out in your internal conversations with your team and collaborators? How is it affecting the overall work of the institution, and do you see any impact on the public? I would say that the real communicative power is probably for a more specialist world, but certainly it has galvanized the Design Museum's sense of mission. Of course, the museum always had a mission, but previously it would have been very much about making the impact of design visible, trying to communicate the value and power of design as a transformative force in the world. In that sense, it was more educational.

Now added to that is this sense that we're in an existential crisis, the climate crisis, and design is one of the key forces in addressing that crisis, and the museum is being empowered to play a role in driving the change that we need to see. This has had an incredibly stimulating effect on the museum's sense of purpose and on the staff, in the sense that people feel so engaged across all departments, and they feel inspired by the work even if they're not directly involved in it.

And then there are more practical impacts on our operations. For instance, delivering exhibitions in a more sustainable way. There's been a tremendous amount of work at the museum on low-carbon exhibition-making, given that exhibitions are ultimately quite wasteful productions. But that's just an example of a stimulating side effect of some of the work that we're doing. I definitely think that, in the UK landscape, other institutions are following with interest and trying to think about what the equivalent contribution might be in their case.

I guess the fundamental question is what civil society can do at a time of political failure? **In my conversations, it emerged how design, especially in larger art museums featuring dedicated departments, has been called up to address such internal logistical/operational problems, but also how it is seen as a potential driver of new publics.** That's so interesting. I find it counterintuitive but also encouraging. Because I often think of it the other way around: that art is a good way to get people into a design museum as well.

Maybe that has something to do with the saturation of the art world in London. I mean, we often feel like we compete with the big art museums for audiences.

But I can put a slightly different spin on it, which is that we are funded by the Arts and Humanities Research Council, which the current government is not particularly inclined to keep funding at all. A Conservative government can see the value of science research councils because they're funding research that might result in innovation and growth. Tory governments are not particularly invested in culture; they are not particularly inclined to encourage diversity; they're interested in very normative behavior.

That's a very long-winded way of saying that Arts and Humanities funding is under threat in the current political climate. Who knows what will happen after the election next month? So, to a government that's interested in innovation and growth, design is very useful. The fact that you could point to this big design research program, which might help transform the economy, is very useful. That's not an audience-focused shift, but it is a major shift for the Arts and Humanities Research Council, which traditionally didn't really fund design at all. And now, I feel the power I have as a program director within AHRC is that design demonstrates its relevance to a government that may not believe in the transformative power of the arts.

This begs the very important question of how we can change and diversify business models for museums, which are tragically and dangerously homogenized.

In this sense, the Design Museum has been recently given independent research status. What does that imply for the future? So yes, and it was very much the Future Observatory that led that initiative.

This means we can apply for state grants, which we're not the first to have achieved. Other museums already have that status, like the Tate, the Science Museum, and the V&A, but we're actually the first independent museum in the UK to have it. So this opens up new avenues of financial and funding support. Ultimately, in order to be recognized as an IRO, you have to outline what your research culture and strategy are, and with most museums, the research strategy is focused on the understanding of the collection, questions of historical interpretation, and accessibility. That's the research culture.

Our research strategy is based on using design as a medium for reflecting the way the world is changing, so it's a much more contemporary and future-facing focus that is not about reinterpreting the past. It's about reflecting change in a contemporary landscape, and now with Future Observatory looking toward the future changes that need to happen.

We said, you know, the purpose of the Design Museum is to make the impact of design visible, and the purpose of Future Observatory is to make design research have an impact. Sure, so it's not necessarily always centering your activities around the material hoarding of items as conveyors or vessels of knowledge, but venturing into producing knowledge or subjects of research. You have launched this new digital journal, and its first overarching topic is *bioregioning*, and you're going to move into more-than-human themes thereafter. Tell me a little bit about bioregioning and how you go about picking these topics. Bioregioning has been in the background of a lot of conversations we've been having at Future Observatory for the last two years. We've done work with an architecture practice in the UK called Material Cultures about bioregional models, like how to build with natural materials from local environments as opposed to shipping materials around the world. And there is the work of Atelier Luma in Arles and practices like Mass Design Group in Rwanda. In our network, we were seeing people trying to develop this model of bioregional design and architecture.

When I started in architecture, the discourse was all about "starchitects" and young designers wanting to make parametric shapes. It was all very, you know, spectacular. And now young practitioners are interested in things like soil, plants, and mushrooms, which is an unbelievable cultural shift and a hugely positive one. I mean, some architects hate it, of course, but I find it tremendously inspiring and reassuring.

Bioregioning felt like a suitable framework in the sense that it really challenges existing systems and cuts across borders and jurisdictions to understand "who" the landscape is. It's a way of challenging governance, raw materials, how you promote citizen participation, and local knowledge.

There's a risk that people might think of it as this slightly parochial localism, a closing off of global perspectives. But the interesting thing about bioregioning is how you network and communicate between bioregions—it's a planetary perspective. You think about what's best for that landscape, and you learn from the way other bioregions and other landscapes are doing it. Jan Boelen has this wonderful line about how materials are heavy and ideas are light. So we decided to make the first issue of the journal about bioregioning—as a verb, an action. And the issue not only celebrates it but also critiques it.

And the next issue of the *Future Observatory Journal* will be on the more-than-human. We've decided to align a lot of our programming around that theme. So the next round of our Design Exchange Partnership grants is themed around more-than-human—which is £600,000 of funding. And then there is a major exhibition, *More Than Human*, opening in June 2025.   There are two things that caught my attention while reading the journal. One is a concept that is very powerful and, to a certain extent, completely undermines the traditional paradigm of 20th-century design, which is the idea of "scaling out" rather than "scaling up."

The other is that there is no obvious mention of technologies that are implicated in the fabrication of the environment. Can you comment on this?   The only piece that addresses technology is the one about the EU Critical Materials Act. The EU is obviously worried about where its rare minerals are coming from and is thinking about repatriating the extraction of those to the EU—things like lithium and cobalt. So there's a piece about what it means to bring extraction back home. You are right; technology is not so far central to this debate. I think that's because of two reasons: firstly, there is no such thing as bioregional technology. What does a mobile phone made in Devon look like? It's just not a relevant question because of globalized extraction and production. Technology just sits outside the frame at the moment. But it is very interesting to think about what a building made entirely in Devon would look like, using local timber, biomaterials, and rammed earth.

What about the scaling issue?   Well, the traditional economic models are all about scaling up. Bioregioning challenges the logic of increased production and growth. You can only scale up within the carrying capacity of the bioregion, and then it's more a question of scaling out—in other words, proliferating good ideas to other bioregions.

At the moment, when you try to think about good examples of that, they might seem almost irrelevant, but I think that the principle is a good one. Let's take, for example, Atelier Luma using sunflower waste to produce insulating panels. The principle is not that you then industrialize sunflower panels for export across Europe. The principle is that you see what the equivalent material is in Italy, and you scale up in a bioregional way. Or, as Jan Boelen would say, if we're using olive pits to produce a material, it's not that we scale up olive pits, but you look at North Africa and say, "Well, how do you use date pits in the same way?" That's the scaling-out principle. It's a logic of proliferation and iteration, not of volume. It's a beautiful principle, but it's difficult to point to lots of concrete examples of it.

This is where the system demonstrator comes in. Atelier Luma is probably the most established bioregional system demonstrator there is, and that's the value of it. But who's funding it? A wealthy philanthropist?

Exactly. How do you create incentives—business incentives—for those that don't have that kind of financial capacity? That's the thing. There's no way to operate these models at the moment using market logics and market investment. There are three main forms of funding: there's private philanthropy, public funding, and business investment. At the moment, 99% of business investment increases carbon emissions, so we have to use public funding and private philanthropy to try to produce system demonstrators to get business investment into non-polluting, non-emitting models. But that's a very good point. It's also about asking how we can build alternative futures for the institution; it is the kind of repositioning that administrators and policymakers should reflect more on. I don't mean it has to be a model for everyone, but diversity in institutional methodologies is a true necessity now to redress the course of action. We're also working on our own system demonstrator. Hopefully, next year, the Future Observatory is going to build a stone frame structure because stone is a very low-carbon material compared to steel and concrete. But no one uses stone structural systems in the UK; it's only used for the finishes, so the skills and supply chains aren't there, and there's too much friction. We're hoping the demonstrator will result in a building code for stone, which will make it easier to adopt as a structural material. A small project can be a major contribution.

If you can get anything created that demonstrates that an alternative way is possible, that is the kind of thing I'm interested in. It could be at a design fair or at a biennale, but that is such an exclusive set of circumstances that it almost confines it to a culture industry framing. It is also true that we must never forget that the power of cultural institutions is in the way they influence the cultural atmosphere. I think cultural institutions help create the weather to some degree. Even if they're only influencing public opinion or the nature of discourse, this is all creating the weather. They are places of tremendous power in that sense.

In the publication celebrating the 10th anniversary of Walk&Talk, the festival organized since 2011 on the island of São Miguel in the Azores, Portugal, Jesse James, one of its founding partners, writes that "being *peripheral or on the margins* brought the concept of autonomy to the center of the Azores' history and identity, where questions of ownership, access, and circulation intersected with its autonomous movement. Walk&Talk's networks of affection, both local and trans-regional, were essential in cementing the relevance of its project and its periphery."[1]

Born from a desire to establish social dynamics of encounter between artistic practices and local communities, the festival has organically evolved from a public art parkour of open-air murals to year-long initiatives connecting transdisciplinary cohorts of practitioners and thinkers—artists, curators, architects, designers, performers, and musicians—with the situated knowledge embedded in the territories and culture of its liminality. Departing from a notion of fluidity and adaptation, Walk&Talk has operated as a platform for social and territorial regeneration by progressively broadening its mission as a cultural and political agent of transformation. The festivalism of the temporary event of the early years made way for more attuned strategies of long-term cooperation with local entities and schools, producing programs that have ranged from creative residencies and summer schools to platforms for knowledge transfer, grants, and mentorships for local creators and cultural entrepreneurs, as well as productive laboratories for artisans and traditional makers, all activated through communal engagement with local residents and agents.

Anda&Fala, the organization behind the festival and its various initiatives, is now permanently operating from the island through Vaga, a space for art and knowledge, and its headquarters. It has become an essential interlocutor in shaping the cultural policies of the archipelago by nurturing a sense of "collective ownership" of its activities. Among other achievements, it has successfully lobbied to revise frameworks of access to national funding from Autonomous Regions and encouraged a civic movement to promote Ponta Delgada's candidacy for European Capital of Culture 2027. The politics of affect and relationality that find expression in the "peripheral centralities"[2] of former colonial territories and natural regions akin to that of the Azores embody potent forms of cultural tooling for attunement to a transforming world, from our relationship to land and resources to social commoning. It is from these emergent networks of knowledge embedded in territories of so-called liminality across the world that methodological practices like Walk&Talk's become a powerful inspiration.

1   Miguel Mesquita (ed.), *Walk&Talk 2011–2022: What you don't know is worth discovering,* exhibition catalog, Anda&Fala, 2024.
2   From a conversation between the author and Jesse James (July 24, 2024).

Ecologies of Institutional Transformation

You have built a career around a strong engagement with artistic and environmental practices, a focused exploration that is a semi-imperative nowadays for many institutions tending to contemporary culture. What did you see emerging when you started and what about now? How has the context transformed? It's hard to fix a beginning point in this kind of work, but I suppose if we're looking at the space of interaction between art and ecology, I can find it about 10 years ago with research that led to the yearly festival Extinction Marathon (2014). The Marathon is a format that brings together all disciplines around a particular theme that feels relevant to the cultural world and society at large in any given year. I was public programs curator at the Serpentine at the time, and I had been involved in a number of Marathon festivals before. I also have a background that is interdisciplinary; I didn't study curating and I didn't study art history. I studied literature, gender studies, and critical theory, so I already had a sort of interest in the ways that ideas move between disciplines and the role that art could have as a kind of amateur, in the sense of a lover of everything, and as a sort of antenna into the movement of ideas. The research toward the Extinction Marathon, which was co-curated with the artist Gustav Metzger, brought me personally to a level of depth of feeling that was much greater than any other I had been involved with before.

In 2014 it was very clear that cultural institutions were not talking about ecology and environmental topics because they were afraid of being called out for their own impact on the planet. Now the conversation has obviously become a lot more elaborate, even though I would argue that it has also become simpler and less deep in other ways. In the span of 10 years, there has been a surging number of initiatives in various creative sectors, including design and architecture, to engage ecocritical discourse.

What have you seen transforming in this sense, and can you also speak to the legacy of the first Marathon and plans for its latest edition (2024)? The first thing that I'm going to say because you've mentioned the world of architecture and design is that I found that after launching the General

Ecology project in 2018, most of the teaching and engagement opportunities that I ever had to bring the subject forward, which is in large part around systems and organizational transformation through ecological and ecologically minded work, came from an architectural context more frequently than the art or art historical context. So for me, without a shadow of a doubt, in the pedagogical sphere, the architecture and design worlds are far more advanced in terms of wider and deeper reflections than the traditional art historical or curatorial study environment.

If we compare the approaches to soil, more-than-human consciousness, and the Earth as a planetary organism to perspectives that emerged from critical anthropology, then we can see that around the 2012/13 mark, the intellectual life around these subjects was profound, with events such as dOCUMENTA (13) in Kassel.

More than ten years later, we find ourselves at a bit of a crossroads again. It matches with a sense of crisis that I myself feel, that is to say that, now that institutions have adopted the ecological discourse as a crucial and fundamental one, then by necessity, as soon as something spreads more widely, it also simplifies in its approach.

So what we're looking at now for the institutions that are focusing their efforts on ecology is that they are messaging the need for effort under two main banners: on the one hand, the carbon and impact reduction of the sector itself, new materials, building solutions for museums, and regenerative practices within the museum infrastructure. And on the other, a nebulous but still incredibly pervasive ideology of art as a kind of awareness-raising tool, where we expect art to have the same effect on people's awareness as a call to action from David Attenborough on the BBC.

What happens, inevitably, is that there's an illusion of individual agency in this approach that gets propagated through this economy of attention, which doesn't take into account the systemic imbalances that are actually holding things in place.

So, the space that I am much more interested in is the space in between these two great attractors. I'm fascinated by art when it does what it does best, although I am not prescriptive about the "how" at all. These practices are sometimes incredibly practical, getting art and culture involved in the transformation of actual systems, in education, pedagogy, food distribution and production, policy infrastructures, and so on. Other times, they can be extremely speculative, devoted to something a little closer to the notion of worlding.

And that's, of course, much more difficult to quantify; it's much more difficult to track; it operates at the level of deep time.

One of the very important conversations that I had at the beginning of the General Ecology project was with Jojo Mehta, co-founder of the Stop Ecocide Foundation. I started the General Ecology project by reaching out to people I admired in the environmental spaces and asking, "How can a museum be useful to you?" And Jojo gave me an answer that was incredibly sophisticated, in retrospect. She said, "As a museum, you have the agency to make the notion of 'ecocide' as much a part of the common language and culture as that of homicide."

For me, Jojo was talking about moving the notion of ecocide actually away from awareness-raising and dissolving it into the world of culture by making it commonplace. From awareness to culture. Awareness is the thing you know about, and it can sit somewhat in a foreign relationship with the way things are; culture, on the other hand, is the thing you take for granted and you don't even see anymore because it structures your world every day.

It's in those spaces, the speculative spaces of culture and worlding and the practical spaces of systems transformation—and all that's in between those—that I think we should be. But as things stand, cultural institutions have become fairly myopic around what kind of approaches can unfold or emerge out of an ecological habit of mind.

And it feels to me that although there are incredible colleagues and practitioners that are very aware of this —a few years back I thought of it as an emergent practice that was going to become more literate about itself and its agencies—in fact, this small cohort of professionals continues to operate in a kind of subculture, whilst at the same time ecology appears to have taken center stage "on paper." **In what way does it remain a sub-culture? In my conversations for this book, there seems to emerge a clear shift in understanding that this in-between space that you talk about, so moving from the institution as a resonating board for raising awareness to a site of action and production, is really taking hold. Not that this makes it mainstream (hence this book!), but what are the stifling factors, in your opinion, that prevent institutions from moving forward?** We need to take this up at different levels. On the one hand, there is undoubtedly the fact that institutions have baggage and appendages and necessities that precede ecological ways of programming or transforming institutions themselves. So, inevitably, there's a kind of business plan incompatibility between the way things have been done until now and the way things could be done. Having gone through Covid, the financial crisis, and the rise of populist governments, most institutions are going to struggle to resolve this.

One of the things that I find most crucial to acknowledge to start doing this work is that institutions are primarily concerned with their own survival. The survival of the institution itself is a very fragile thing, and I don't think any director in their right mind would be willing to take an existential risk at this moment, right?

But to achieve real transformation requires a systemic rethink that, as a result of today's precarity and fragility, inevitably boils down to funding. It is not the only issue, but it's a big one. So to avoid risk, institutions too often rely on marketing and communication to "cover" their ecological bases, so to speak.

I have nothing but respect for all of my colleagues who work in that world, but a museum's engagement with ecology doesn't rest on what said museum communicates to its public about ecology through announcements. If it does, then that's where we find sentences like "we're working to reduce our carbon footprint," and where we get told that art is great for spreading the word.

The problem, of course, is that the visionary work of artists, designers, or architects is much more complicated to communicate; sometimes it's completely impossible, and sometimes it rests in the depth of incomprehensibility for ages before it can be worked through. I'm a public programs curator by training, and I love saying things to the public, but I don't like giving answers or spoon-feeding audiences. I far prefer to organize ideas: put together forms of engagement (gatherings, publications, podcasts, exhibitions, whatever) in which we can address extremely complex things, but in sexy and engaging ways, so that nobody's trying to talk down to or educate anybody. Rather, we're trying to have a shared experience.

And this is where, for me, the experience of speaking with the public is much closer to that of creating a ritual or a ceremony than it is to creating press releases or statements.

This dynamic mirrors elsewhere: the survival of the institution in a world that is essentially defined by perennial transformation asks how to keep a stable object in an unstable planet. Too often, in order to maintain its stability, that object will isolate itself and make borders, which in a museum context is essentially its communications infrastructure. If you think about governments, they do the exact same thing. As soon as they feel anxiety or unrest among citizens, they start to put emphasis on, and then police, their borders, which is where the refugee or the migrant becomes the archetypal figure of the externality, of what needs to be kept on the outside in order to ensure stability.

There might be a bit of a generational issue at play, too, in the sense that I see with joy that a lot of peers that I find visionary are now finally taking the reins of institutions, and those institutions are changing in weird and interesting ways. But that transition is happening as we speak, and, of course, these are colleagues who are inheriting quite precarious situations.

Lastly, as much as we try to make structural changes to an organization, these impulses, initiatives, and intuitions are very personal and very close to those people who look after them. Much as there is always an attempt to distribute the activities or the initiatives among a wider group of people, the minute an individual leaves, institutions do tend to kind of reabsorb that energy back and return to exactly the way things were. Hence the need for greater risk-taking and greater willingness to change.

So, if we agree that there is a certain oversaturation with programs that tackle ecological or environmental practice, what about formats of public engagement? What strategies or changes are necessary to keep a level of criticality in knowledge transfer with your publics? Are, for example, Marathons still valid conduits to speak to your audiences?

In a former interview, you mentioned that when you started the General Ecology program in 2018, one of your primary goals was to "foster a community of interest." Who are your audiences now? The formats of public outreach are definitely changing. The Marathon, a household format at Serpentine, found a hiatus at the end of 2018, which was extended with the Covid-19 pandemic. Since 2023, we have been running a version that is completely different from before, in response to the changing emotional and political landscape of the world. To begin with, in lieu of presenting the Marathon as a single weekend, the completion of a long period of research, we decided to make part of that research process public. So, in October 2023, we ran an event that was positioned as a "prelude" to the Marathon: what once was done in a closed-door context (convening advisors and gleaning research potentials and participants from brainstorming sessions) was instead done in the open.

It became clear, though, even as we stepped into a space that was intentionally positioned as tentative, that the format itself of a long-durational, frontal event presented its problems in the current times, which are so marked with unspeakable pain. The atmosphere was very raw. Then, mid-event, filmmaker Manthia Diawara asked, "How can we foster spaces for the sacred to be able to exist today?" which connected with something I've been thinking about very deeply and that I'll share later. So, in that moment, I realized that the most compassionate interactions that the prelude was having with its audiences were the ones that may fall more under the rubric of ceremony, conviviality, sharing, and ritual.

As a result of this direct learning, which was not done in a book, or in theory in a boardroom, but literally felt through being there, in place, and trying stuff out, we decided not to host the large-scale event that we were planning for July 2024. Instead, we stretched the Marathon as a program over the entire year, all of which would follow a more poetic and deep narrative of engagement and pay more attention to the metabolic process of the Earth. In July, a gathering was dedicated to planting, seeding, and burying, and to artists' relationships with the land. In September, another gathering focused on worlding, planting, and composting. These are real, environmental and human/more-than-human relationships. They are also epistemological movements: we compost leaves, and we compost thoughts and ideas. There is continuity between the two. At any rate, instead of one big festival, it's becoming this more distributed set of little circles of storytelling and ceremony.

Fundamentally, what we're doing is trying to be responsive; to rely a lot less on statement-making or taking a position and a lot more on holding space and convening emotions, visions, bodies, exchanges, and forms of intimacy.

The interaction with the public is something I always find really important. It gives me an enormous amount of energy, particularly in the way that in that interaction we find ways of telling each other stories. I suppose that both in pace and in situation, I find myself leaning a lot more on the history of ceremony than that of conferences.

So, do I understand correctly that you are shifting focus in terms of your direct audiences into fostering these networks of people with whom you want to think, feel, and create? As a cultural programmer in an institution, you have the power to pick and choose which stories to champion. How do you think your public has changed? I'll tell you a story. In December 2018 Filipa and I presented the second festival in a research project on interspecies consciousness titled *The Shape of A Circle In The Mind of A Fish*. The first iteration had focused on language, and for this second one, which we subtitled "we have never been one" in honour of Bruno Latour's book, we convened an interdisciplinary group of practitioners around the notions of swarm organisms, interior multitudes, bacteria, and planetary symbiosis, so anything from nanorobotics to metabolism and Gaia theory.

There were about 800 people in that room. Backstage, I had a conversation with a friend and colleague, Ben Vickers, who had been involved in these subject matters for a long time, especially through the prism of how these matters emerge in the space of advanced technology. I remember him being a little taken aback, saying he could not imagine that a few years ago you would have been able to convene so many people around this kind of material. I suppose he wasn't wrong. That, I think, resulted from the confluence of a number of factors. Firstly, certain subjects that might appear very niche can indeed be communicated, shared, and presented in ways that are seductive, appealing, and accessible, without at all simplifying anything or patronizing one's audience. I explicitly place this methodology in direct opposition to the now-ubiquitous and populist domination of marketing-friendly concepts and language coming out of cultural institutions today, when they believe that to shore up against this incredibly precarious time, they need to become what they refer to as "audience-led" (and mistakenly, in my opinion).

Fostering a relationship with your audience is, for me, not at all about reducing the cultural institution's language to that of social media influencers or—even worse—relying on the latter's endorsements to "bring the public in." For me, a lot of the relationship with the public is a relationship of intimacy: can we create a community of practice together? Can we commit to each other, to telling each other stories, to staying, to returning? The idea is really to organize spaces and situations in which we might be able to have a shared experience around an incredibly deep question, one that may be stuck at the back of all of our throats—and to do that with responsibility, discernment, coherence, and tenderness.

The community of General Ecology built itself. I didn't purposefully build it; it just gathered itself, following an interest, a yearning, an intuition. That same community is still the backbone of everything that we do with Ecologies at the Serpentine, and it emerged, bit by bit, in these rooms, in these one-off gatherings in which special things happened, in the intimacy of a couple of series of podcasts that met our public mid-pandemic in their homes, in their ears, close to their bodies and all of our loneliness.

Let's get a little bit more into the practicalities of Ecologies at the Serpentine. As you have explained, it was a conversation that morphed out of a series of curatorial initiatives into more of a holistic, systemic, and structural intervention within the institution as an entity. So what does it entail practically? The evolution from General Ecology to Ecologies is one that the Serpentine itself hasn't yet fully externalized, but that's what we're currently working on.

General Ecology is a curatorial project which, whether I wanted it to be or not, was primarily tied to me, although of course there are some really crucial colleagues who have participated since the get-go—Kostas Stasinopoulos and Holly Shuttleworth in the first instance—and crucially some non-Serpentine friends and colleagues, Filipa Ramos more than anyone, who really shaped its beginnings. It holds a series of research questions that are fundamentally interdisciplinary, rooted in more-than-human theories, in critical anthropology. The ultimate goal, or sort of speculative horizon, of that part of General Ecology that concerned itself with organizational theory was to embed ecological purpose and principles within the very structure of the Serpentine as an organization. Becoming Curator of General Ecology was a sort of performative gesture towards that embedding, because suddenly you have a curator of ecology, and that did not exist before in a contemporary organization. This was 2018. There is, of course, no need to be the first, but it was still very much a performative rarity.

But if one aim of the General Ecology project was to embed environmental responsibility within the fabric of the organization, then a curatorial project heavily identified with one curator was never going to fully succeed. First of all, because as soon as that person goes away, the project itself goes too, and second, because you can't pull the rest of the organization behind one person.

Toward the end of 2022, I started to have conversations with the directors at the Serpentine about creating an Ecologies department and representation for that department at the level of senior management. It's maybe a little bit like companies that put "nature" on their board: I wanted Ecologies to be a department that has a position within the organization but that also works in completely distributed ways, following a strategy that develops protocols for the implementation of environmental purpose across the entire infrastructure in ways that are consistent with each department and area of activity's best potential. So: you work with buildings? Our interaction may then have to do with airflow or energy consumption. You work with production? We may talk about material use for exhibitions. Do you work with live programs or public outreach? We may be thinking about facing climate breakdown, climate justice, artist-led approaches, and meeting our public where they are. We've worked with the restaurant, with our landlords at The Royal Parks, and so forth.

The strategy of Ecologies at the Serpentine is fundamentally that each area of activity can embed environmental purpose in its fabric, but it needs to do so in ways that are consistent with what that activity is, not just imposing a, say, 50% carbon reduction across the board, for example.

So, in order to start to implement this, in June 2023 I re-joined the Serpentine after a brief hiatus as Head of Ecologies. The idea of having an identity that is plural—Ecologies—is so that it's not associated with any particular curatorial identity or area of activity or action, and therefore can be more resilient and can be flexibly adopted by the rest of the organization.

One of my current most focused points of interest is the organization itself as a kind of audience. We've developed artist-led projects for embedding a sense of environmental belonging in colleagues and collaborators, running workshops that are specifically aimed at them. Vegetal meditations, resonant music, role-playing games on monocultural plantations, movement workshops, and so forth. What we're trying to build now, out of all of this, is a sort of ephemeral collection of artworks that remain as leftovers of these workshops, to be included in a kind of welcome pack when someone joins the organization: your own private collection of artist-created ephemera that gets you closer to the planet in ways that don't sound like what Green Teams in organizations usually do (carbon calculation, recycling, and so on). This is all super important, but just not where we want to be in terms of work culture.

Sounds like an incubator of rituals or methodologies that you can replicate. So, if you weren't tied down by material and temporal constraints, what would be your long-term goal, your ideal picture with Ecologies at the Serpentine or anywhere else, really? If I take your question in the vastest possible sense, what I think needs to happen is that we change the "business plan" of the human-made system of this planet and make one that is consistent with planetary boundaries and with environmental belonging. By "business plan," I just mean the way that we operate and what we are aiming toward in terms of organizational and organized behavior. I'm also deeply convinced that there is an unstoppable and large-scale transformation taking place at present—what some call "the polycrisis" —and that we are witnessing the end of a particular kind of world while refusing to face it. In helping to foster spaces where we can face it—I am humbly in debt to Vanessa Machado de Oliveira Andreotti and the Gesturing Towards Decolonial Futures Collectives for this—we may make space, as they suggest, for whatever may be birthing next. To that end, I'm particularly interested in the role of culture as a kind of midwife or doula, as something that accompanies a society or civilization, a species, through a period of intense transformation and that does so with the groundedness and the presence of mind to be able to witness what is happening as it is happening.

To encourage this interest, I recently did a little bit of training as a death doula and a bit of training in psychotherapy with a focus on mourning. Both of these are skills that I wanted to develop in order to further support a "genre" of cultural initiative that aims to create spaces that may help hold what is unbearable and what is just born and still too fragile to stand alone. If we think about an independent project, *Songs for the Changing Seasons* (an exhibition curated for the Vienna Klima Biennale with Filipa

Ramos, 2024), the idea was to notice the ways that more-than-human species prepare for the changing of seasons and to learn from them what we can about this massive change, our current interregnum, this end that we are witnessing. Trees shed their leaves before winter; bears hibernate, and animals store food.

The planet prepares for big shifts in ways that humans also do but don't acknowledge. To me, the space of culture is our human equivalent of civilizational, seasonal preparation: it is the place where we conserve, where we protect for later, where we encode, and also where we choose what to let go and grieve it.

Another particularity of today is that transformation is happening at a faster speed than our capacity to hold it cognitively: we need to make space for that fact. In the words of a friend and colleague, Aslak Aamot Helm, "People don't want to die in a landscape that they cannot describe." It's a sentence I find devastatingly sad, but I absolutely love it as an analysis of how the symbolic systems by which we are holding the world in place are being left behind by a kind of chaotic transformation that is, in itself, a kind of ontological-symbolic system hybrid that we are not at all equipped to interpret.

You are gesturing towards the idea that as we witness a moment of systemic collapse in many ways, our conduits for apprehending, representing, and speaking back to these transformations have to change as well. And so, institutions of culture should too. In this sense, I want to pick up on something you wrote in an article entitled "Senses of Purpose."[1]

"Over the past years, but most sharply in the past months, I have come to be convinced that this work of connection, this weaving practice—a kind of cross-disciplinary translation and tools for mutual understanding—may be so fundamental as to point towards a new field of practice in and of itself."   I wrote that text several years ago, and it was published only quite recently. Hearing you read it again changes my interpretation of it from how I intended it back then, and I think that could be

1   Christos Carras (ed.), *The Handbook of Cultural Work*, Bloomsbury, 2024.

a huge gift that this conversation is offering to me. Keller Easterling, who is a thinker I deeply adore, talks in Medium Design (2021)[2] about "the matrix or substance within which things are suspended and in which they change over time" as the space of contemporary action and praxis: the matrix is the medium.

I think of culture in very much the same way, as this medium or matrix. Culture is the invisible part of what we know: it is what structures what we don't know we know, and out of which come the ways we hold our worlds in place on a daily basis. I also think about the spaces between disciplines as a kind of thick yet invisible space through which ideas circulate. In this context, ritual and ceremony are a thick, saturated, communal space through which the experience of the present harks back or points back invisibly to something that is more cosmic or more universal or planetary.

All of these are kinds of "medium design;" they all follow a method by which we choose to be operating at the level of "the thing between things." At its best, in my opinion, a work of art draws out of you something you already had inside but that was stuck and needed to come out, but you didn't have the tools, the experience, or the language to let it out. When you see it in an artwork, it says to you, you exist; the thing that you feel is real. The thing that you feel exists, and you exist. It roots you into a relationship with the world that is fundamental, intimate, and deep, and potentially paradigm-shifting.

So, sensing into that invisible yet thick space of imagination, ideas, and immateriality; between disciplines but also further afield, between everything, is where "the work" takes place.

I'm obsessed with the attempt to sense the things that are here but we don't see, like a kind of haunted curatorial method. Filipa always reminds me that intellectual understanding provokes a kind of physical pleasure, so in a way, I'm actually a seeker of pleasure in this too—if I'm completely honest—in the midst of all the metabolizing and everything else.   Well, that could be a great message for institutions as spaces of pleasure! Rescuing a little of the grief that comes from looking at the picture of where institutions are nowadays, besieged by overburdening bureaucracies and over-politicization, defunding, etc.

You are working by intervening or parasitizing into different realities, although you do have this continued commitment to one specific institution. What is the relationship between the two courses of action?   The answer that I give you might need to change over time. With the General Ecology project, the Serpentine behaved as a kind of incubator that allowed it to develop somewhat unsupervised. This allowed it to feel genuinely experimental, and will, I think, remain the greater legacy of the project over time.

The Serpentine is also a home and a base through which to experiment with elements of institutional transformation or prototyping that you can only do when you know really deeply all the loopholes and all the idiosyncrasies of an organization. This can sometimes prove extremely frustrating, especially when the "desire" for this kind of work wanes according to other priorities (funding, audiences, etc.). At other times, something just cascades into something else, and before you know it, you've achieved more than you could ever hope to. It's up and down.

The independent projects fulfill a tactical distribution of those ideas, a testing out of some of the propositions incubated through the research-led aspect of the Serpentine work, in contexts that are radically unfamiliar. It also allows for collaboration with peers and institutions that I deeply admire. So, for instance, I'm now working on a project called Sites of Practice (2024) convened by E-WERK Luckenwalde, as a form of microfunding and a support structure for art and design-led experiments across ecology and pedagogy—and hopefully, in time, it will become a pedagogical unfolding for philanthropic institutions that want to work at the deeper level of cultural and systemic emergence.

It was made possible by an EU-specific funding called Arising Quo, and E-WERK Luckenwalde itself, as an organization, was a perfect convenor because of its experimentations with energy and with its own infrastructure.

2   Keller Easterling, *Medium Design: Knowing How to Work on the World*, Verso, 2021.

I'm always drawn by love and by connection. If there's a project that's floating about and that I would love to do, I'll always do my best to find a place for it that's as adherent to its needs as possible.   One of the goals of these conversations is really to try to enucleate perspectives and approaches that hopefully could become of inspiration for others.

The pandemic was really a watershed in that it created a whole new history for institutions, as it cannot be understood purely as an externality, a moment when I fear we have missed an opportunity to affect real change. Unfortunately, I see a system reverting back into old habits by creating really polarized scenarios in a risk-averse culture that is everywhere. And this is happening also in spaces of culture because they are places of political agency. What advice would you share with your peers?   I'm going to try to answer your question from two different standpoints. The first is practical, compassionate advice to individuals and colleagues who are trying to weave this work into institutions. I will "gift forward" a piece of advice that was, in turn, gifted to me by Grégory Castéra, a friend and professional I very much admire, whose practice focuses on commoning. He came to London at a time when I was particularly grumpy because of the increasing precarity of institutional funding for this work and the impoverishment of public attention for the ecological due to the inevitable power of the populist version of it all. In the face of all of that, I was complaining about how broken it all seemed. At that point, Grégory interrupted me and said, "you've been doing this work for 10 years, so you are more of an expert in this space than the latest and loudest. Remember this and remember to stay the course."

That is exactly the advice that I would offer to any individual who is interested in doing this work. It's going to be frictional. It will always feel like an uphill battle because you're trying to have a deep relationship with this work, whereas in order to be recognized, popular, and well-funded, you need to say what is wanted of you, not what is needed by the wider metabolism. That sense of purpose that you hold will steer you through these obstacles and is really important.

For institutions, I have nothing but the most abstract of advice, and that is to try and make the exercise of focusing on the ultimate sort of mission something really far away and really unachievable. Say a museum's mission was to strive for planetary justice and balance and to do it through art or culture. How would that affect the museum's aims and implementations in its long-term strategy? How would it affect its decisions at more practical strategic levels? Going through this kind of exercise would, I think, make a huge difference to institutions that are currently, as all are doing, prioritizing their own survival over the thriving of the whole metabolism.

NON-EXTRACTIVE ARCHITECTURE

Principles and labels of sustainability aim at reprogramming the language of making, from agriculture to textile manufacturing, by pressing scrutiny over the environmental and social impact of material chains of production and distribution. The negative toll that the building and construction industry adds to the anthropogenic exhaustion of Earth (37% of total carbon emissions globally) calls for a radical rethinking of architecture's systemic dependencies on resource extraction and the establishment of remedial frameworks that move beyond the bureaucratic arbitrage of energy-efficiency certifications. As a worldwide reckoning with the imperatives of mitigation, repair, and reuse becomes increasingly vital to contrast ecosystemic collapse, on what values does an architecture of renewal and regeneration build itself?

Attendant reflections demand a reconciliation of architectural practice and discourse with an ethical framework of purposefulness and an agential reorientation of its methods toward a stewardship of the built environment that minimizes waste and depletion, and tasks itself with integrating material and technological solutions that support processes of territorial and social inclusion. The Non-Extractive Architecture platform, initiated by the research studio Space Caviar since 2021, has deployed a variety of cultural formats to collectively investigate the varied ramifications of these assumptions. The project started as a process-led exhibition in the spaces of the now-disbanded V-A-C Foundation in Venice, upon the invitation of its then director Francesco Manacorda. Supported by his desire to contribute critically to the conversations instigated by the city's Biennale cycles, the project operated through a concatenated series of initiatives that, through an international research residency, discursive events, material labs, editorial and public programming, disclosed the ongoing research process with a multidisciplinary community of experts and practitioners, as well as publics. The eponymous book[1] is a "collective manifesto" by participants and contributors around its titular investigation "on designing without depletion." Non-Extractive Architecture advocates for an architecture of resourcefulness based on circularity, adaptive reuse, and material choices that honor the ingenuity of ancestral and vernacular knowledge, as much as the adoption of technological breakthroughs, all the while demarcating a role for architecture to truly perform as an agent of economic and social transformation. The currently operative instantiation of the project is the Non-Extractive Architecture(s) Directory, an ongoing digital platform developed in collaboration with the non-profit re:arc institute, which collates practices and findings categorized along five investigative themes and can also be browsed by physical location. It is, most significantly, the embodiment of a widely distributed network across global regions, evidencing how alternative paradigms to a corporatized architecture of scale, fame, and exploitation already exist.

The Directory, which will be further activated and replenished with case studies in its next-phase development, belongs to an increasingly emergent group of independently run initiatives that invest in knowledge-building and connective infrastructures around urgent research agendas that most professional and pedagogical establishments are failing to offer. These include subjects like placemaking and community building, adaptive reuse and restoration, intersectional studies, and decolonial practices that address topics of labor, gender, and racial equity.

1   Space Caviar (eds), *Non-Extractive Architecture. On Designing Without Depletion*, Sternberg Press, 2021.

Expanded Pedagogies

IV

Advocacy across Art, Design, and **Science**
Conversation I

I'd like to start by describing in broader terms the evolution of TBA21's institutional ecosystem. Starting from Francesca Thyssen-Bornemisza's interest in a specific modality of collecting geared towards supporting creators whose work explores pressing social and environmental issues, until today when it has evolved into an art and advocacy foundation that does truly unique work akin to a form of cultural activism. Can you walk us through the core early steps?

TBA21 was founded in 2002 by Francesca, who marks the fourth generation of art collectors in her family. Francesca's understanding of what art can do is deeply influenced by a sentence her father wrote in the introduction to an exhibition catalog where he states that he is convinced the exchange of cultural goods will lead to the opening up of audiences' horizons, facilitate cultural diplomacy, and contribute to the process of world peace. Fast-forward to 2002, Francesca founded TBA21 as a collection that was always meant to live in the public sphere, as a public service. She wanted to work very closely with the artists themselves, not just buying objects but really being involved in the process, developing ideas, and realizing more and more complex works. Daniela Zyman joined as chief curator and artistic director very early when it became clear that the emphasis was on non-Western positions, starting from Eastern Europe, then the Indian subcontinent and South America. Obviously, when you start being engaged with artists that have a research-based practice, whose work is heavily process-oriented, you quickly become very engaged with political people, individuals that work in a political public sphere.

So they started doing something that became integral to how TBA21 evolved, which were yearly convenings in Lopud, a small island in Croatia, 45 minutes from Dubrovnik. This was itself important because during the siege of Dubrovnik, Francesca opened a restoration lab in the old city where they would safekeep and restore Renaissance paintings of the city. The seminars would consist of around 40 people, with no press or public, during which they would present the programming and the thinking of the next year to a group of expert friends and colleagues.

What was the turning point when you joined in 2019, and can you explain how you decided to tackle the ocean as a discursive environment to guide the actions of the foundation? When I entered the foundation, I was really struck by the openness, which was based on having your ideas scrutinized by a group of people in a very intimate setting in a way that everybody could be very candid and didn't have to worry about what was on social media the next day. This scrutiny affected the programming of the next year. So, you had an organization that was willing to open up its thinking to a collectivity and was agile and dynamic enough to incorporate what it was hearing and responsive enough to change itself if needed.

When we were approaching the ten-year anniversary, there was a request to imagine a new project that would operate very differently from what was done before, which was mainly commissioning groups of artists, producing, and exhibiting them.

At that time, there was already the Anthropocene Observatory at HWK (Haus der Kulturen der Welt, Berlin) and other projects that opened up the question of the environment, and so we reflected on the key concerns and values of the foundation to shape a new brief that became more political in a sense, because a lot of artists were working from the micro to the macro politics of domestic violence, the questions of peace in a really global or larger sense. At the same time, there was also a keen interest in opening up spaces for transdisciplinary exchange.

We asked ourselves what system within the environment embodies this change, this fluidity, and this is how we came to the idea of the ocean as a fluid system that is intricately interconnected, where you could trace the causes and effects of change. The ocean became both an arena, a topic, as well as a conceptual tool to untether ourselves from land-based linear binaries and really think with fluidity; that's what the ocean invites you to do if you take it very seriously. And to do so, we then were able to use a boat to think from and with the ocean, from and with change, rather than sitting in studios, offices, or laboratories of universities; this field immersion was super important. And then the other aspect was to avoid immediately going into production, having this experience and producing something and somehow falling into the trap that every impression immediately needs to be converted into work.

This was the birth of TBA21–Academy, which is the research arm within TBA21 that, in the beginning, dedicated its program exclusively to the ocean. We would invite artists working on the ocean to the boat to be there for at least two weeks at a time. And around their interests, we would assemble teams of scientists, environmentalists, legal experts, etc. **It would be valuable to explain this paradigm that seems to me to have kept informing the organic evolution of TBA21. It is this mode of encounter and collaborative construct that originates in the scientific expedition. This attempt at building transdisciplinary cohorts of people working together has later deepened into your methodologies. What were the values early on that you believe you have retained?** I think the biggest values are time and personal connections. What I mean is that all we do is based on relationships and time. If there is an interesting practice, an interesting artist, an interesting conversation, we would engage on the smallest scale possible and give that relationship the time to grow, understanding more and more about people and their interests. We were able to put people together with others to stimulate and support conversations that were moderated, mediated, and facilitated. That was one of the realizations, and the other was working long-term. That very much stayed, and I think in that moment when art and science collaborations were very fashionable, we knew that despite the use of the same language or terminology, the meaning was completely different. You cannot just put some people from different disciplines together and think they will figure it out somehow. It was very clear from the beginning that we wanted to support research-based practices, and we became the facilitators of these practices. And as facilitators, we needed to ask ourselves, is it enough to just produce works and exhibit them? Or do we have a different responsibility? That is where the advocacy part of TBA21's work started.

This advocacy work has become a parallel element, as we aimed to open up different channels and avenues to engage by creating conservation sites, by officially becoming the first art organization to be granted Observer Status by the International Seabed Authority, by creating educational programs, and so on.   I am interested in this facet of the initiative, willing to make itself a valuable public asset. TBA21–Academy was born in 2011, and a few years later, you opened a physical site in Venice, Ocean Space. With regard to the issue of audiences today, and the clear rise of research-based practices, how do we create engagement with the public around this type of work, aesthetic sensibilities, and modes of storytelling that confront the planetary paradigm? How do you deal with the layered communities you have now long engaged and craft a sensible communication with such diversity?   It's on a case-by-case basis. On the one hand, we have our commitment to Venice through Ocean Space and various other spaces we engage with and try to create meaningful dialogues between these.

Like The Current, which is a curatorial fellowship program we have been running now for ten years, first throughout Oceania, the Mediterranean, and currently the Caribbean, The Current has been thought of as a catalyst to trigger even longer trajectories and processes beyond its runtime of three years. For example, Ute Meta Bauer was the first curatorial fellow of The Current, which led to TBA21 commissions with Armin Linke and Joan Jonas, but also to independent and still ongoing research projects investigating the relationship between the climate crisis and cultural loss. Last season, we presented the findings in a research exhibition at Ocean Space, including a special edition of the *Comparative Law Journal of the Pacific.*

At the level of policymakers, scientists, etc., these are completely different audiences, and I think there was, and still is, a question of validation. By becoming hyperspecialized, it is very difficult for members of different disciplines to meet, build trust, and work together.

Again, it is a question of time and personal relationships. We have found incredible collaborators over the years from science, policy, and conservation, but it has taken a dedicated effort on all sides to build these relationships.

The Ocean Space wants to act on the hypothesis that art and culture can be these accelerants in transformative processes, but that these processes are based on relationships between people and their environment. In Venice, obviously, we didn't have to make a case for working through the arts and with artists. And Venice happened (2019) when we opened a very prominent frontline of climate change in Europe. Public programs of contemporary art centers have the freedom to bring members of different disciplines to the fore to unfold the topics embedded in the exhibitions. The question becomes how to make it relevant for the different audiences we are trying to engage and serve. Therefore, we work through different activities and involve different communities of practice. This includes conservation efforts in the lagoon, food practices, involving local associations in the programs, as well as close collaborations with the local marine institute, universities, and art schools. We experiment with more-than-human governance forms like the zoöp, which is based on regenerative principles. This is how we try to build engagement.

Can you explain the connection with your pedagogical and research explorations (The Current) and the advocacy work that you have been clearly getting more and more engaged with in recent years? The way The Current is structured now is in three-year cycles. Each year is made up of two moments: a moment of collective and collaborative field research and a moment of sharing, which takes the shape of a small festival. This fourth cycle (2023–25) is investigating emancipatory processes in the Caribbean and the role of the ocean. In the second year, we focus on the network and prepare the ground for the exhibition in year three. In parallel, we run an online educational program called Ocean Uni, which is dedicated to art, activism, and science that invites fluid thinking with the ocean as a way to move beyond the binaries of land and sea. Ocean Uni's curriculum provides students, researchers, and the public access to wide-ranging ideas and explorations through regular live sessions, reading groups, small-scale workshops, or activations. It is accessible through the online platform Ocean-Archive.org.

Year three is the exhibition, which usually features two new commissions that are developed and produced in parallel to the ongoing research. This opens a window, mainly for Venetian communities and international visitors to the exhibition. Because there is an abundance of relationships created, topics surface from these encounters. Working along these long-term engagements between many different disciplines gives us the opportunity to find practices, concerns, and avenues to engage with.

These are the topics that we try to commit ourselves to within this framework of conferences, COPs, United Nations Ocean Conferences, and so on. So the question then becomes, how do you bring this kind of thinking, which embraces complexity—these slow, relational practices—into emergence? **So, is this a way for you to measure impact? Are recognitions like the one from the International Seabed Authority forms of assessment that supplant metrics of ticket sales, for example?** Yes, the advocacy work, the European projects, and the international policy projects become avenues to demonstrate the question of impact. In the beginning, getting there was not a marker for us, but retroactively, when you look at it, we're the first and only cultural organization that leads a work package within a Horizon Europe project. We are the only cultural organization that was on the advisory board for the mission Healthy Ocean of the European Commission. All of these things are markers of impact. I believe, as a private foundation, we have the opportunity to challenge the role that organizations play and bridge the gaps between disciplines. **Absolutely, and it is the purpose of this publication to start gathering experiences and perspectives around why it is so essential that we recast institutions of culture within the wider civic and political system, where they are recognized for the social and economic value they can produce.**

When it comes to the specifics of the cultural field, what are the new alliances and collaborations that can support this argument and reinforce the value of culture in democratic discourse? And what is the most urgent, critical facet that cultural institutions need to act upon today? Two things. On the one hand, there are the governance structures of cultural organizations. The way most institutions and organizations are built is based on an idea of competition.

Public funding has been decreasing dramatically over the last few decades, and therefore many cultural organizations have to become tourism businesses, which actually not only perpetuate a completely unsustainable overtourism effect but also become reliant on this model. Beyond that, institutions need to compete with each other to have a profile and a unique selling point. This is ingrained in the structure of many museums. Creating structural conditions for multiscalar collaborations will become increasingly important, and our institutions are not built for that.

I think it is time to reshape the governance of collaboration, support engaged practices, and rethink the roles of collections. It is important to involve artists in this thinking to serve them and for cultural institutions to become more responsive and remain relevant. For me, the public-private cooperations remain interesting because of the different dynamics, which are often difficult. This means that everyone involved is willing to experiment and take risks, as well as being prepared to face difficulties. I think that is what we're currently seeing within the Bauhaus of the Seas program, a large-scale Horizon Europe project where the consortium is trying to create the conditions for co-creation among cultural, academic and educational institutions, and municipalities. In these experiments, it's helpful to be clear about everyone's role and understand which partner can mitigate risks for the others. This demands trust, though, and with very short delivery timelines, that is difficult to establish.   There are two last topics I'd like to tackle. First, what real potential do you see in this New European Bauhaus program, where you are one of its so-called six Lighthouse projects, i.e., pilot programs to test these interdisciplinary, trans-sectoral coalitions?

The other is the motivation that brought you to establish *Organismo*, the new project launched in 2023, which attempts to take this research-oriented, transdisciplinary approach into the generation of real-life outcomes with other partners, public and private. I am interested in its connection with what I see as an emergent and necessary remedy to reinforce processes and conduits that can function as aggregators of collective knowledge to deliver impact-driven results—something that the corporate, academic, or political systems alone clearly cannot deliver.

Ultimately, knowingly or unknowingly, the New European Bauhaus has opened a door to make this kind of collaboration possible. Critically speaking, all experimentation and innovation are stifled if you have to declare what the result will be three years in advance.

There seems to be an understanding that to engage with the converging crises, we need to change the ways we operate, but there are structural challenges that make radical experimentation within the public sphere increasingly difficult. And so, this is why we don't simply become an advocacy organization. This is where working with artists offers us opportunities that we otherwise wouldn't have, and being a private organization gives us the possibility to integrate our learnings more structurally, which in turn we can leverage in collaborations. At the end of the day, artists materialize ideas. They capture moments, and I mean not moments like in a photograph but political, environmental, societal moments.

As for our experimental independent study program, *Organismo*, it connects research, theory, and speculation through a series of focused case studies—regenerative interventions that explore different forms of alliance. The project aims to explore new methodologies and configurations of actors when working in the service of ecological transformation. Its foundational hypothesis is that the work of artists reinvigorating interdisciplinary projects has great potential to contribute to cultural paradigm shifts that can instigate new ways of inhabiting the planet and embrace both complexity and inclusivity. It tries to collapse the timeline between thinking and doing. Usually, there is a long moment of explanation, where theory gets translated into practical application. We wanted to collapse this timeline and have a space where thinking and doing happen in the same space, in a kind of very open intergenerational moment of co-learning that we co-design with a number of partners.

This is another experiment in radical collaboration initiated by a private foundation and a national museum but involves the ministry of culture, associations, commercial entities, and foundations. It is led by us in the sense that we are providing a dedicated team that facilitates the conversations and programs the public moments, but it's a massive collective effort.

Advocacy across Art, Design, and **Science**
Conversation II

Tell me about your relationship with the city of Madrid. How has its cultural landscape evolved in the past few years, given that you have been involved with it on different levels and within different institutional realities, and how does TBA21 fit into this picture now that you have joined it? I am interested in the fact that your work has often challenged conventional institutional formats.

My first experience with a public institution was at the Centre de Cultura Contemporània de Barcelona (CCCB —Barcelona Centre of Contemporary Culture), where I worked as director of exhibitions and curated several projects. These weren't just focused on contemporary art; they touched on architecture, literature, and cultural studies —fields that are part of my academic background. I've always had this natural drive to connect different disciplines.

Over time, I realized that these public institutions can often feel rigid and slow to respond, so, with a group of curators, we started experimenting with the idea of "temporary platforms" or "temporary institutions" within the institution itself. The idea was to investigate a specific theme or concern for a certain period of time through exhibitions and public programs, bringing those conversations to the media and to other less evident contexts of the city, with the communities close to CCCB acting as loudspeakers.

At CCCB, our goal was to function as a research center of the present—to explore its conflicts, crises, and open dilemmas. We wanted to use cultural resources and various knowledge-producing communities as tools for interpretation and diagnosis. But more importantly, we aimed to provide a space for deep political and ethical debates and for testing possible responses—ideas that could point towards alternative futures.

That's how I started a series of interdisciplinary projects called *Serie Beta*. This initiative brought together artistic and cultural creation, scientific research, and social innovation. Some examples include *Big Bang Data* (2014–15), *More Humans: The Future of Our Species* (2015–16), and *After the End of the World* (2017–18), which tackled the climate crisis through art, speculative design, literature, and research.

For instance, with *Big Bang Data*, we explored the topic of big data—something that, at the time, very few people were working on. We created collaborative formats, bringing together educational institutions, universities, companies, and practitioners—basically anyone engaged with the subject. That's when I understood the transformative power of cultural institutions: their ability to bring relevant concepts and issues to the forefront of public discussion, using participatory and collective approaches. These "temporary institutions" didn't just engage communities; they also helped to evolve the institution itself.

When I came to Madrid, I found a very different city, one with an enormous substratum of independent collectives and a thriving community of artists focused on participatory initiatives already in motion. Many of these were connected to the 15-M political movement, with several organized around the Center Medialab.

I was appointed artistic director at the Center for Contemporary Creation Matadero, Madrid, where there was a particularly interesting program called Intermediæ, which had been running for over 20 years. It brought together what felt like an army of artists working with diverse communities across the city. At the same time, Madrid had a very progressive government under Mayor Manuela Carmena, who sought to decentralize culture, focusing on better understanding neighborhoods and their unique needs. Recognizing the potential of the Intermediæ program as a vehicle for this, the government significantly reinforced it with additional resources. This period marked a moment of cultural mapping—an effort to understand the city's needs in terms of cultural infrastructure. It was an incredibly productive time, with a renewed emphasis on connecting artistic practice to the everyday lives of Madrid's communities.

When I arrived, Matadero was a lively, festive place but not very speculative or reflective in its approach to programming. I tried to develop research lines to work with, one of them on critical ecologies. I was then connected to the people from the environmental department of the city council as they wanted to be associated with a cultural institution to engage with climate-awareness topics that were pushed through the 2030 European agenda.

So, in 2019, I put together The Mutant Institute of Environmental Narratives (IMNA) to work with different people inside the city council, and I got the Polytechnic University of Madrid and various creative communities involved. And because we did it in partnership with the university, we ensured its continuity even after I left, which was part of my vision to emancipate the program itself. IMNA is the artistic laboratory for the climate of the city of Madrid. It proposes new ways of storytelling to address the environmental challenge through formats such as exhibitions, podcasts, or workshops, and this is very important, urban naturalization strategies.

You need to be very strategic from the beginning when you are working for specific public institutions and understand that everything can suddenly change because it is very connected to politics. In these kinds of municipal centers, like Matadero, there is no space between the municipality and you; there is no protection, like a board, or a long-term shared vision and strategy.

You are now in a private context with TBA21—what was your expectation in joining the organization, and what potential did you see there for what you wanted to do? First of all, working in a private foundation offers independence and flexibility, allowing you to respond to needs in real time. TBA21 is both visionary and adaptable, unlike many top-down foundations that require reality to conform to their structures. I appreciate how we work with artists, creating spaces of care and supporting their research in collaborative practices.

Together with Markus Reymann, we're shaping a new direction, in the awareness that now is the moment for collaboration. For our activities in Madrid, this also means becoming key partners of the Thyssen-Bornemisza National Museum, with whom we have been collaborating for several years through a joint program of exhibitions.

TBA21 is an international foundation that established its headquarters in Madrid two years ago (2022). When developing new programs, we understood the importance of bringing in TBA21–Academy, the foundation's research arm focused on ecologies, by deploying it as an incubator for collaborative inquiry, artistic production, and environmental advocacy with the practices it has been cultivating for over 15 years. We understood our role would be to act as the glue for initiatives already taking place within the Spanish context. There is an abundance of talented people working in interdisciplinary fields—from architects and designers to researchers and philosophers—who deserve to be supported and connected to our international network.

This is how Organismo: Art in Applied Critical Ecologies was conceived. It is not only a program of independent studies that we run with the Thyssen-Bornemisza National Museum, but also an initiative driven by our ambition to create a movement of collaboration focused on transitions related to ecology and social change. For Organismo, we have invited participants from the arts and sciences as well as other fields. Through applied case studies, we aim to bring together diverse entities and institutions in Spain, such as museums, art and science foundations, and universities, that are curious to explore how these practices can benefit them and how they might be integrated into their structures.

This is especially important to us: not to create new institutions but to help transform existing ones—those that have already worked hard to connect with audiences and communities, involving artists for their capacity to radically reimagine our current planetary systems and our way of inhabiting.   What I find interesting is that TBA21 has built an institutional structure organically, founded on a methodology of work that has been present ever since the beginning, which is connected to this idea of generating alliances between not just disciplines but with the particular experiences that creativity carries with it. Like the dimension of the scientific expedition (which was part of the projects commissioned by the foundation in the early 2010s), it is based on small clusters of people who share a mission intensely.

In this moment, when you are engaged on so many fronts—with the creative community, with governmental or public entities, and with private ones—how important is a reflection on defining your audiences? I find this is a critical aspect, particularly now that many institutions are increasingly asked to perform for audiences at large, and so they are pressured to behave in ways that are not necessarily integral to their original mandates.   TBA21 brings to Madrid artists and practitioners who are not part of the Spanish scene, mostly from nonEuropean contexts. We want to be complementary and instrumental to the city's cultural ecosystem. We aim to connect our international network with the local context, which is something that is needed.

Also, when you design projects collaboratively, like we do with Organismo by engaging agents from different contexts and disciplines, you already have the audience because you bring many different contexts together with their communities.   Organismo is the last instantiation of this course of institutional transformation that has been really shape-shifting and, more importantly, not necessarily anchored to one individual space.

So, who are your interlocutors or end receivers? Organismo seems to predicate itself on the idea that we are in a moment when we cannot really support and communicate the importance of culture unless we transform the perspective of those who are already supporters of culture.   Yes, absolutely. Organismo works with real-life cases in ecological transformation, highlighting how important and disruptive it is to bring creative people, in the widest sense, into the conversations. So, this is our goal as a foundation: to affirm the presence of the artists in conversations around the past, present, and future and show a different idea of what an artist can do in such a context.

Some of the institutions involved in the case studies were initially taken aback, but as you mentioned, our operational approach is firmly rooted in conviviality, collaboration, and experimentation. This is something that many people within public institutions cannot afford to do, as there is often no room for risk-taking. Instead, we are the ones who can take those risks: we actively seek out creatives to collaborate with and build new contexts by introducing innovative ways of thinking and doing.

We have a proven track record in our trajectory, which has earned us trust. People recognize that the projects we undertake are ambitious and that we are committed to building advocacy around the transformative potential of culture.   You have built your institutional governance to rethink and affect systemic work, and that is an act of design in the sense that the multivocality you bring to certain real-life projects is led through research-oriented processes founded on the proposition that no real impact can be generated unless this polymorphous cluster of know-how and perspectives can be brought to the table.   An anecdote: when I was leading the Mutant Institute, we jointly presented a project with the Polytechnic University and the City of Madrid for a European initiative aimed at combating climate change. The organization highlighted that it was the first time a cultural institution had been involved in such a project, which are typically led by urban planners, engineers, and others. Their response was pivotal: "We will support your project because a cultural institution is involved. After many years of work, we've learned that the challenges we face are not technical or economic; they are cultural. We need a cultural change." This is the key point: addressing climate change cannot happen without a cultural shift.   In recent years, you have also increasingly worked on positioning TBA21 across relationships with intergovernmental institutions that build awareness and lobby for change at a higher level in the political sphere. What difference can TBA21 make at these kinds of tables, given the plethora of international events and organizations that already exist in tackling topics around social and environmental justice? What is the added value you can bring?   Change can be triggered on a small scale, as we do hyper-locally with these cases in *Organismo*, or it can be done on very important platforms, which, however, still work in silos. In the current context of polycrisis, working on advocacy and creating synergies between disciplines is the only way to address global challenges. There is a clear need and opportunity to create a new mechanism that consolidates fragmented knowledge from multiple reports and numerous stakeholders to address the priority needs of decision-makers.

For several years now, we have had observer status in international organizations dedicated to ocean legislation and have participated in numerous working groups at international conferences. We have a gift: the support of our President, Francesca Thyssen-Bornemisza, who has relevance in many contexts and wants to use it to facilitate our participation in these international platforms because of the need to bring culture and the arts into these debates.

The mandate received from the French government to lead the work on art, science, and philanthropy for the UN Ocean Conference to be held in Nice in June 2025, for example, represents a timely opportunity to develop this work. This international appointment, together with other institutional roles in the EU and UN frameworks, entails a high level of exposure for us and a huge responsibility.

You are also part of the new European Bauhaus program with the Bauhaus of the Seas Sails chapter. Recently, you were part of a relevant closed-door meeting in Brussels titled Archipelago of the Future (2024), and I know you came away with a degree of skepticism around its outcomes. Why? I've been working in this context for 30 years, and I sometimes see that practitioners of culture are trying to create silos again. I saw this again with the Art and Science and Technology division, and it feels like we are still in the 20th century. Also, there was no diversity at all; we were the usual suspects, the same people who have been working on this for the past 20 years, so it's a pity that we cannot find 20-year-olds involved in these very subjects. Even the artists that were presented were almost all in their 40s, so where is the new generation?

Also, the language that is used within these kinds of networks is very restrictive for me, and I think that you can find qualities and people doing important work who do not self-describe as fitting into the art, science, and technology configuration.

It's like the new people doing new things are there but don't have access to these very complicated European programs, and so they do things without support. And I think that is why participation in the Organismo program was so high.

The institutions that were there at the meeting didn't seem to be very connected to these notions; they were proposing new spaces for new institutions for these kinds of novel practices. I don't think we need need more institutions; we need to transform the ones that we already have. As soon as these practices are institutionalized, they lose their sense of risk and opportunity. So, I think the way we need to work is by supporting the collectives that are already making things happen. This more organic distribution needs to be protected; the life that runs through these networks needs to be protected.   I find this extremely important, the idea that transformative action comes from within in recurrent cycles, because the moment you try to institutionalize it, it becomes averse to change.   This is a lesson for me. I think it is very important to choose the place where you can enact change. You don't need a big scale. It is not necessary to establish a new institution with a huge representative building; it's better to occupy an existing reality and just go out and make things happen. It is a moment to think and do at the same time. This is crucial because, otherwise, the temporal reality of the institution and that of society are never connected.

The thing I love about TBA21 is this idea that we don't mind if we cannot say what we'll be doing in five years. We don't want to know it. This is how the Foundation has been working since the beginning: reacting and trying to sense the needs out there. One thing that I tried to explain in this Archipelago meeting is that private and public partnerships are now more important than ever. This idea of bringing people from different contexts also opens up to different audiences—I really dislike this 'preaching' approach of talking to the converted.

This European project, the Bauhaus of the Seas Sails, in which we are involved with many other partners, can be productive because we work with municipalities and people who have never connected with our approaches. So, if at the end of two years, say, the municipality of Oeiras in Portugal (which is part of the program) decided that instead of building the Museum of the River Tejo, the river itself could be a museum, it could be intercepted, lived in, and cared for through a program in a more experiential way "without bringing a new thematic construction there," then we'll have succeeded.

"Architecture is political by default." This statement by Cruz Garcia, one half of WAI Architecture Think Tank, which together with Nathalie Frankowski is the studio behind the establishment of Loudreaders, encapsulates the wider theoretical and practical implications that the project aims to tackle and the historical acriticality that ensconces architecture's deep imbrication with the political and socioeconomic manufacturing of Euro-American hegemonies.

Originally incubated as the collaborative work of the Post-Novis Collective presented in an exhibition held in 2019,[1] the initiative officially launched during the outbreak of Covid-19 in 2020. Loudreaders is an independent pedagogical platform and itinerant school taking aim at the structural asymmetries that still support the architecture profession and its educational system as products of colonial oppression, which perpetuate protocols of access and research founded on narratives of racialized difference and exclusionary spatial practices of planning and policing. Loudreaders targets head-on the implicit biases of architecture academia and its elite culture, proposing educational curricula and methodologies that support inclusive, relational forms of learning across multidisciplinary articulations.

The project takes its name from the performative exercise of *lectores* that, at the turn of the 20th century, entertained fellow tobacco workers across the Caribbean from the monotony of their daily job by reading out loud, only to become a widespread itinerant practice of vocational education that nurtured networks of political and communal solidarity infused with anti-colonial, anti-capitalist sentiments of emancipation. Taking inspiration from this self-organized form of pedagogical resistance, Loudreaders is organized as a series of curated seminars, workshops, talks, discussions, and cultural programs of hybrid nature that support various researchers, thinkers, activists, and practitioners devoted to building scholarly and programmatic knowledge that champions histories long suppressed, marginalized, or instrumentalized by dominant narratives and institutions.

Their *A Manual of Anti-Racist Architecture Education* (2020)[2] is a manifesto and toolkit of decolonizing measures that center intersectional studies in re-examining modern architecture history, exposing the relationships between racialized and class precarity and unequal parameters of access to quality work and education in the field. "My dream university is one that has a white studies department," stated Garcia during a lecture at Columbia GSAPP in 2023, addressing how the polarizing implications of white supremacy, settler colonialism, and racism, which are still pervasive in our contemporary socio-political debates and ecosystems—zoning laws, access to services, resources, infrastructures—remain part of a common history that has been arbitrarily normalized.

Having successfully registered as a non-profit by raising funds from institutional grants and donors, Loudreaders piloted the first annual Trans-Caribbean School in Puerto Rico in the summer of 2023. Garcia and Frankowski were also the first recipients of the Association of Collegiate Schools of Architecture's (ACSA) Faculty Fellowship to Advance Equity in Architecture. Through the grant, they will be able to further amplify their outreach and collaborations, which already include publishing books, the biannual *Loudreaders Journal*,[3] and the online platform where all archival documentation is made freely available.

1   More on the collective at https://waithinktank.com/Post-Novis.
2   The manual and other imprints are downloadable at https://loudreaders.com/.
3   More about the journal and the development of Loudreaders at https://e-flux.com/architecture/loudreading/.

Black Atlantic Speaker Series

In 2017 Lesley Lokko launched *FOLIO: Journal of Contemporary African Architecture* during her tenure as director of the Graduate School of Architecture at the University of Johannesburg, which she had established two years prior. In her first op-ed, she wrote: "The aim is to present a view of a continent bound not so much by the conditions, challenges, and contexts that define it, but by the sheer range of positions *that don't*." The explorative and somewhat unconstructed dimension of potentiality and self-determination that this sentence reveals is where her indefatigable efforts to reshape the canonical narratives and methods of architecture education reside. A pluri-awarded educator and writer, Lokko has taught in the UK, USA, and Africa for almost 30 years, advocating for structural reforms in Western pedagogical institutions by championing histories and practices from the Global South, supporting modes of learning, thinking, and building that are civic-minded, purposeful, and inclusive, and making themes of culture, identity, race, and gender part of the curriculum.

The African Futures Institute (AFI), which she founded in 2021 in Accra, Ghana, where she grew up, is an educational organization that channels her intellectual rigor through programs that both serve the booming continent and its future professionals, as well as position the African experience into global conversations around urbanity, citizenship, and planetary co-existence centered on decolonizing and decarbonizing practices. The Institute anchors its actions around clusters of knowledge from Africa and its Diaspora, and by rewarding the connective energy of peer-to-peer support, transgenerational exchange, and practice-led learning, it builds its own foundations on the transformative premise of shared ambitions, goals, and values. As the composition of its boards (trustees, patrons, advisors) demonstrates, the Institute aims at reconfiguring the hierarchies of knowledge and conversations among various stakeholders involved in what Lokko has termed the "laboratory of the future"[1]—from engineers and builders to academicians, established and emergent talents.

First programs have focused on dialogue—Pan African and Black Atlantic Speaker series (2021–23), among others—and archival projects like The PinPoint Directory, an ongoing list of practitioners and thinkers in Africa that critically address the built environment, concomitantly producing research around archival work and representation. Speaking History is instead an academic initiative that redresses and augments the Eurocentric canon with quality research and resources around urban and architectural studies of Africa and the African Diaspora. The creation of the African Architectural and Urban History Network is tasked with giving lasting impact to such efforts.

Lokko speaks affectively of educators' critical role in shaping the spaces, tools, and interactions that can truly inspire younger generations to believe in their collective agency as builders of their own future, from the perspective of their layered stories and situated experiences. The Nomadic African Studio, whose inaugural iteration is scheduled for the summer of 2025, is AFI's first attempt at a teaching model informed by Lokko's well-rehearsed principles of relational pedagogy.

1 Title of the 18th International Architecture Exhibition —La Biennale di Venezia, which Lokko curated in 2023, by spotlighting Africa and its generations of talents for the first time in the history of the Biennale.

Instituto A Gente Transforma

The Instituto A Gente Transforma (We Transform Institute) was formally established as an NGO in 2016 by the designers Marcelo Rosenbaum and Adriana Benguela, who deploy design methods in developing social programs of territorial and economic regeneration for the Indigenous communities of their native Brazil. Over 300 ethnic groups are custodians of the ancestral lands that are home to the world's most diverse biomes, the largest river system, and the most extensive virgin rainforest. They also remain gravely underserved peoples whose precarious livelihood, abated by enduring socioeconomic inequality and diatribes over land ownership, is a historically unresolved predicament that the country continues to battle.

"Today these communities are my only clients,"[1] says Rosenbaum, a designer of celebrity status who, since the early 2000s, has run a commercially successful practice servicing the private and corporate sectors.

The Instituto effectively took shape after the designer participated in one of the so-called 'immersions' organized by the Laboratório Piracema de Design, conceived since 2003 by the designer Heloísa Crocco and the artist Juan Alberto Nemer. This pioneering program brought interdisciplinary cohorts of creators into intensive sessions of cohabitation and collaboration with remote artisanal communities to co-create projects that would leverage socioeconomic impact in the long term. Inspired by this experience, Rosenbaum and Benguela started their first project under the aegis of the Instituto in 2011 in Várzea Queimada, a small agricultural settlement in the state of Piauí. To date, their activities have extended across 11 states, bringing to life 15 projects with over 170 partners. The Instituto promotes the crucial role of living traditions, ancestral techniques, and know-how as instruments for social emancipation and as generators of sustainable economic autonomy that can tie communities to their land and thereby contrast their material and cultural impoverishment.

These multi-year processes are shaped in close cooperation with local Indigenous leaderships and realized through the integral involvement of governmental agencies, cultural and financial institutions, philanthropic ventures, foundations, companies, and civic organizations. The Instituto is the agent of transformation and connection that enables design-led approaches to respond to localized needs and challenges, bringing pluri-disciplinary knowledge (from design to business strategy) into the careful definition of purposeful interventions which integrate buildings, products, pedagogical and cultural programs, trade ventures, circular manufacturing, and distribution planning. For example: two housing buildings for 540 children and teenagers at the Canuanã Farm School in Tocantins; the Projeto Menire focused on developing a Kayapó women-led economy in the Indigenous land of Menkragnoti built on community-based tourism; a project in Maceió for the upcycling of sururu shells, which have long posed an environmental hazard, turned into construction materials and products; Jalapoeira Apurada, a collection of objects created as an outcome of a partnership with WWF and three quilombola associations which brought together, for the first time, 37 women to revive the golden grass craftsmanship of the Cerrado region; or the Coleção Molongó, a brand of educational toys created by the Nova Colômbia community in the Mamirauá reserve to support children's development and locals' upskilling.

1   From a conversation between the author, Marcelo Rosenbaum, and Adriana Benguela (November 1, 2024).

Designing Alliances for Holistic Growth

Education has been central to your varied professional activities, and I would like you to share some reflections on where we are today with pedagogical practice and design. What are the key challenges, and especially what of the relationship between practice, pedagogy, and theory, and where are interesting interactions happening nowadays? I am very critical of current design education in general. Of course, you see interesting things happening, interesting students, and so on. But I don't see forward-looking educational models being implemented. New developments are, for me, not coming from traditional educational universities and schools. The problem has to do with the model that was elaborated over the years and is copy-pasted from one institute to another, which created a kind of bureaucratic, managerial approach, driven by a form of efficiency thinking in education. That is a general remark about education, by the way; that is not specific to design in itself. In a certain way, current design education is blocked because it's not bringing up new knowledge, so we have to rethink the model. I don't have an answer to what it could be if you ask me now, but let's say that the Black Mountain colleges of the 21st century—where curiosity, skepticism, and conviction as an attitude are fostered—still have to be born. Do you think that is connected to a form of identity crisis of design in general, which is always seeking a certain positioning within the wider field of so-called creative practices? No. I think an identity crisis is a very productive mode, as you really continuously question yourself. The problem is that the students are looking for that identity crisis, but the institutes that are there have a quite rigid definition of what it should be, and rather than provoking questions around it, they pretend to have the answer and take part in the discussion. Replying to the question of what design can be, what role it can play, what it can contribute, and what possibilities are opening up, that is something the bigger educational system is failing to deliver. More than many others, you have truly engaged with education in its meaning as "production and transfer of knowledge." Curatorial models that you have set forth in the past, like those for the biennales of Ljubljana (BIO

50—24th Biennial of Design Ljubljana, *3,2,1...Test*, 2014) or Istanbul (4th Istanbul Design Biennale, *A School of Schools*, 2018), are a clear example of that. How did they embody a true reflection or response to the times and contexts they were set in? Would those curatorial approaches still be valid nowadays? The quality of a biennial is that you can always reformulate a new proposal because it's this temporary, ephemeral institute that is very performative in producing statements, and the traditional educational systems you are referring to miss that flexibility. They might do it from time to time to the level of an assignment, but not as a structural way of working.

So, the biennale is a temporary zone that can be created to use the exhibition format as a place of experimentation for educational practices, and this is indeed what happened there. But they both were a kind of response to specific situations, at the same time very local and very global.

If we take the Biennale in Ljubljana, it was originally born out of a design competition between East and West, and what I tried to do was turn it into a collaborative project instead. It was and is important to move away from the idea of competition and rather promote cooperation. It was a time when new digital tools like Skype and Facebook were becoming widely used; we could start sharing documents and so on, and they were available for everyone to exchange internationally. At the same time, we were doing this biennial in a country, i.e., Slovenia, which was in a huge economic crisis, where designers did not even have a space to work. So, I thought to bring local and international creative communities together around topics related to everyday life. It was six months, 120 people, 11 teams. We created a very condensed situation to build international connections—after 10 years, many of those people still work together. They've built a network. That is the kind of impact that I would love to see after these events, something that can live forward. The image that I use often is the image of permaculture—it is based on a completely different model than the one we use in our Western contemporary society built around efficiency thinking.

For instance, our society is convinced that you have an efficient forest to maintain and exploit, like a standardized, predictable environment. We know at what time we have to harvest the monocultural forest with the same trees; they grow in the same way, and we will have a high profit. But that's an illusion because when there is a storm or a disease, they will all probably have that same disease. When you have a permaculture forest instead, you probably have five different trees, you have bushes, birds, you have bees, and many species, and when the disease or a storm arrives, what you still have afterward is a resilient, diverse community that keeps on supporting itself and communicating.

What I want to say is that many of the things I do are related to designing connections between different stakeholders that most of the time don't know what or how they will build together. So, there is no master plan, and it's very ambiguous what you put in the middle.

What I find interesting is also that these models allowed the Biennales' projects to emerge as practice, but also as critique and as a theory.

A few years later, you activated a similar strategy in Istanbul with the idea of enabling networks and communities. What was the context there?   When I started with Ljubljana, the status of the biennial itself was quite low. Although it is the oldest biennial of design in existence, it was not seen as an important event in itself. The Istanbul Design Biennial had a completely different impact.

One of the things I always ask myself with projects like these is how to frame them better, so I ask—what is the need? Why are we doing this? Why should we do this? In Istanbul, I accepted the job only after an extensive field trip in Turkey. I wanted to see the country, meet designers, and the architecture and craft communities; I wanted to feel what could be a need, and it was quite clear, after a short while, that education in that country was a big issue. Education as a place for plurality, for diversity, as a place for helping different opinions, as a place for doing things differently. This idea of the educational system had been step by step completely erased. Now we know that there was an agenda there; they were trying to shape a generation with one single opinion and standardize and normalize that course.

I thought it was highly political to do "a school of schools" to show that there were many possibilities of organizing educational processes and to use the exhibition as a free space for people who wanted to present something they could not do in the traditional state-organized institutes and to inspire the students, teachers, and professors who were step by step eliminated from that very system.

The thing was not to communicate this beforehand, not even during the Biennale, and just to do it and to say that 99 years after the Bauhaus was founded (the centennial of the Bauhaus was being celebrated the year after the Biennale opened), maybe it was time to think about other models. So, that is how I try to connect a very deep local need with something that goes on internationally. I thought it would be good to possibly set the discussions and the discourse for the year after so that we would not look back to it as something to simply celebrate.

Also, because John Dewey, a very inspiring figure in the field of art pedagogy who was already talking about that bridge between theory and practice back in the 1920s/30s, was officially invited by Turkey back then to develop possible ideas for the country's education. So, I found it very interesting that it was one of the first countries worldwide to come up with and even formulate new models for education, which were then erased almost entirely.

So how do we communicate to-day the importance of design in our societies, its impact and role? Are these temporary zones of cultural manifestation still places where some form of exercising in thought and practice can be made? And if not, what else has come in their place? What role do traditional institutions play to this end?   I will elaborate on the last five to six years, but to do that we need to go a little bit back to the beginning of the 2000s when the big discussions were about art and design, design as an icon, and the design piece as an object that could be sold as art at the Miami Basel of this world, etc.

Moving further, also due to the digital revolution, the object and the icon became not something to sell anymore, but tools to critique something, so critical design emerged. The digital realm started to transform design with notions like sharing. We were getting more and more into the process-driven and understood that we had to start talking about scenarios. So, we began to speculate because we were also starting to deal with biosynthesis and the idea that we could design life. As a practitioner, I tried to be as close as possible and even instigate or make visible these kinds of evolutions in the design field. This happened with the show *Critical Design* in 2007, then founding the social design department at the Eindhoven Design Academy. And that is like what you said in the beginning; we have this permanent identity crisis, where each time you reformulate possibilities of what design can be and can become.

I was trying, as an educator, curator, and director of an institution, to give that a platform—that could be educating, teaching, publishing—and trying to see how that could lead to changing the role of design overall.

Having done that and being there and creating a lot of awareness and discussions and probably a lot of provocations, I also saw that at a certain moment it was not enough anymore for me. So, when I got invited by Luma in the very early stages of its formation, I thought it would be good to just put words into practice. Take past experience in order to maybe say, okay, you can critique society, but if you have the chance to start from scratch, from the molecular level, what and how would you build it up? The economy we have now is wrong, and design is functioning in that system, so you have to fundamentally rethink it.

But if we are to rethink systems, aren't our current cultural infrastructures also in need of being reimagined? Are we in a moment when the platforms we once built, the museum, the kunsthalle, the design week, the biennale, these modern models, are no longer effective?   Do they still have a function to play for design at large and its public life? What of their role in the future?

There are many thoughts that come up when you say this. The idea and approach of bioregional design practice that we champion through Atelier Luma is informed by trying to understand what it means to be "localized;" that when you are in a certain region or context, you can discover something that is of value and that modernism, through mechanization, automated transports, etc., disconnected us from.

So, each time, what I try to do is indeed to answer a certain need in how we could reshape that world by design and use rather than an object, the institution as a tool to make that happen. I think cultural institutions are crucial for that because they are still kind of neutral grounds where different players can come together. They are not a company, and they are not the academic world. They are in between. They are this kind of third place of research gathering different minds, out of which possible new worlds can be created because it is very difficult to do that in the traditional academic world today. And it's almost impossible to do that in the corporate world.

Ten years ago, I might have said real innovation would come from education, and today, I would say it comes from the cultural world because it's, for me, the last place of hope. It's the last place where we can formulate alternatives, where we can think beyond bureaucracy, beyond only profit-driven models, and even rethink the economic model itself. I see a free space where I can maneuver.

I think, in general, cultural institutions are incredibly traditional; they want to conform. And I'm sometimes disappointed at what I see because they don't take their task very seriously, and by doing so, they lose sight of where it all started.

For instance, design museums started as places of learning. For me, the museum was a library where I could go as a designer, copy the models, and take the models home to my studio to see what I could do in my project with it. But now we are not to touch it or take it home because it's all belonging to the conservators. And the logic is visitor numbers, and it's not, instead, how can we empower people with this knowledge; it's to conform. It is to show what we have, but not what we can become.

The institution could become a place where we fundamentally rethink, for instance, how we communicate. Is there, next to the analogue and the digital, another way of organizing and creating different worlds? What would be that third world? I'm interested in institutions as possibility machines.　　But do you really think that an institution is a neutral ground? How is it less politicized than the corporate or academic world?　　It's at least more neutral than that. It's a place where dissent can still be performed. Try to protest in a company; try to express your political opinion in a university.

So, going back to instistitutions as places where you can support and empower the production of knowledge, I think that your activities at Z33 in Belgium were among the first to push forward the idea of the cultural/design institution as a research-based entity.

Because you were also involved then in the making of its new building, could you speak a little bit about the relationship between these two elements? So, the idea of dematerializing the activities of an institution through that process-oriented, research-driven mission and how does that enter into collision with the institution as a physical site?　　You touch upon an interesting conflict or a paradox, you could say.

It is that the exhibition machine and the research entity have a different time frame. They have another temporality. That means that one has a very clear timeline, while the other could be something that goes on forever.

But if you're a public institute, you want to share with audiences. It's very interesting to share things with the public that are literally not finished yet, and to bring research into a space for people to come to work together with the staff and the organization itself. You create these kinds of in-between spaces, between presenting, making, and thinking, where students and residents can come and study and contribute. You see all these layers of new knowledge adding up.

And I'm also doing that in Atelier Luma at this moment. What we did there, and which is also very important, is that the production and the thinking, the making, and the conception of the exhibitions and the cultural program are intertwined. In the spaces of Atelier Luma, I tried not to have doors between spaces; it is all fluid corners, gestures that make those in-between spaces—proximity, no divisions, and fluidity make things possible. And of course, it's about an attitude.

All of the subjects that we have touched upon so far converge into what you have been doing now for the past few years in Arles at Luma. So, it's the summer of 2024, the space is finally open; where are you now with Atelier Luma? What has happened in this one year that you have been finally public? What happened is that we have shown that this way of thinking and working with a bioregional approach is possible even in a complex setting.

As I said to you before: I just wanted to do it, to put it into practice. Yes, we can build with leftovers. Yes, we can build with straw. Yes, we don't need air conditioning. You need to be able to show the world that it's really possible with all the rules and regulations that are there. So, that means putting in one single building, which is a regulation bomb, an exhibition space, offices, a clean room for bacteria, workshop spaces for metal and wood—you can.

And on top of that, we said we want to do that with natural materials—that is kind of utopian. So, we showed the world it's possible. That means that many people came to look. And many asked, "Can we have these? Can we buy these materials?" And we are not selling them; what we sell is our expertise. We can work together. We can look at what this bioregional approach could mean for your region, for your company, for your environment. This is what is going on now with partners in Korea, the Emirates, Denmark, the Champagne region, and Austria. This is what is slowly getting on the road. So, you have active collaborations now with other realities? Can you name an example? Sure, those that I can disclose still belong to the cultural world, which might be interesting here again; others in the commercial field I cannot openly share at this moment.

What we try to do is to give the notion of scaling up a new definition because most of the time in the economy or the capitalist economy, scaling up means "more of the same," and we are interested in "more similar approaches in different parts of the world." For example, in the framework of the Klima Biennial (2024) in Vienna, Austria, we have set up our idea of producing locally—materials are heavy and should stay local, and ideas and people are light and should travel. This is kind of the baseline of our philosophy, and that is what we are looking for each time. Can we produce something locally? What can we produce locally? How can we build ecosystems with that? In the framework of the Klima Biennial, we had 100 students for 100 days for the *Biofabrique Vienna*, a pilot project we co-developed with the Vienna Business Agency in partnership with the TU Wien (Institute of Architectural Design).

And although this was part of a cultural event, it was commissioned by the business agency of Vienna. So, it's quite interesting that you start building these bridges throughout the hard walls in society.   So, you have embedded this type of collaborative network that extends from practitioners and people to the resources of the land and the bio-communities of the region, where thinking, testing, and making happen simultaneously, almost. You were figuring it out as you moved along. Are you thinking of starting up some pedagogical or educational service in Atelier Luma?   Residencies, workshops, and internships—these formats are already part of what we do, but they will be differently organized in the future, also because we have the infrastructure for that. But there is also, then, the data and the science around this and what we can do with it after these years of experience. Two weeks ago, we officially started a collaboration with MIT for the next 10 years. The idea is that, using this bioregional model, we will look into the Mediterranean, the desert, and the Amazon regions, as well as other typologies of geographic and climatic conditions that form and shape ecosystems and the consequences of globalization.

The program is called Global Commons. We start with the Mediterranean because it is where we have the most knowledge at the moment, with researchers and students, a dedicated professorship, etc.   We live in a critical moment where polarizing positions endure around design and its understanding as discourse and practice. There is certainly a vocal and dedicated network of people with a future-projected understanding that acknowledges we need to somehow abandon the systemic frameworks we have long worked with and open ourselves to new epistemological paradigms that are undoing the parameters on which modern notions of design have been built. On the other hand, the commercial nature of design as a product and solution is more and more falling prey to branding and marketing, which we see increasingly parading at events like Milan Design Week with a stronger presence of corporate interests from the likes of the luxury industry. If you were a younger or less seasoned practitioner trying to navigate the system, you would be rather confused by this picture.   The only thing that schools really should learn and teach is a critical attitude where curiosity, skepticism, and conviction are fostered. Embrace curiosity and humor; a critical constructive attitude is always necessary. It is about asking the questions in terms of knowledge production: Am I interested in it? Is it important? Is it meaningful? Is it helping the world?

I think this is the problem where design institutions, whether schools, universities, or museums, are not doing their job because they are not educating this critical attitude. They are just conforming to what we already have. They are not really fundamentally questioning it; they're not shaping or empowering their public.

What if design is a human right? What would happen then? Because we are not supposed to design, produce, and distribute ourselves today. I don't know if you realize it, but we are not supposed to design ourselves. That is really blocking a lot of people and a lot of creativity. Only certain people with certificates and licenses, patents, and certain diplomas are allowed to do things. Others around the world are excluded from this privilege.

Design institutes *have to and can* rethink this position, that privileged system that they are co-creating and establishing.   Tell me more about how this is specifically embedded in the conceptual architecture of Atelier Luma, because what you are saying is very potent—the idea of design as a human right, the idea of global commons empowered by design. How are these values already present in, or how have you built them inside, Atelier Luma? I mean the idea that you're not simply designing a system on the drawing table but you are also learning from your processes and the people that you are involving in the process, because that's the whole added value.   I have to be honest.

I know where I want to go, but I'm not yet fully there. Let's say that these kinds of insights also come step by step.

I really believe, and now I'm sure, that you can "find things." What I mean by that is most of the time today, research is overestimated. You just can find something in front of you—but you do have to "see it." And this is all based on the idea that we all have our intuition, we all have our capabilities, and being aware of that, being open and curious and critical about the world, is enough to start with.

And that's the basis, not only of education. You have to observe, you have to look around. You have to cherish what is there, embrace it, celebrate it. So, the key is in the methodology of doing things. Finding is the first; then what you find, you have to connect with needs, with history, with the past, with science, data, arts, culture, the non-human, the economy, and technology.

And then you have to prototype; it has to be physical. Then you can bring more and more people around it. If you're able to prototype that possibility in a shape and a form, you can check if you can implement it, and you can start playing and developing scenarios around it. And then let it be an actor in something that you formulate together with a group of people in a community. That means that from product design to material design, to urban design, you see that social, critical, and speculative design methods in more and more complex processes are crucial. They all have a moment in that they all contribute to that larger constellation of the development of something. This needs a kind of guidance in a framework that you allow or let exist to share it with the world and to transmit knowledge. And so depending on the content that you are producing, you need to choose the right medium for that message. Is that the movie? Is that an exhibition? Is it a book, a text? It doesn't matter as long as you create these kinds of loops and iterations, which is the very traditional design process, to let something evolve.

I don't know if that is an answer to your question, but this is what I would say is a way of working, of dealing with issues that are around us and that, as a team at Atelier Luma, we try to establish with our partners. In a way,

I think that the people of MIT know almost too much; they have a lot of solutions, but they don't have the problems. So, we find something for them, and we try to connect them to reality, to the real problems. And this generates interesting discussion and confrontation.   I agree that we also need to completely rethink what the object of research is and, therefore, what the new objects of knowledge are.

I suspect this in a way connects to what you were saying about research being overrated; it is because we kind of keep moving research across the same trajectories, and the real act of design there is to redraw the perimeters of what exactly it is that we need to know or want to know, and reflecting, therefore, on its outcomes. The crisis that educational institutions find themselves in is connected to the fact that they still perform within obsolete paradigms, typologies, and definitions.

Exactly.

Purpose-
fulness
& Pluralism

Institutional Practice as **Field-Work**

Director and Chief Curator
Giovanna Borasi

In the aftermath of the Covid-19 pandemic, there has been a strong surge of pressures originating from civil society, and more vocally in the context of the United States, where museums have become both targets of critique as well as platforms to voice social dissent that calls for diversity and pluralism and that often reflects wider geopolitical contestations.

Could you comment on this phenomenon? How is this situation manifesting where you are in Montréal, and is there any particular difference in the way it is addressed between Canada and the United States? I think what happened in the last years has deeply shaken and questioned all institutions for many different reasons. On one side, the traditional idea of an institution rests on amassing and gathering the knowledge of others, and so on what terms and on whose authority this can happen has been questioned. Also, the idea that the traditional structure of institutions is a kind of top-down system that tells you what is knowledge, what you should look at, and what you should think about challenges the very nature of the institution.

On the other side are the questions of who is running the institution, who the institution is representing, and who is participating in the formation of ideas, so pointing to the whole question of diversity in terms of ethnicity, race, thought and social and economic conditions. And I think certainly Canada, which has the principle of pluralism inscribed in its Constitution, has been shaken by this question too, but somehow has been able to provide more of a prompt answer.

I think with the States it was the murder of George Floyd that opened up this wide conversation on representation and transparency, and what is more particular to Canada is the relationship with the Indigenous community and the horrific stories of the residential schools.

Prime Minister Trudeau launched a process called Truth and Reconciliation in 2012 to address what the government had to do to recognize the facts and reconcile with the Indigenous community. But in this new context, every institution had to deal with the issue of creating a dialogue with the Indigenous or other communities that are less visible, less present in all kinds of cultural manifestations.

So, I will say in Canada that has been going more in the direction of really thinking about Indigenous communites, and obviously, it is a difficult relationship because they have been colonized in all kinds of ways, and for them, institutions mean control, power, and that they are not free to be who they are. It's a very complex dynamic that Canada is still trying to figure out. **Can you tell me about your own initiative in this sense, with the Living Land Acknowledgment program and what your goal is in the long term? Are there inter-institutional conversations around decolonizing practices, issues of land and cultural dispossession, that specifically look at this from the perspective of architecture and the built environment?** Land acknowledgment is something very common in North America and means that every time you start a conversation with a gathering of people, you acknowledge the fact that you know you occupy land that was taken from the Indigenous community, that it was their land. So, it is something that you do verbally to acknowledge that.

But what we thought in conversation with some members of these communities is that somehow this form of acknowledgment is always referring to the past, the land "was" their land, while they are still living on these lands. And so we decided to create a different kind of program, and that is why it's called the "living land" acknowledgment; it is about today and about the contemporary and about what the condition of the land is today. We have a group that we work with continuously to study and understand the way they see all these issues. We also created a fellowship where a person comes and works with us for two years doing research related to the land the CCA occupies. And so it's a way of making evident what their connection to the land is today and somehow the fact that we're still occupying it without their permission. This creates a kind of live dialogue with the community, and it's not about being in the past; it is about stepping out of the way and giving them support to direct discourses about our occupation of land and how it's affected them.

In relation to the dialogue about architecture, even the word "architecture" for them is a Western imposition, because for them home is the land. And so the architecture they live in, in the north of Canada, for example, is again an imposition of the government, who just came and said, okay, you need this kind of house—but that's not the way they would choose to live.

So, we did an exhibition a few years ago that was curated by Joar Nango, Taqralik Partridge, Jocelyn Piirainen, a group of Inuit and Sami curators and artists, along with our Associate Director of Research Rafico Ruiz, that was called *Towards Home* (2023)[1] and was really looking at what "home" is for them, trying to define questions of what home means in the future and to give agency to Indigenous architects to actually establish their own way of building architecture.

The idea was not to define a kind of Western distinction of geography, but to focus on an area where the Indigenous communities through the north of Canada, Greenland, and northern Europe have shared values and beliefs. We created a group of young architects who are in the process of getting their masters. They're all Indigenous and have worked together to understand what Indigenous architecture is. I think this is starting to come more and more into practice, as practices that are rooted in an Indigenous way of thinking in relation to the land and the community and how you will make decisions.

So, for example, even the question of copyright is contentious because knowledge is passed on orally from one generation to the other. It's not something that you own; it's a community's. Therefore, they will not be able to sign a release in the way we imagine that you are a person and you have your known rights about what you are saying. So, all this is part of what, institutionally speaking, we call decolonizing. But here in Canada, we speak more about Indigenizing, which is to really try to

1   Joar Nango, Taqralik Partridge, Jocelyn
    Piirainen and Rafico Ruiz (eds.), *Towards Home
    · Vers chez soi / ᐊᓪᒋᕐᒡᒍ / Ruovttu Guvlui: Inuit
    and Sámi Placemaking / Conceptions Inuites
    et Samies du Lieu, Valiz*, Canadian Centre for
    Architecture and Mondo Books, 2024.

understand and be changed by this way of thinking and how different it is.   So many contemporary topics have violently emerged onto the stage of public institutions, posing pressures on their roles. This has been happening also across institutions of education. I wonder how you see the relationships between practice, pedagogy, and theory in the field of architecture transforming when it comes to the role that cultural institutions play.

There is clearly a shift there that places them in a new potential zone of intervention.   Very good point—we touched on some of these questions a few years ago in a publication we did called *The Museum Is Not Enough* (2019),[2] and we are actually doing a second volume of it now.

Other institutions, like, for example, libraries, have changed dramatically in the last decades to become neighborhood centers where you have all kinds of activities that go beyond reading a book, and there is the idea that all ages are represented there. They have become much more of an anchor, at least in North America, in neighborhood life. Other sorts of institutions as well have changed their relationship with the public to really transform themselves and understand how to engage with its needs.

I think that's what museums need to reflect upon, and I think the combination of the pandemic and all these other upheavals really demands that the museum becomes a very different place than just a place to collect, show, and pretend to have the knowledge to pass on.

Even public programs, which in the past were a way of having a much more direct relationship with the public, don't work anymore if it is just a lecture where a person is unloading their knowledge on you. People are interested in dialogue, to voice their own concerns; they are interested in positioning themselves in the room and saying, "I'm curious about this because of the person I am," so there is this other new reality.

The institution can take this as an opportunity rather than thinking that it's just a crisis that we have to go through to come out the other side the same as we were

2   Giovanna Borasi, Albert Ferré, Francesco Garutti, Jayne Kelley and Mirko Zardini (eds.), *The Museum Is Not Enough*, Sternberg Press and Canadian Centre for Architecture, 2019.

before. I think it's really a chance to establish a very different dialogue, a very different way of thinking on so many different levels, and we have seen in this moment that all the weaknesses of the museum show up. For example, funding, especially in North America, comes from certain groups, so you will have certain pressures about what you show and how you talk. We start to see also the friction between the institution and the people who run it or work in it. I myself might have an opinion as a director of the institution, but the institution as a whole might have a different one because the institution as a whole is everyone; it is the board, it is the staff, it is everyone involved. And so this is where I think this dynamic starts to fall apart and the institution cannot have just one voice anymore.   **The cultural agency of the CCA, ever since its foundation, has been drawn to transforming the approach to the discourse around architecture for architecture and architects, or those that wanted to seek engagement with the discipline. I wonder if what we just talked about is somewhat changing the public for architecture?**   From the beginning, when Phyllis Lambert established the CCA and started to think about what the role of this institution was, she always imagined it as a kind of provocative voice. And that is linked to the idea of being independent—you are not a government body, nor are you a body that proposes the way of thinking of a certain group, so you can maintain your independence and can also be against common opinion or the status quo.

The idea of using the name Centre "for" Architecture, in English, meant the mandate was to make architecture a public concern, so the idea is that everyone should be concerned about the built environment, the space around you, and that everybody can contribute. You might not design it, but you can still understand that the way the city is built might change your way of being.

I always think that architecture is the first public for the CCA; it contributes to posing questions to the field and what is important, what issues to think about. By posing this as an ambition, you influence those who are doing architecture, and then a kind of ripple effect happens.

So, for example, last year I visited a hospital in Bogotá designed by Giancarlo Mazzanti, and he told me that he designed it in a completely different way from what he initially thought, because he read our publication *Imperfect Health* (2012),[3] which was really thinking about the way you build a hospital not as a medical machine but as a space for healing, considering what patients are looking at, the way they are looking at a tree or looking at the city —this gave them a kind of energy and affects the time of their recovery.

I think the reason we are here is really that it's not about showing architecture at all, and I think even the archive, the collection that we have, is an incredible repository of ideas that people can go back to, to think about the present. So, it's not about preserving the legacy of these people, these architects, only, but it's more about how those ideas can be interesting for a kind of fresh start today.   The CCA has really shown throughout its history a unique consistency in producing its own legacy as a practice, too, of self-reflection. Across the many projects you have initiated involving the use of the collection, there is always implied an interest and sensitivity around those ripple effects that thinking and practicing architecture can have on our lives and our shared environments.

In line with this legacy, what are the urgent horizons of work at the moment for architects and architecture?   There are a few things that are overall crucial for the CCA in these years. One is what we call "diversifying the perspective." To me, that is a kind of larger direction and is also an internal need for diversifying the line of thoughts, and housing diverse materials at the CCA, but it's also about how we can be an international center and not an encyclopedic museum.

Now we are talking to a world that is more and more divided, parcelled around very different ways of thinking, and so the idea of diversifying the perspective is manifest-

3   Giovanna Borasi and Mirko Zardini, CCA Montréal (eds.), *Imperfect Health: The Medicalization of Architecture*, Lars Müller Publishers and Canadian Centre for Architecture, 2012

ed, for example, in how we deal with the collection. Historically, the CCA has been collecting very much by following what was the power dynamic in architecture, so white men, mainly European or North American. Diversifying is important in terms of other voices that we can collect that were present but overlooked.

Diversifying is happening through the land acknowledgment program and through the work we are doing in Africa, and the way we are doing it, which is really not about us going there and saying what is important. It is giving agency to architects, students, and researchers there to tell *us* what is significant for their history that therefore we should look at.

This "diversifying the perspective" has different facets for the CCA, and it is fundamental in really understanding the position of the institution and what it means to be international, which doesn't mean being global. For example, with the project we're doing in Dakar, we are extremely local because we are there with the local curator; we are thinking about what is important for the culture there and in Senegal. But because we bring this into the CCA, then it becomes an international subject that everybody should look at somehow.

The second thing is that the CCA has always tasked itself with looking at what the urgent questions are, and this is thanks to the work that Phyllis did, or that Mirko [Zardini] did, or all the other curators and directors before me. And now it has gained a certain authority. So, if we say this is important, somehow it becomes important, and we also need to be clear and responsible about this.

It is about how to think not only about the urgent questions but also about the way we look at them.

After many years of investigating the environmental crisis, it is time to look at the role of the architect. The show I did with Mirko in 2008, *Sorry, Out of Gas*, which was about the oil crisis, was a way of starting to think about this. The project we are doing now, *Groundwork* (2024), curated by Francesco Garutti, really wants to look at how the architect's role, their way of being and doing, should change in relation to the crisis, to the point of asking whether we even need to build. The ecological crisis has been central for the CCA, but now it's really at the top of our concerns, and because we are the institution we are, we will not address this by doing an exhibition showing the most recent technological developments or green façades; instead, we will show transformational projects or practices that are dealing with a very different approach to this question.   **You personally have had an on/off relationship with the CCA for quite a long time. Now, in retrospect, how do you see that relationship evolving? And the question after that is about the temporal factor connected to institutions, meaning: do institutions nowadays need stability and long-termism to really be effective participants and contributors to the narratives of their own times, or not?**   Yes, true, I've been with the CCA on and off for nearly 20 years, although I never really thought it would be so long! But I really love the CCA because of what we are able to do—because it is of the right scale. It is small enough to be very agile in ways we can decide on something and act on it quite rapidly, and at the same time, it is big enough to take on some long-term and ambitious projects.

I also insist very much that those who come to work at the CCA do two jobs at the same time; one is their job, and the other is building the institution.

You always have to be yourself and bring your own ideas, and at the same time think about the long term of the institution. So, is that idea sustainable? Can it be repeated, can it be modified, can it evolve into something? I think this institution will not perform well if every year there is something completely new and different and somehow also very much related to one person.

I always say—what is the CCA? It is us, now, deciding where the boat is going. To me, the institution is the people who make it, and in my 20 years at the CCA, I have already seen five or six different CCAs.

In my experience at this point, I can say there are two types of people who come to work at the CCA. There are the institutional makers and the institutional users—you have people who are really there and understand that they can advance their individual work or be themselves and at the same time build the institution, and there are others who will use the institution to actually do their own piece and then go somewhere else. Both are necessary for the institution because both are advancing and pushing it.

What do you think is happening today in architecture, especially with younger generations, and considering how you have recently used filmmaking, the narrative medium par excellence, is there a connection with the challenge of recounting or telling stories about architecture nowadays? There is clearly a challenge now. Architecture, I find, has disappeared from generalist media. *The New York Times* used to cover it; maybe it is still in *The Guardian*, but it's so connected to the one individual writer that if he/she is gone, then there is no one left.

Architecture is not discussed anymore. Before, it was about the star architects, so it was kind of easy for journalists to point out how great the person was and what they were doing, and today we have not found a way of talking about these issues in a more discursive way instead of talking about bibliographical data.

On top of that, magazines of design and architecture at large that were once a reference for the majority are gone too; then digital ones came about, but now they are facing the same financial challenges that paper ones did. Now either you pay 10,000 or 15,000 dollars for an article, or they're not covering you. This has made architecture disappear from the general conversation, and it lives in other forms. Obviously, social media is very present, but that is not editorial work. I think it's highly problematic. Now architects have their social media and websites, and you just check there.

The conversation has been flattened a lot, and so I think for the CCA it is important to address "how" to talk about architecture and—again, going back to the idea of architecture as public concern—how you make those issues present. So, for example, in the recent series of documentaries that we created, for me the question was about how globally we are facing problems of loneliness, more people living alone, the housing crisis, increasing numbers of people living on the streets, and how all these things are connected. And there isn't a simple answer, but certainly housing is central to it. So, the question is how to make people understand that, on one side, architecture is not the solution nor will it solve the problem in itself, but that it is part of the conversation and is a lens through which you can actually understand some of the challenges that this population has. The idea was how to tell that story, and to me it was not a book, not a show, but a much more agile medium like the documentary, which can be present in so many places at the same time. With the arrival of social media, you are where the people are, so if they are on Facebook or Instagram, you need to be there.

So, one thing is the increase of attention to moving image formats in this moment, but also it is about rethinking the relationship of the institution with those topics.

If you do a show or a book about, let's say, homelessness, there will be a degree of separation from the subject because we will present the photo of someone who has been on the street of Los Angeles documenting the homeless crisis, but if we are there with movie cameras then this degree of separation is cut off, and we are the people hearing the homeless talking to us in a kind of direct way. So also, as a curator, I have to say, it has been an incredible change because suddenly you are the one reporting. It is going for direct sources instead of secondary ones.

This has brought an immediacy, and considering this discussion that we have now about transparency or clarity and so on, I think this has added value by saying, OK, you actually have been there, you have seen it, those are real people who are telling their own story and there is no mediation. And I thought that's the approach that the CCA should have now: to say we are really invested in this, we are showing you what we are seeing.

Groundwork is our current three-chapter film/exhibition series, and it is continuing this approach—we are there with the architect while she's doing her research, while she's doing the preliminary investigations on her project. And so you also document the hesitation, the questions that people ask the architect in the same way you are. You are really there, and that to me is a way of responding to our general mandate, but also to the kind of change of context of today.　　　When it comes to the realm of architecture, do you find that the need or the demands coming from the transformations within the practice also affect the work of those—like curators—that articulate its forms of fruition as discourse?

The number of applicants to architectural schools has plummeted in recent years, as a symptom of how people see perhaps architecture not as a conduit to really impact the world. Do you think that the need for new institutional paradigms is also a reflection of how the practice itself is being approached by younger generations?　　　It's a very good point. I think we are still fighting against the fact that everybody thinks of architecture as a building.

Many architects come into the CCA saying "but this is not about architecture" because they think: here is a centre for architecture, so it should be a place where you see a model of a building, etc. At the CCA, we have a much larger and blurred idea of what architecture is. So, I find that certainly the new generation, which is very engaged with values in thinking about how they contribute to change or give direction to what will happen next, finds architecture not the solution somehow. Many new generations are thinking of ways to provide a response to the issues that we have, and maybe, yes, if you take literally architecture as a built form, then it is not the answer; it seems like the opposite of an answer somehow, as it continues to be so much in the hands of real estate developers and a way to divide more or to add social and economic injustice.

So, if you don't think about architecture as larger than a built form, then you think there is really something not right. A lot of the work we are doing is really to change the idea of what architecture is about and the variety of its forms. And again, if I go back to this, you know the work of Xu Tiantian, the architect we're featuring now in the first chapter of the *Groundwork* film series—she was asked to do a museum on Meizhou, an island in China. And she refused to do a building because she saw it was really not necessary after discovering how the community works, learning about their fishing practices, etc. The challenge we have now is to make people understand architecture as a much larger entity and discipline.   Picking up again that comment you made earlier about the crisis of specialized media connected to design and architecture, where do you think the horizon is moving? Culturally speaking, where do we get the pulse of where design and architecture are really going? Is the cultural infrastructure the way we know it—the spaces of biennales, triennales, museums—still the place where discourse and practice meet?   Yes and no. I would say yes if you are able to visit as many as possible. If you are a general member of the public and your experience is only, say, the Venice Biennale, you have a very one-way mode of seeing the world. If you can do Venice, but then also go to Sharjah or other places, then—because the public is different, and because the architects exhibited come from different geographies, they come with a very different discourse—then it's valuable because you have very different pictures of the same world.

The discussion about biennales, triennales, and the crisis of these models has been going on for some time, but I don't think we have yet found another model to abandon those, and I have to say that maybe what we underestimate is still the kind of social connections that are happening beyond what is exhibited—these encounters and dialogues are still, and especially after the pandemic, very valuable opportunities.

Because even for us… we are trying to be very present digitally, and I always think somehow the idea of the CCA is bigger than what actually happens in Montréal. Like so many people I know, they've never been to the CCA, and at first, I was myself very frustrated about this. Now I'm totally fine because I think the important thing is that it's understood that this institution wants to find a way of putting itself out there. And so, to me, these multiple voices, this pluralism, will be the answer.

Once, for example, I had a meeting with a group of smaller institutions in North America, and they were lamenting that they were very small, smaller than CCA —but I told them, what if we all decide that in five years we will all talk about the environmental crisis? Let's say that all places in the world that are dealing with architecture will do that. Each one in its own way, but that we are synergetic. Then maybe you will have an impact because of this kind of global coordination, where everybody is pointing at the same time to the same issue. And importantly, that requires not to be competitive. I launched this idea; I'm not seeing it coming because, as I said, there is also this competitive nature around institutions.   The CCA has adopted this multipronged approach since the very beginning, also because of the remoteness of your location compared to other more trafficked urban centers in the world. You have pioneered ways of using the collection as a repository of hidden stories and creative manipulations, what others bring to it in a way to expand it. I know you have been running a pilot project with machine learning. I wanted to know more about how you are entertaining this relationship with the shape-shifting world of the "digital," and what about, for example, digitally produced environments that can range from cinema to gaming, and how the CCA is dealing with those.   The digital at the CCA, as in many other institutions, has different facets. So, on one side, you have the digital infrastructure for communication and access to our resources, but from a project that we developed with Greg Lynn that was called *Archaeology of the Digital* (2013), the idea was really also to think about the digital as content in itself and what is the digital material that makes sense to acquire and preserve. That was 12 years ago and was followed by a huge investment in understanding how to treat the born-digital and give access to it and all the kinds of questions related to that, as it was also important historically to really look at how architecture had changed because of the arrival of the computer.

We continued this work not only for born-digital content but questioned how to use digital tools to provide more access to our collection—somehow the big contradiction is that it is a very visual collection, but still, to find things you have to use words. If I have the digitized drawing of a floor plan and want to look for the toilet, I won't be able to find it because the word "toilet" is not in the description anywhere. And this is a massive task that a machine that is actually able to detect elements in drawings could do. What you find on the market is much more advanced in terms of photography, as there's been a lot of work on facial recognition or object recognition in photography, but in drawing, not so much, as it is much more complex. So we did a pilot project with Sylvia Lavin at Princeton University School of Architecture to look into drawings—she was interested in a more complex issue, which is finding trees in drawings, since there is not really a codified way of drawing a tree, so you have to teach the machine to recognize them in their variety. So, we had to ingest into the machine thousands and thousands of drawings.

It will be a very interesting tool to use in the future, where you will be able to do a lot of things. For example, a researcher could check out of the thousands of drawings the CCA holds, the ones where there are elevations with bricks. So, we are looking at a way of complementing the work that our human catalogers are doing to really see if there is other work that machines can do.

For the rest, I have to say we have been trying all these new tools, ChatGPT, etc., but for us, it doesn't do the job yet, but I'm positive that at one point, those tools will enter into the realm of the museum. **Going back to your employment of new narrative tools, the film, documentaries. The distribution of these types of content follows different networks than the usual ones; I am interested in how this affects the possibility of creating different forms of institutional alliance.** Yes, the first network is film festivals. And that is great because the institution becomes present in a very different body of places simultaneously, from Korea to Copenhagen or Rotterdam, and gets exposed to all these different publics.

As soon as the film festival circuit is done, we do institutional presentations, a lot of screenings in universities or other institutions not necessarily of architecture but that are interested in the topics addressed. So, the movie becomes a prompt for a conversation, and that, I think, is an interesting way, again, for the CCA to be kind of an activator of a conversation, and ultimately, they end up on our website or YouTube, and then they are there for everybody to watch. So, we are not yet done, and I think it will be the work with the next series of really partnering with a larger streaming platform—we haven't really explored that yet. **What about the next edition of *The Museum Is Not Enough* that you're going to publish? What would be a key change from the previous one?** The first was really a way of introducing the concerns of the CCA on various topics: the idea of education, the self-criticism of the institution, but somehow, even if we invited other outside voices into the conversation, it was still very much featuring the CCA as a main subject.

What we want to do this time is to bring in many other voices sharing different topics. One is the use of film and moving images and what it means for institutions, as we are not alone in this. The second issue is the question of national museums or international museums, and I think the idea of the national museum is very much in crisis while we are also redefining what a nation is and who the voices in that nation are.

Another topic is rethinking or redescribing what we call critical cataloging. And again, I think everybody is facing this—it is really looking at how things were described. We did an interesting exercise to take one image and give it to 20 different people to describe it, and the result is interesting because you have just this one image, but somehow each person, because of their background, their expertise, their role, or their race or ethnic group, describes the image in a very different way.

This is also about questioning the predominance of visuality in our cultures and how much we think that everybody is seeing the same thing, while it's not the same thing because of their personality, their position, and so on.

The other issue is that of the post-custodial, which is very much what we are doing now in Africa. When we started this idea of diversifying the perspective, we said we had to really invest in acquiring things that come from different modernities or different places that we might not have looked at. But then, speaking with the network of scholars in Africa that we had created, they pointed us to how that was wrong because it meant extraction again. So, this is why we created this new program where we collaborate with people on the continent, we identify an archive, and then we support the research of local scholars to look at it. They identify what is important for them, and we support digitization, and we put all this in Wikimedia so everybody can access it.

So, the next chapter we're dealing with is this position of the institution going from collecting to connecting.

I'm pushing for thinking of the institution very differently as a place where knowledge can be shared, where you are the facilitator of moving that knowledge around more than saying, "I take everything, put it in my basement, I digest it, and then put it out for you to learn from it." So, that's also a kind of transformation that I think museums should look at.

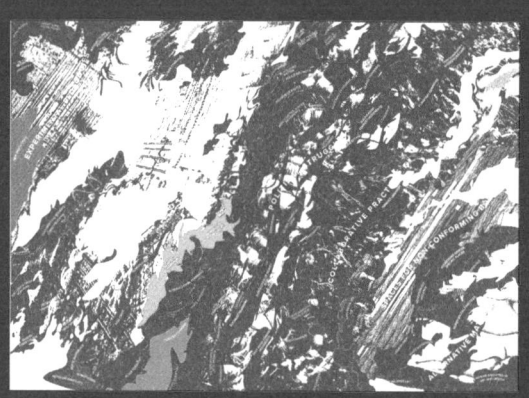

"Feminisms are myriad and countless. In every region, specific movements and discourses about gender emerge, entangled with local political struggles and cultural histories."[1] This is the opening statement that Bryony Roberts and Abriannah Aiken penned for the online project and research that originated Feminist Spatial Practices, of which they are co-founders. Birthed from a commission by e-flux and the Jencks Foundation for their collaborative research program "'isms and wasms," it has since become a participatory archival project counting over 100 contributing members from a global expanse. Roberts and Aiken are design practitioners and educators whose work has long investigated modes of architectural engagement with publicness and inclusivity, having taught studios (Columbia GSAPP) and developed research around the spatial implications of reproductive justice, mental health, and gender- and neurodiversity. The mapping project, which in its first instantiation took the shape of a visual diagram, laid the groundwork for the open-source platform that launched in 2024 and whose process of making aimed "to be a feminist practice itself, one of building community and celebrating global, situated perspectives." The growing repository tasks itself with unpacking the vast spectrum of practical, pedagogical, and theoretical articulations of feminism as a politics of radical care, commoning, and equity beyond gender specificity or identification, and in so doing elicits the resonances of localized experiences across times and geographies. The platform can be consulted through temporal and thematic frameworks, featuring practices, projects, events, and publications across art, design, and architecture whose conceptual or agential remit engages critically with the built environment.

What Roberts and Aiken began with a group of like-minded collaborators already invested in relevant scholarly and practice-based work rapidly evolved into an expansive collaborative enterprise motivated by the unprecedented potential of this generative tool. While other existing projects of similar archival nature or spotlighting diversity in design and architecture[2] have been appearing over recent years, Roberts and Aiken felt there was no centralized system through which not only resources could be shared, but ultimately common research agendas, projects, and mutual advisory could be developed.[3] The platform welcomes open submissions while gathering its growing members by means of ongoing public activities, labs, and partnerships with external entities that its autonomous character could maximize.

Its existence is also factual evidence of the need and urgency to rehearse reflections and empower programmatic transformations across the pedagogical and policy landscapes attendant to architecture, through which novel bodies of knowledge, generational skills, and sensibilities can be nurtured and ultimately deployed to support the creation of equitable and inclusive spatial dimensions of public life that have been fast eroding in urban societies.

1 Bryony Roberts and Abriannah Aiken, "Feminist Spatial Practices, Part 1," *e-flux Architecture*, March 2023, https://e-flux.com/architecture/chronograms/506357/feminist-spatial-practices-part-1/.
2 See some examples quoted in the introduction essay of this book (notes n. 7, 16), and in "Feminist Spatial Practices, Part 1" (ibidem) and others like https://womenwritingarchitecture.org/ and https://cyberfeminismindex.com/.
3 From a conversation between the author, Bryony Roberts and Abriannah Aiken (November 1, 2024).

If many of the projects and ideas contained in this book similarly gesture toward less immediately legible outcomes of design than materially finished objects, spaces, or tools, the non-profit re:arc institute has, over the past three years, invested in establishing a support structure for its financial and vocational viability. It tasks itself with nurturing an ecosystem of capacity-building, practice-led initiatives in the field of architecture that see themselves as transformative agents advocating for the discipline's ecological and social responsibilities and evidencing the need to establish an alternative operative and discursive framework for their sustainment as producers of socioeconomic and cultural value in an era of climate breakdown.

re:arc was created under a mandate from the Inter IKEA Foundation (the parent company that holds the intellectual property of IKEA) for the establishment of a philanthropic venture at the intersection of architecture and climate action. Currently managed by a team of nine and assembled by Carla Cammilla Hjort, who formerly established SPACE10, the now disbanded research lab in Copenhagen, re:arc operates through three concatenated program chapters (grant-making, practice labs, public discourse) that champion community-oriented initiatives leveraging grassroots knowledge, collective participation, and social empowerment, with a focus on historically underserved groups and vulnerable territories.

If monetary support benefits NGOs, activists, and organizations already invested in pedagogical and solidarity-based actions voted to strengthen localized networks founded on equitable work, safeguarding biodiversity, and eco-social care, the practice- and discourse-focused legs of the activities aim at generating a virtuous cycle of knowledge-sharing among an emergent generation of critical spatial practitioners. This network-building effort, while the least tangible, is a fundamental feature of the institute's unique mode of work, one that makes evident the systemic transformations that the architecture industry must address in light of its environmentally degrading impacts and its contribution to reinforcing structural inequalities.

The practice labs are shaped in close collaboration with practices on carefully selected projects from ideation to completion (24 under realization since 2023 and mostly located in the Global South), supporting and funding their development and physical construction, thus highlighting the ineffectiveness of existing subsidies and philanthropic models in architecture that are no longer responding to the needs of today and tomorrow. The "hyperlocal" practitioners who are advancing actions rooted in communal work and social mutuality are the new frontline workers that sustain an architecture of purpose, rather than specialization, which finds no stable operational routes in the current building industry and therefore hardly enters the heritage systems of professionalized learning.

The re:arc institute offers proof of how practices are today the places of knowledge in architecture and supports "a mode of work that's more in alignment with their values."[1] It is through their localized innervation that ameliorations in the rituals and habits of coexistence for "planetary wellbeing" can be effected, and new bodies of knowledge can be created for future-facing institutions of education. Next in the institute's plans for the upcoming three-year cycle is a shift in geographical focus to Latin America and the Caribbean, the regions that hold 50% of the world's biodiversity.

1   From a conversation between the author and Alice Grandoit-Šutka (re:arc institute), (November 29, 2024).

ArkDes, Swedish Center for Architecture and Design
Stockholm, Sweden

Impact-Driven Agency:
the Museum
and Public Life
Conversation I

Director (2017–23)
Kieran Long

Not unlike many of your peers who are included in this book, prior to joining the institutional field, you practiced as an independent writer and curator. Some of your colleagues mentioned that at that time (2010s), they felt like the critical capacity of specialized journalism was shrinking. That was roughly when you joined the V&A as Keeper of Design, Architecture and Digital, a newly created division. You have stated that within that specific context, covering contemporary design needed a new approach able to cut across some of the departmental divisions.

Why so? What were your reflections around the state of design at that moment? What defined that new approach?   Back then, I didn't see that the possibilities in journalism were necessarily narrowing. I think many of us were outgrowing the narrow audience for specialist magazines. Also, the ambitions of magazines' owners did not always align with ours. I was looking for a broader platform to have a conversation with the general public, and the V&A was that. We had 3.6 million visitors the year I joined (2012), and the museum was undergoing a period of growth in general. That was driven by large-scale exhibitions like *David Bowie Is* (2013) and *Alexander McQueen: Savage Beauty* (2015), which had a huge popular cultural impact.

I still had the discipline of journalism in my backbone, and that generated two provocations in the collecting and exhibition practices that I tried to bring in. One was to simply observe that there's a slightly surreal situation in large institutions like the V&A where certain fields get a lot of attention and have a long history of collecting and research, but those fields are culturally marginal compared to others that have no profile at all in the museum. Some of those new fields that I was working with were driven by emerging technologies, video games being the primary example, about which we made a huge exhibition, *Videogames: Design/Play/Disrupt* (2018). Video games are a technologically and culturally sophisticated field, and they are definitely an applied art. But the V&A had half a dozen art glass curators and no games curator. They also had a whole division for ceramics, which is a great strength of the V&A, but no one looking at advanced materials or plastics. So, my first instinct was to investigate the tensions of these imbalances. It was hard then to map the spectrum of design and applied art fields of the V&A onto what I saw as the most compelling fields of design out in the world.

The second provocation was about collecting. National museums collect with a very long horizon in mind. Christopher Wilk was my first boss at the V&A and an incredibly inspiring person; he is the long-standing head of furniture, textiles, and fashion. He would say that collecting at the V&A was not just about the generic object and its artistic importance. He would say that often the V&A knows which things it wants to collect, but that they wait for the right one, the specific example that has meaning beyond its form and authorship. And if that right one takes 30 years to find, they'll wait 30 years. So, when I arrived at the V&A, we didn't have an Arne Jacobsen Ant Chair (the Model 3107 chair, designed in 1952) in the collection. As part of the research for the *Plywood* exhibition in 2017, Christopher collected one made in 1967 that was from St Catherine's College, Oxford, which is a Jacobsen-designed building. The Ant Chair is in every collection in the world, but the V&A works incredibly hard on finding "the" Ant Chair, with a provenance that is meaningful. This is a great way of collecting and should never stop. But my idea was to say there are some objects that are more important now than they will be in 30 years, and I don't see why they shouldn't be in the museum too.

We started the Rapid Response Collecting initiative in 2013 (led by Corinna Gardner, with important contributions from Louise Shannon, Rory Hyde, Kristian Volsing, and others), and we were acquiring things directly connected to current affairs and to moments of contemporary history where you see the world clearly through design. For example, we acquired a pair of Primark jeans to try to access a conversation about textile supply chains, fast fashion, and labor-related aspects of globalization in the Global South. And we acquired Cody Wilson's 3D-printed gun (The Liberator), which had to do with advanced materials and distributed manufacturing. Or the MacBook Air on which *The Guardian* newspaper stored the leaked files from the NSA that Edward Snowden illegally sent to them. We were working with established collecting logics of provenance, but in a different temporality, with a much lighter emphasis on authorship and with a bit more urgency. It was incredibly motivating for our new team and department. We were buying things and getting them on display in days, which the museum had never really done before.

It made the collections feel more directly relevant to the world we live in and started to critically question some of them. For example, the V&A collection of Indian textiles is one of the greatest in the world; when we added the Primark jeans (made in the Rana Plaza factory in Dhaka, Bangladesh, which in 2013 collapsed and killed 1,134 people), we were putting ourselves in critical relation to the historic collections and forcing a relationship between the V&A and the contemporary world of design and making. **How did this effectively upset or disturb the departmental or disciplinary environments of the museum? That is, how did this new approach reflect the way you understood design at the time and how it was transforming or responding to its own times?** I did and still see design as a broad practice of the imagination that is not confined to professionals. I was influenced especially by people like Arjun Appadurai and other sociologists and philosophers who saw the work of the imagination (as Appadurai phrases it in "The Future as a Cultural Fact") as the decisive factor in our lives as people in society. For me, that was a good way of understanding design. The work of the imagination might well be designing a very fine sofa, but it also involves being a good parent, a good politician; your imagination is involved in being a good protester or democratic citizen. Protest was a big topic around 2012 and in the following years, especially in London, whether it was about tuition fees, immigration, or Brexit. So we collected objects connected to protests. The brilliant exhibition *Disobedient Objects* (curated by Catherine Flood and Gavin Grindon, 2014) was also a paradigm-shifting project in terms of how we treated vernacular creative practices that affect the future of society.

That time at the V&A also coincided with an extreme democratization of the tools of design. There were many more people who could design and manufacture in three dimensions. SketchUp had been a thing for several years. We saw 3D printing emerging as an accessible phenomenon and not only in a "positive" way, in the old sense of design as an agent of modern progress. I continued this idea when I went to ArkDes in Stockholm, where we made exhibitions with memes, apps, and materials from protest movements that were designed to have a political agency. All of these, for me, are squarely works of design, and they became possible and interesting then because everyone had access to those tools.

Because I come from a working-class background and have no art history background, I have little interest in established historical categories of design. I'm interested in the resonances between design culture and popular culture. I was educated in English literature at a school very immersed in post-structuralist theory, and I found it liberating as a young student to erase the hierarchies between Shakespeare and the packet of cornflakes in the famous formulation by (one of my then professors) Terence Hawkes. So, it was quite natural for me to come and see design as a broad field and as a spectrum of practices, professional and otherwise. The thing is that the V&A reacted extremely well to this; it never tried to put me in my place.

The example I always give is the destroyed Snowden laptop. When we proposed that acquisition, I took it to the acquisitions group, which consisted of the six heads of department, of which I was one. I remember the head of sculpture saying to me, "I completely understand this. The laptop is a work of iconoclasm, exactly like the acquisitions we make around the English Civil War or the Reformation." He understood it as a double work of design: an Apple product ("designed in California"), redesigned by the British security services when they destroyed it—an obviously symbolic, artistic act.

The V&A was not resistant to this because I was working within the traditions of the museum, but with a different methodology and on different raw material. I think our team brought some forgotten collecting traditions and logics of an old museum into the present day in a way that has had a long-lasting effect. **You have stated that when you arrived at the V&A to establish this entirely new department, you had an interest in looking at design and its relationship at all scales of public life, and this notion of *public life* is something you have made central in defining the broader vision and mission for ArkDes. Can you tell me how this idea germinated and how it moved across your practice?** It's not my notion; you can see its genealogy very clearly in the work of writers like Richard Sennett and Joseph Rykwert: they have a way of seeing the city as a terrain of practices of citizenship. Particularly, Rykwert was important for me; I was lucky enough to convince him to write a column for the *Architects' Journal* while I was editor there, partly so I could have lunch with him once in a while. "The Seduction of Place" is the foundational text for me about the city as an order of civic virtue. You also see in that book how practices of citizenship can be radical and upend hierarchies, but also how we are creative within existing hierarchies or societal structures. Through these ways of conceiving citizenship, I emancipated myself from the idea of chasing the formal innovations of avant-gardist designers. I think that notion has had its day. What I'm interested in is the extraordinary creativity at every level of society that we see among citizens and among artists of different kinds.

This idea of public life comes strongly from my upbringing as a writer about architecture. Architecture is always in a double bind, believing in its own agency as creating platforms for creative citizenship but constantly being critiqued by citizens' own lives in those spaces. That is an endlessly fascinating dynamic that allows you to look at those things from many different scales and points of view.

I don't see museums as repositories of knowledge; I think they are repositories of evidence. Every object in a museum is a piece of evidence, and that makes it possible for us to interpret it with the knowledge that, in the future, others will interpret it differently. One of the wonderful things about the postcolonial critiques that are now coming to museum collections is that they are possible because the collections are there. Without those collections, the critique would be much more difficult to articulate. The objects and the unjust and morally reprehensible methods of their collection make possible the civic-scale conversation we are having now. These pieces of evidence can be ripped from the context they had in the 19th century and given a new one in the 21st.

When we collected the pair of jeans, for example, it was with the sense that one day there would be an exhibition called *Manufacturing in the Global South in the 1990s and 2000s* or something like that. Someone will get to grips with the structural injustices of the global capitalist system in manufacturing and design's role in it. And they will need the evidence to tell that story in the future. What you're setting up as a curator is constantly the possibility for future reinterpretations and new storytelling.   Staying with that notion of public life, once you arrived at ArkDes, how did you create an understanding or a platform for its communication? You moved from a place like the V&A, where design was part of a broader remit of cultural practices, to one that bears design in its name. What was the mandate and, thus, the mission presented to you when you joined?   ArkDes is a national museum, and in Sweden, to be its director means that you are a senior civil servant. I reported directly to the culture minister, so that was a new dynamic. There are laws in Sweden that are robust in ensuring independent decision-making in cultural institutions. But to be in that system was a big learning curve, especially coming from outside the country. I went through seven different culture secretaries during my time as director and three or four different culture ministers. The one who hired me wanted me to change ArkDes completely. It was perceived as an institution that had lost its clarity of purpose and mission. And the reason it had lost that was due to what we're talking about.

ArkDes, like several museums in Europe, had grown out of an institutional collection of architectural drawings. The Institute of Architects in Sweden (Sveriges Arkitekter) created the museum for its collection back in the 1960s, and its mission was to continue collecting, especially the work of modernist architects in Sweden who were dying at that time. So it amassed archives, just like the NAI in the Netherlands or the RIBA in the UK.

And halfway through its life, it suddenly became a national museum. That shifted its responsibility away from serving the profession of architecture toward being a public museum. The word "design" was later added to its remit, and it became the National Center for Architecture and Design, but it has no design collection and no government mission to collect design at all. So, there was this bureaucratic label without any real idea of what the category of design included and what it did not.

I chose to take this idea of public life with me from London, and what it does is it situates these professional fields in the world and gives us the possibility to say: "I am not interested in what architects and designers do or in teaching the world and the public what they do. I am interested in the way we see our lives through what architects and designers do." That might sound like semantics, but it's a very important distinction for me. It was to say we don't tell people how great architects and designers are or follow that agenda that some architecture museums still feel a duty to. We're going to say, if you look carefully into the objects of architecture and design in the public realm, you will see the dynamics of our society. And you will see them perhaps more clearly than in any other artistic field.   **Give me an example of a project that embodies this idea.**   The first exhibition I made at ArkDes was *Public Luxury* (2018, curated with Daniel Golling and Marie Louise Richards). We made it at the time of a general election campaign in Sweden that had a lot to do with public space and institutions and was the beginning of the electoral success of the far-right party Sverige Demokraterna. We found examples where design allowed us to see into these emerging dynamics. For instance, public protests against works of modern architecture that were run by the far-right party, which ended up winning a lot of power in the 2018 election. On the other side, we found grassroots campaigns that were trying to save public spaces or make projects resisting top-down dynamics of city change.

We found other ways to exhibit the kinds of creativity and public life that are not normally considered professional, and we put them in the same show with the best designers, architects, and artists in Sweden and beyond. We had, for example, Johan Celsing's project for a mosque in a northern suburb of Stockholm. We built a one-to-one model of its dome in the museum as a gesture during an election campaign dominated by the conversation around immigration from the Muslim world. We wanted to invite people to come to the museum and walk under the dome of a mosque, maybe for the first time in their own country, because there are more or less no custom-designed mosque buildings in Sweden. What is this cultural artifact? It is both an accurate depiction of an unbuilt building, a design tool, and a piece of evidence that shows us how society is changing at the symbolic level. The exhibition tried to help the public ask questions about that change. **So, how is this approach you just described helping or supporting the practice and practitioners of design and architecture itself? Do museums have to serve this role? And if so, how do you enable that through programming?** That's a very good question because it is the question that is most holding back design institutions around the world, I believe. Because we can't escape the feeling that there's a lot of pressure on institutional leaders, and there was on me too, to go and tell the world how great architects and designers are. My answer is that, unfortunately, only 10% of any artistic discipline at any time in human history has been any good. Is it our duty to campaign for the 90% who are not doing good work? Do you want me to go and advocate for those people? Does the government want that?

I don't believe they do. But at ArkDes, we had a certain responsibility to do that. So that's why I created the ArkDes Think Tank, which was a policy unit initiating practice-based research projects around the country. The think tank had as its topic the application of architecture and design skills to complex problems in society. And in that context, I have no problem at all in saying you need design; society needs more design professionals. We need more architecture in complex processes of urban change. And ArkDes today does that very effectively. We brought in tens of millions of krona to do research and fund open-ended design charette projects looking at how the north of Sweden is changing in the context of resource extraction, Indigenous people's rights, new technological industries, etc. These were practical projects bringing design talent into that machinery.

Carlos Mínguez Carrasco, who was the chief curator at ArkDes throughout my time there, made the exhibition *Kiruna Forever* (2020) about the city of Kiruna in the north of Sweden. It took in all of those dynamics in a way that's open-ended. Our audiences, including our professional publics, have the opportunity to come to a place where their minds are not already made up; they can decide for themselves whether the many kinds of transformation coming to a place like Kiruna through these practices are the right ones for that place.

So, the exhibitions could be critical and open, while at the same time, in the think tank, we were in the business of advocacy. We were working together with people like Dan Hill (then at Vinnova, the national innovation board in Sweden), the national architect (Helena Bjarnegård), and many others to create broad stakeholder participation in design projects that had real outcomes on the ground. We found a way to do both things. I think it was important to have two brands: one saying the work of a museum is to allow everybody to make up their minds about what good architecture or design is. The public should be free in museums to make up their own minds. But when we're in our policy mindset, working with municipalities and government agencies, we need to be advocating hard for the best of what design can contribute to society.

That's why it was so important that I had a chair on the National Council for Sustainable Cities, where I was able to influence the National Housing Board (Boverket) and other agencies like the National Energy Board (Energimyndigheten) or the National Research Council (Formas). It was our duty to influence those organizations in terms of what design can offer them.   **It is certainly an incredible setting, one where you can implement real-life impact. Yet I wonder what you think are the** limitations of operating within that kind of governance structure, with full public subsidies. One could argue that regardless of the source of funding—state, philanthropy, or commercial sponsorship—nowadays museums can easily fall prey to all sorts of manipulations, whether motivated by private or corporate interests or political agendas.

That's a really good question and one that we all think about a lot today. I think the dynamics have changed and are changing. The first thing to say about ArkDes is that, however I might complain about the Swedish public sector and its difficulties, the Swedish civil service is a robust, transparent system with very low corruption and with significant independence given to experts.

So, the government could not instruct me on how I should set my priorities within my institution. That's a principle of the whole Swedish civil service. I was, in Swedish, a "myndighetschef," a director of a national authority. Without that formal status, I would not have had a seat on the National Council for Sustainable Cities. I would not have been able to persuade the National Innovation Council or the National Housing Authority to give millions of krona to design-related projects on the ground. It was a tremendous advantage, especially for the more advocacy-based work that we were doing, to be a real public sector organization.

For me, as a creative person, I felt, in the end, that the problem with the Swedish system is that you get very adapted to it. You start to understand the kind of answers the public sector wants, and you can't avoid the feeling that sometimes it's easier to just give them those answers. As soon as I started to feel like I was doing that, I knew it was time to move on.

The other side to your question is that I think when I started in the V&A, we all felt public money was more morally pure than private money, like there was something inherently better and less corrupt about public funding and public space. But there is nothing inherent that makes it morally better. We see that particularly now in the cultural sphere in relation to the Israel-Palestine war and the chilling impact it is having on publicly funded institutions. The success of an institution does not depend on public or private money but on how it governs its spaces and practices. I think the picture is much more complicated than we thought back in 2012, especially with the way that far-right political parties are trying to instrumentalize cultural policy in Europe. **You have said it now and did before on other occasions that you believe curators are public intellectuals. Being in a leadership position, where you are crafting the narratives and spaces to exercise that type of agency, how do you support or empower this notion through programs, actions, and within the internal mechanisms of the institution?** The idea that a curator is a public intellectual was, back in 2012 and even today, a provocation designed to articulate a set of responsibilities that I think curators, especially in public institutions, have.

A good example of that is from the exhibition *Public Luxury*. That show was trying to be responsive to lots of different new dynamics, and one of them was the sudden appearance of terror attacks in Sweden. The day I moved to Sweden in 2017 was the day of the Drottninggatan terrorist attack, where somebody hijacked a truck and drove down the busiest shopping street in Stockholm, killing several people and injuring many more. It was a traumatic experience for the city. Stockholm had no security director before that event, and, of course, the first thing they did after it was to hire one. And then the security industry turned up to start selling products to the city to prevent these kinds of attacks. What we did was commission three designers to make prototypes of a bollard, an object in the public realm that stops cars from driving down the street.

We invited people from outside the security industry to ask how we might use this moment to create not just new protective functions but also propose an alternative to a new infrastructure of cameras and barriers that makes us feel that we're in a police state. We built these prototypes with real materials, we exhibited them, and we invited the security authorities from the city and abroad to come and have a discussion with us about those things and meet those designers. We started a debate in the national press. The City of Stockholm commissioned further prototypes, which we eventually put in the public realm, and today those prototypes stand on the same street where the attack happened.

That's my interpretation of what a public intellectual is: you lead a public conversation but also bring the creativity of your field with you. Through your own ability to communicate into the mainstream of the public debate, you create space for others.   All you have talked about speaks to the idea that an institution should remain as closely as possible embedded in its own locality, serving its own public.

I want to tackle this issue of audiences, particularly considering that in Europe we are going through very violent waves of radicalism. In your view of the institution serving public life and the curator being a public intellectual, how is this shifting the role of both? Ultimately, how is the definition and relation between the "local" and "the rest" transforming?   I think one of the reasons that in the end I didn't want to continue after seven years in Sweden was that the local pressures were too great. When you're in that system, it gives you tremendous agency at the local or national level, but less agency beyond that. The V&A is a museum of the world, one of a small group of international institutions that have the muscles to act globally everywhere, and it's an amazing experience to be there.

I think institutions of design played a really important role in the late modernist period when they first started bridging local and international practices and opening up those practices for local practitioners. These were often small, highly refined "institutions" showing work from overseas for the first time. Now, the networks are much easier to maintain internationally than they used to be, and international work is much more visible. If, as an institution with international ambitions, you are simply on a merry-go-round of practitioners who are the flavor of the month at MoMA and then end up showing everywhere, you're not serving any purpose at all.

Being in a smaller country, I think there is a role in a well-resourced institution like the one I run now (Amos Rex, Helsinki) to bring things that otherwise would never be in Finland. But the point is not just to buy in those people.

The point is, how do we make meaningful exchanges of knowledge, meaningful practice-based collaborations with those practitioners, creating a meaningful context here for them and a way of nurturing the local context?

Carlos has this brilliant phrase that we used to use a lot in Sweden: he talked about "terroir," that the conditions of a given place give rise to a certain character of artistic production. He used to say we're a national museum of architecture and design, so we should ask what people expect to find when they visit. If you're a tourist, then you expect to find Gunnar Asplund; it would be perverse not to show that. But you also expect to find other aspects of that "terroir," not just a Valhalla of national heroes. In Carlos' formulation, it is not national identity that is important.

To think of this in this way helps you escape reductive national identities. "Terroir" has to do with the particular conditions that prompt a certain practice, a certain flavor of a practice in a particular place. But these are not defined by nation-state boundaries and certainly not by ethnicity, because anything can be planted in a given terroir. You want to discover that; you want to feel that; you want to taste that a little bit when you come. As an overseas visitor, you want to somehow find Finland when you come here. But you want to find a kind of Finland that is not trying to define the boundaries of Finnishness. You want to find a Finland that is open, where you could plant your own vine, and it could grow in unexpected ways.

You have now moved to Amos Rex (2024), a private contemporary art institution. How will design and architecture enter your narrative? Do they have a place there?

I'm interested in a reflection on how we reconcile this idea of disciplinary, specialized knowledge with a mainstream entertainment culture that more and more is occupying the territories of the trans-, inter-, and cross-disciplinary that are pollinating contemporary creative discourse.   A couple of answers. My first motivation for coming to Amos Rex was that it is an extraordinary public space. The museum is inside a very prominent and important modernist building here in the center of Helsinki, with an underground exhibition space and a courtyard above it, which is one of the most trafficked pedestrian spaces in the whole city. In July, we had 1.6 million pedestrian journeys across this courtyard.

My trajectory here will be to work with my colleagues to go on a journey from being a very good and successful Kunsthalle to being a Fun Palace: Cedric Price's concept of an institution with many moving parts and many temporalities of programming embracing a spectrum of high and low culture.

What kind of public space is a museum? Of course, a museum is very often a room with fine objects, but it's also everything else you find in a city. It's a public toilet, a place for dating, for sunbathing, for hiding, a place where you can drink wine with your friends or where your child can meet theirs. There are infinite, very precise social phenomena that can happen in a museum, and that's what I love to work on. Now, if you agree that the museum embraces a huge spectrum of what the public realm of the city can be, then some of the best practitioners to discover that potential will be designers and architects.

They understand these dynamics. So, for me, the agency of working in a really central public space in a European capital city that also has a strong architectural character is to invite artists, architects, and designers to plant things there that can unlock new aspects of what a public space can be.

ArkDes, Swedish Center for Architecture and Design
Stockholm, Sweden

Impact-Driven Agency: the Museum and Public Life
Conversation II

Curator Contemporary Architecture and Design
James Taylor-Foster

In the opening article of a six-part column you wrote exploring "spatial and design imaginaries through the lens of the body," you refer to a term first coined by Jennifer Brundle—"interstitionary"—which describes the "often over-looked work that keeps a system, such as society, in harmony"—things that are not tangible nor substantive but are "softly world-shaking nonetheless." That speaks to how "ideas" have increasingly become the object lessons of design. The idea of dissolving canonical boundaries between the field of design and "everything else" can be traced along institutional lines to the likes of Paola Antonelli (*Broken Nature*), Beatriz Colomina and Mark Wigley (*Are We Human?*), Kieran Long, and the Rapid Response Collecting initiative at the V&A or *Public Luxury* at ArkDes, among many others.

What perhaps differs slightly in my own practice is precisely what you touch upon—the interstitial, even less easy-to-grasp aspects of design that float around us and shape the ways in which we are creative, social, inter-dependent, and so on. It has become less about *dissolving* established boundaries and focused more on the possibility to elastically pull something from the "periphery" to-ward the center, if only briefly. I'm less interested in relo-cating ideas from the edge of a discourse to a spotlit center, or from a subcultural space to a "mainstream" one; I'm excited when an opportunity comes to hold an idea tangibly but momentarily—for the length of an exhibition or an event, for instance. Once its moment has passed, it's always fascinating to see whether, or how, an idea might organically enter another kind of discourse. These exer-cises are about playing with the capacity for institutional power to absorb and affect culture.

Perhaps the clearest example of this gesture is visible in the exhibition *WEIRD SENSATION FEELS GOOD* (ArkDes, 2020; The Design Museum, 2022)—an exploration of a feeling: ASMR (Autonomous Sensory Meridian Response). We were seeking to shine a light on an emergent cul-ture, community, and creative field that hadn't, until that moment, entered the space of a museum.

It is an overlooked power of the exhibition to be a vehicle for embodied experiences. I do want to invite audiences to *feel* something, to linger in a space or with a work, to come back for another visit with friends.

Too many institutional exhibitions fail to hit this mark—not because they can't, but because the people or structures behind them seem uninterested in doing so.

Let's roll back to that idea of bringing peripheries into centers, allowing them to somehow disturb a certain narrative that the institution inevitably represents. When you arrived at ArkDes, Kieran Long was appointed director and tasked with giving shape to a national institution dedicated to Swedish architecture and design. What were the priorities that you set for yourself within that wider mandate? The museum had been in a rut for a time; visitor numbers were low, and the museum's positioning within the local and international cultural sphere was flatlining—and Kieran Long had been appointed by the Minister of Culture, Alice Bah Kuhnke, to steward the place toward a new era. It was exciting to me that a minister of culture cared enough about discourse around design and architecture and about an institution to place trust in the right person at the right moment.

I remember an internal conversation in early 2018, perhaps, in which someone asked, "Shouldn't an architecture museum build architecture?" It's a fair question! We looked at the buildings that house the museum—a combination of military exercise halls that were renovated and expanded by Rafael Moneo Architects at the turn of the millennium—and we soon saw the importance of adjusting them in order to house an ambitious exhibition program. This became a two-pronged project—one long-term and another more improvisational effort. The first and most pivotal adjustment was the commissioning of a new studio gallery that sat at the core of the museum, which we affectionately called BOXEN (2018–23) and was designed by Dehlin Brattgård Arkitekter. Seeing as we couldn't extend the museum's display environments by building outwards, the best option was to densify the spaces that we had.

BOXEN turned out to be a special space, largely because of its scale and flexibility. We imagined it as a platform for fast-changing, experimental exhibitions with considerably lower budgets and resources than the headline exhibition program. It was a powerful piece of architecture in its own right: a 150sqm double white cube environment made of steel, metal mesh, and plywood, with a vast oculus and a ramp around its perimeter. Positioned amid a now long-gone permanent display, the gallery rather poetically appeared as an inhabitable "model" among a sea of models tracing the history of Swedish architecture. Through working with it, I came to understand this room as a curatorial engine of sorts —a space to do things that might not fly anywhere else. It felt as though we were able to fail here, too. Over time, BOXEN became the site for some well-attended exhibitions—from Space Popular's *Value in the Virtual* (2018) and an exhibition about the craft of Swedish videogame design (2019) to *Cruising Pavilion: Architecture, Gay Sex, and Cruising Culture* (2019) and *WEIRD SENSATION FEELS GOOD* (2020).   **ArkDes defines itself as a "museum, a study center, and an arena for discussion about the future of architecture, design, and citizenship." Over the past six years, how have you mediated between these three vectors around architecture, design, and citizenship?**   The revisioning of ArkDes incorporated this broad notion of "citizenship" into the museum's core, government-mandated mission. In a single word, it foregrounded the civic agency of architecture and design, a reminder that these are highly political, social, and cultural spaces.

We've had the privilege of inviting architects and designers to imagine new public spaces, build them at full scale, and let them operate as a part of the city on the island where ArkDes is located. Studio Ossidiana created a public space designed for birds and humans, the collective Swedish Girls built public furniture, Linda Tegg created a biodiverse meadowland, and MYCKET has co-created a more-than-human play environment at the museum. Over time, ArkDes has become an institution with knowledge of what it means to work with creative minds to propose new types of public space. The conceptual anchor of "public life" has proved to be a flexible concept and a bellwether as we have worked over recent years.   How do you mediate your contribution as a citizen and as a professional in this ambition to turn the institution into a platform for societal debate? This is a very potent role to play as a cultural practitioner, but how do you reconcile the two?   The conflict between the fact that I am an individual who embodies certain beliefs and ideologies and that, in my role at ArkDes, I have represented and worked within a government body is a continual negotiation and an interesting dilemma. There have been incalculable moments over the years when I have been in direct conflict with myself, the institution, or both —whether that is politically motivated or a challenge to the system at large. The oversimplified truth is that I believe it's (mostly) possible to inhabit conflicting roles simultaneously; you steer your way through by way of micro-decisions in every project you are working on, in meetings and deliberations, and in questions of communication.

The collaborative energy within institutions is what helps any cultural practitioner navigate such complexity. As a curator, there are two types of role I tend to take: one as the facilitator and the backgrounded conversationalist, and the other as a more prominent spokesperson who must embody the essence of a project. I work just as hard and diligently for both types, but the ways of being are different. There is, perhaps, a third model that has appeared more recently to me through working with Joar Nango and his collaborators on the presentation of *Girjegumpi: The Sámi Architecture Library* at the 18th Venice Architecture Biennial in 2023. This project required a more facilitative curatorial role but also involved a large amount of labor in what might be called "defending the space." In other words, to negotiate between three co-commissioning institutions and the institution of the Biennale in order to carve out a space where the artists could work as uninhibited by rules and bureaucracy as possible. Being a project led by Indigenous perspectives, this is a body of work that I could never speak *for* but only about. Working collaboratively to develop a project of this scale and nuance also meant tending to a new territory of operation for ArkDes, too—one that continues. We need to put an end to understanding the role of a curator as one of binaries in which you're either yourself or you're not. If there's one irrefutable truth, it is that we are bodies of feeling—and an institution can never be. So much curatorial work is embedded in deep and real relationships and networks, and the practice at its best is defined by a person's capacity to bridge, connect, hold, and edit.   **Let's talk about publics and what you think you have achieved over these past six years since you started. Besides supporting an appreciation of design and architecture in our contemporary society, there is a need to reinforce the role of institutions within the wider context of civic and social life.**

These two issues are coterminous and resonate with what you just mentioned—this risk zone that one always inhabits when working within a cultural institution, where the personal becomes something else. **What are your thoughts on this?**   When the project to reimagine ArkDes began in earnest in 2021, I co-edited a series of essays under the title *Solicited: Proposals* with *e-flux Architecture*. We wanted to blow open this question of transformation by parsing the architecture exhibition—and, by extension, institutions—to untangle and rethink its meaning and its potential, all through a series of elements. One contribution, penned by Vasif Kortun and entitled *The Threshold*, I return to time and again. In it, he argues that the threshold "is not about accessibility, fluent information, charming socialization spaces, attentive staff, or guards who do not hound you." It is more about the conditions of how the two parties come to trust each other. "It is a fluid contract," he suggests, "not a once-and-done deal. It is also not merely about the 'offer,' but how the institution acts upon the world, its demeanor, its decency, how it levels with a situation, and how it treats the user as wiser than itself."

There is, as you point out, a great deal of confusion today about what a cultural institution is, should be, or could be. Beginning by thinking through the threshold as a concept, rather than a revolving door or a window display, is one of the keys to emerging from the mire. The trick is not to batten down the hatches and try to defend the dogma and infinite permanence of an institution as a bastion of knowledge or authority, but to find ways of embracing slippery ideas and societal friction.   **Let's talk about the reopening of ArkDes, which took place in the autumn of 2024 after a year-long overhaul of its spaces. What new approaches are you trying to weave in as gestures that pollinate the new framework of the institution?**   The hardware and the software are entwined. The revamp of the spaces, which are heritage-marked buildings, has been undertaken by Arrhov Frick Arkitekter. They have engaged with a puzzle piece of epic proportions, reappropriating around 70% of existing material in the museum from the likes of BOXEN and former exhibitions. From this, they have designed highly versatile vitrines and displays, movable spatial structures, and furniture. Reorganizing the interior has allowed us to reopen a historic entrance, which in turn opens into an interior public space for orientation, events, and hanging out. Sequentially, visitors can then enter a new temporary exhibition space and a large-scale collections exhibition, which presents more than 500 original and rotating works from the Swedish state architecture collection. A key aspect of all of this has been the work of A.M. Stockholm, which created a new visual identity for ArkDes that spans the physical spaces of the museum to the city and online. It is, in many ways, an impressive symbiosis of design skills to create a coherent presence for the museum.

The software manifests in a series of experiments that are tied to the environments that ArkDes now accommodates, and the museum is now capable of absorbing new ways of meeting visitors. One such experiment we have called "Unboxing"—a station within the collection exhibition where material is uncovered, organized, digitized, and discussed. Every day, including weekends, at least one curator moves from their office and is out in the public spaces of the museum opening folders. The curiosity of the thing—part performance, part real collections work—draws visitors in, and conversations emerge from seeing objects that might never have been seen before.   **What about your own current research? A lot of your work has dealt with digital life and culture, and I know that you've been looking into Live Action Role Play. Why do you want to bring this**

into an institutional context?   One of my current preoccupations is in trying to think through the ways in which we are all imagining alternate worlds, and the research hinges around the creativity and culture of Live Action Role Play (LARP). Similarly to ASMR, LARP and other sophisticated worlding practices have not yet been embraced fully by an institutional setting, and certainly not through the multifaceted lens of design. I imagine that the eventual exhibition will outline the shape of a practice that blends visual art, design, performance, fashion, and more—and will involve some serious reconfiguration of the institution as host. I'm interested in worlding practices that reach beyond binary thinking in order to help us grasp the plurality of the ways we connect and how we might nurture ourselves, our communities, and the world we are in.

This research was prompted by a symposium called *The Limits of Our World* which was held at ArkDes in 2022. This project has also come to embody an important shift in my own thinking: namely, that there is no longer any meaningful distinction between so-called "digital" and "physical" creativity. The two are now largely blended —and will continue to meld. Exploring the design of the self through virtual avatarism is synonymous with character design in a LARP, for example. A key thread among many that binds LARPers and ASMRtists and creative agents is also something that sits at the root of how I want to make space for the expanded field of design: that both can be done by anyone, with or without any specific form of training. This is fundamental to my belief in the civic power of design.

The "More-than" Realm

VI

The Museum as a Testing Ground

Director
→ Aric Chen

Let's start by talking about the state of things with design now. Not unlike many of your colleagues currently working within institutions, you come from a career of active independent practice, from journalism to curatorial work done across various geographies, engaging with contexts and typologies of projects of various scales and natures. It seems to me you have all along framed design as a global conversation. So, where have the epicenters of this expanded dialogue moved over the past 10 to 15 years? What defining characteristics do you observe nowadays across the landscape of design, and what has changed?   I think what has actually *not* changed is that every place, irrespective of where it's geographically located, is both a center and a periphery: a center for its own cultural practices and a periphery for someone else's. I don't think that has changed as much as our *awareness* of it has. What has led to this greater awareness is, of course, globalization. You, I, and most of the colleagues you refer to have, in many ways, been shaped by this period of (now unravelling) globalization that began in the 1990s. It was this ethos of ever-dissolving borders and fluid mobility that, alongside new bodies of postcolonial thinking and theory, led to a focus on narratives and perspectives that were underrepresented in the traditional, mostly Western centers of institutional discourse. Perhaps even more consequentially, it spurred new institutional and other practices in places that may not have had them previously.

This kind of flattening of the world, or polycentrism, was a direct response to Euro- or Western-centrism. To the extent that it amplified once-hidden or marginalized voices, I think we're all richer for it. Of course, it also makes for a messier and more chaotic landscape, just as we're seeing in the broader political and geopolitical spheres. Changing power dynamics always produce a sense of unease, especially among those who feel de-centered, and that is something we are all contending with.

Which leads to your question about how things have changed in design. It's interesting that you started by asking about "the state of things." In 2009 I was on the curatorial team for the inaugural exhibition of the newly built Design Museum Holon, just outside of Tel Aviv. It was a global survey of contemporary design—a kind of Design 101 for this new audience of a new design museum —and we called it *The State Of Things*. Ten years later, the museum asked me to curate its 10-year anniversary show, which I did with Maya Dvash, its chief curator. This time, we called it *State Of Extremes*. The implication was that design had shifted from being about objects or "things" toward a greater intertwinement with increasingly complex conditions. In this case, we looked at design as a mechanism for responding to, and sometimes exacerbating, the cycles of backlash, pushback, and spiraling feedback loops that have more and more pushed our world to extremes, from extreme weather to extreme inequality and polarization.   In this broadened spectrum of the way we understand and therefore need to communicate what design does and is, what are the inherent challenges? One could argue this was always the case, even in the mid-1900s when "good design" needed to be valued for its socially and economically beneficial character.   What I love about design is that if you ask 100 people what design is, you'll get 100 different answers. I find this kind of malleability to be one of design's strengths. It opens up a lot of possibilities, but that, of course, also brings up challenges in describing what design is, and, in following, what it can do.

Personally, I am not so concerned with definitions in the parochial intra-disciplinary sense, except to the extent that they hinder potentials. We are limited by the knowledge and institutional infrastructures of design, which are still very much rooted in the 20th century. I don't think we've developed the vocabulary yet for what design has become; much less have we evolved our institutions—our schools, museums, and professional organizations—to adapt to design's expanded parameters and capacities. And so we find ourselves in a kind of disciplinary limbo in which there is a growing gap between design discourse and design practice, design institutions and the design industry, and between all of them and the broader public, and that is our biggest challenge at the moment.

Before moving to Rotterdam, you were part of a team that

was building up an institution from scratch, which is M+ in Hong Kong, where you headed the architecture and design curatorial division. China and then Hong Kong also provided you with a particular vantage point that speaks exactly to the dynamics you just mentioned. What opportunity did you see in leaving that context for Europe, and once you installed yourself at the Nieuwe Instituut, what priorities did you set for yourself? As much as I hate to admit it, I think my main interest nowadays is in institutional infrastructures and how they can be maneuvered to create new forms of cultural production. I say that I hate to admit this because I've never thought of myself as an institutional creature. But perhaps that's the point: I'm intrigued by how one might infiltrate, or even hack or co-opt, if you will, institutional frameworks to advance new modes of thinking and working. And I think it's exactly this that drew me to my current position in Rotterdam, coming from my experience in China and other parts of the world.

Looking back, having bounced around from museums and biennales to design fairs, design weeks, journalism, academia, and so on, the common thread has always been a desire—or even compulsion—to see how we can push these structures and formats to do more, to rethink their formulas. Some efforts have been more successful than others. But I guess what has tied China to Rotterdam and the Netherlands for me has been the ability that both places offer to experiment with institutional practices.

When I was approached for the job at Nieuwe Instituut, what drew me was the realization, in my mind at least, that there is quite possibly no other institution like it in the world—one that brings together the three disciplines (architecture, design, and digital culture) that broadly represent the spaces, things, and interactions by which we construct the world we inhabit; that bridges a remarkable historical archive and collection with a mandate for experimentation and innovation; that explicitly works at local, national, and international levels; and so on. We present exhibitions and public programs, of course, but also a broad range of research trajectories while supporting talent development efforts, contributing to national policy developments in the areas of culture, creative industries, spatial planning, and heritage; and furthering international exchanges, whether by connecting Dutch practitioners with their peers in Dakar and Indonesia, commissioning the Dutch pavilion at the Venice Architecture Biennale, or curating the cultural program for the Netherlands at next year's World Expo in Osaka (2025). Our complexity as an organization is somewhat an accident of our convoluted history, but it has resulted in what I see as powerful potential for rethinking what a cultural institution is and what it can do.

The history of this institution, ever since its foundation—predating its naming as Nieuwe Instituut in 2013 —has always been subject to very strong political framing. At M+ in Hong Kong, you added a voice to a global conversation, making the museum an incarnation of a vantage point that looked at the world from an Asian perspective. With the Nieuwe Instituut, at the time you arrived, you were confronted with somehow doing the reverse: redrafting or updating the institution's mission, originally built with a strong national mandate, to enter a dialogue with a post-pandemic world of unsettling dynamics of change. You're right that I was attracted to the Nieuwe Instituut for the possibilities that this incredibly complex institution offered, as well as the ethos of experimentation, the fluidity of thinking, and the commitment to social and ecological urgencies that were already deeply embedded in the organization. I've been quite fortunate in inheriting some very strong foundations.

However, to the extent that we were criticized in the past, there was a sense that we had become too inscrutably advanced and inward-looking, to the point where many stakeholders—from the public to the architecture and design communities in particular—felt alienated. To be frank, I do think we had become a bit too dogmatic and totalizing in our approach, in a way that other progressive organizations can perhaps relate to.

So, the first thing was to step back a little, re-engage with the disciplines of architecture, design, and digital culture in ways that are more familiar to more people, while opening our doors to a wider range of stakeholders and collaborators. The immediate priority was to become more outward-facing and, in doing so, bring a broader array of voices and perspectives into contact with each other.

This goes beyond simply engaging more communities and drawing more visitors. It's about more fully connecting with the world, questioning the role and ability of a cultural institution to have an impact outside its walls. And this leads to the idea of the cultural institution as a testing ground.

For me, this is absolutely critical, and it points to a crisis in relevance for cultural institutions generally. As a field, we have, to some extent, relegated ourselves to being places for discussion, debate, and presentation, for organizing talks and exhibitions, perhaps commissioning research and installations, and producing the occasional publication. All of this is important—it's not a matter of either/or—but in this era of perpetual crisis, is it enough? The way most cultural institutions have addressed the many social and ecological challenges we face—and this is not a condemnation; it's really just an observation —is that we've mastered the art of posing questions and raising awareness. But I think we can do more. Beyond platforming and producing new research, ideas, and speculations, can we also actually *enact* some of them as testing grounds?

We occupy a privileged space—a kind of third space. That is to say, though we're all set up differently, by and large, we're not government per se, nor are we the private or commercial sector per se. We inhabit a kind of in-between space that, crucially, interfaces with a wide range of publics in ways that give us the ability to create "real-world" scenarios for testing new propositions in ways that government and industry couldn't or wouldn't dream of. We all talk about the need for radical change, but who's going to be the first to jump? So, why don't we take some of these propositions that are floating around, which we discuss in our auditoriums and exhibit in our galleries, and actually enact them?

Our problem is not a lack of ideas, nor is there a shortage of platforms for discussing and displaying them. We also have sprawling bodies of existing research to draw from. The problem is what to do with it all, how to take it forward. This is where the notion of the cultural institution as a testing ground comes in. If we can't try some of these things out, who can? What is the risk for us?   **Give me some concrete examples that embody this approach. On other occasions, you have spoken of this idea of the museum as a testing site through the concept of "enacted speculations."**   One example is the Zoöp. This is an idea that was initiated by one of our researchers, Klaas Kuitenbrouwer, and that was first presented at Nieuwe Instituut as a speculation in 2019, under my predecessor, Guus Beumer. Essentially, it's a governance model—building on Indigenous knowledges, the rights of nature movement, more-than-human discourses, etc.—that brings non-human interests and voices into an organization's decision-making processes as a way of furthering more ecologically regenerative practices. It's a methodology developed through extensive research, workshops, and collaborations that includes appointing a "Speaker for the Living" to one's board of directors, forming an internal working group to identify and implement more-than-human practices in annual cycles, and so on.

And so my question was, "Okay, this is a fascinating idea. Why don't we stop talking about it and start doing it?" So, in April 2022, we became our own guinea pig. We spun the Zoöp off into an independent non-profit foundation and institute and formally signed on to become the world's first Zoöp. The speculation became an enactment. To some, the idea sounded strange or even silly: a national museum appointing a "Speaker for the Living" to represent birds, plants, and microbes on its board of directors. But here's the thing: once you make something a reality, it suddenly starts to seem less strange. As we finish this conversation (in late 2024), we've measurably increased the biodiversity of our campus, greatly improved our sustainability efforts, and, perhaps most importantly, shifted our mindsets and those of others toward making the cultural changes, however modest, that will be needed to ensure a habitable planet in the long term.

Four other organizations in the Netherlands have become Zoöps, with 6 to 8 more to be added imminently in the coming months. Dozens more have committed to working their way toward becoming Zoöps. And perhaps most remarkably, earlier this year, on two separate occasions, the Municipality of Amsterdam began the process of implementing Zoöp principles in the regeneration of neighborhoods and a major park in that city. In less than three years, what sounded to some like a silly speculation has started to become government policy. It's still early days, but so far, so good, and all it took was for a cultural institution to take the first step in making it real.

I hope our New Store will be another example. As you know, for years, we've seen an almost endless churn of speculative projects by designers questioning the role of design in the capitalist commodity system that requires more extraction of resources and generates more waste, etc. So, in graduation shows, in biennales, and in award competitions, we've seen designers questioning their complicity in these systems and proposing new relationships between production and consumption, new ways of defining value, and new modes of exchange that aim to be more socially and ecologically regenerative. And so, having seen so many of these proposals, we ask, why can't we test them out with real customers in a real store? We just soft-launched the New Store at Nieuwe Instituut, having already mounted a couple of pilots: one at Dutch Design Week last year in Eindhoven and another earlier this year at Milan Design Week.

In Eindhoven, one of the projects we tested was Arthur Guilleminot's Piss Soap. Arthur makes soap out of human urine—urea being a natural disinfectant that's already used in commercial skin care products—and recycled cooking oil. In Milan, we organized a pop-up hair salon at Stecca 3.0 where you could get a free haircut by a professional stylist as long as you gave more than 3 centimeters of hair and agreed to have it sent to Human Material Loop, a Dutch studio that has developed a process for turning human hair into yarn. Now, these are all slightly provocative projects, and purposely so; when you're at a design week, you're competing for attention. But there are learnings from doing this that can apply to other cases in more scalable ways.

Now that we've opened the New Store on a long-term basis at our home in Rotterdam, we see the store as a node in a nexus of ongoing research, enactment, and feed-back—a collaboration between us, academics, designers, their (local) ecologies of making, and our visitors/custom-ers that challenges assumptions about production, con-sumption, and behavior and asks if such a thing as regener-ative consumption is possible within some approximation or iteration of a market system.

This is the value in taking this on as a testing ground. You know, everyone is so afraid of failing. But how do you define failure here? We don't need to make a profit —this comes from our research and programming budgets—so in the worst case, we call it an interactive performative installation! (laughs) To me, the only form of failure is a failure to try. **How are you thin-king through these mission-oriented goals and your relationship with audiences? Who are the publics of these novel directions you're giving to the institution across these diverse facets? For example, how are you redressing certain biases ingrained in your collection, or how are you building new alliances with other institutions and professionals? So, who are your publics in this ex-panded sense?** That is the big question that everyone is asking, and I will once again go out on a limb and say that we've all been trained in a kind of corporate marketing way to think in terms of target audiences. That is to say, you can't be all things to all people; you've got to know your customer, and yes, all of that is true. But in addi-tion to that, I would argue that while we can't be all things to all people, we have to be many things to many people, because if we are to think of cultural institutions as serving society, society is a complex web of diverse yet intercon-nected agendas, perspectives, histories, etc.

Part of this requires relinquishing a certain level of con-trol. You mentioned redressing biases in our collection. Our acquisitions policy has evolved from an emphasis on authors—the traditional canon—toward themes and prac-tices, which have included everything from feminist activist collectives to squatting. We've also been developing tools, including one we call The Asterisk, that allow us—and others—to annotate our collection records with decolonizing and other perspectives as a way of perpetually adding new layers of interpretation in an accretive and co-creative, rather than revisionist, way. This has been made both visible and interactive in the new online collection platform that we recently launched.

But to go back to the broader question about audiences: because of the way Nieuwe Instituut is structured, we not only have to programmatically engage with many publics but also with policymakers, professionals, institutional and academic peers, and others; the key is to articulate the areas where we can bring them together.

In an ideal situation, we can create a virtuous cycle in which policy and public agendas, as well as private and professional agendas, can come together and strengthen each other. So, I would say it's not so much about choosing target audiences or even target stakeholders. It's about developing targeted initiatives, like New Store perhaps, that bring the needs and agendas of the various stakeholders together. **So, what are your performance metrics? What are you required to deliver?** We are not in a golden age of Dutch cultural funding, and, like elsewhere, the situation is only becoming more precarious. But for now, at least, we are still fortunate to be working under a subsidy system that allows us to take risks and focus on the tasks at hand, where fundraising and selling tickets are not existential matters. (This does not mean we neglect visitor numbers; we had our most paying visitors ever last year, at 21% above the pre-pandemic year of 2019, and are set to exceed that again in 2024.)

But being so reliant on subsidies comes with its own risks. We're trying to diversify our income streams, though that also complicates accountability. For now, like all public institutions in the Netherlands, we get most of our funding approved every four years under various subsidy schemes, for which we have to present a four-year plan, and we are essentially evaluated on that. Of course, we'll have our visitor numbers looked at, the collaborations and projects that we do, the number of designers we work with, the initiatives we've undertaken, and so on. That's all there.   Can you speak of how the idea of using the institution as a prototyping platform fits within new policies of expansion of your network and collaborations? I find this a very important aspect of institutional agency that needs to be transformed in view of our current challenges as societies and for the role they play in them. The cultural politics of institutional cooperation must move beyond the itinerancy of shows and the exchange of artifacts.   That's another important point. Institutions cannot stand alone, nor act autonomously, the way we once may have. For one thing, in an age of fragmented discourse, we simply do not have the singular authority we used to, and the issues we tackle are too complex to *not* work with broad networks of knowledge. More pragmatically, we will increasingly have to rely on sharing resources in the way that art museums are no longer simply loaning works to each other, but also sharing ownership and custodianship of them.

What's more, as testing grounds, I would say we have a lot to gain from collaboration. For example, right now there's a big debate in the Netherlands about the marginalization of architecture in the country's spatial planning efforts after decades of neoliberal policies that have heavily favored market-driven approaches. So, we've found ourselves faced with a housing crisis, growing spatial inequality, a range of stalled energy and mobility transitions, and other issues, without the tools or mechanisms to adequately address them.

Many of these issues are not new. Over the years, a wealth of ideas and proposals has been floated for addressing them—and many of those are in our archive. So last year, on the occasion of the 100th anniversary of our collection, we mounted an exhibition called *Designing the Netherlands: 100 Years of Past and Present Futures* (2023). This was in collaboration with the Board of Government Advisors (the office of the State Architect), which has been organizing a series of "Future Ateliers" with contemporary practitioners speculating about how we can start designing now for 100 years into the future. By bringing visions from the past 100 years from our collection together with the questions of today and the future, many useful resonances were found. Everyone saw how much there is to learn from the archive; we don't need to constantly reinvent the wheel. And so we've continued this collaboration with the Board of Government Advisors by opening a long-term space in our building where some of the discussions, workshops, and debates that the show prompted can continue on an ongoing basis. We're also embarking on new collaborations with a network of smaller, local architecture institutes across the Netherlands to develop this initiative at a regional level.

The point, once again, is that no one can take on the big questions of our day on their own. As you know, before it was merged into the Nieuwe Instituut, we used to be the Netherlands Architecture Institute, which is remembered as having been the flag-bearing, one-stop shop for all things architecture in the 1990s and 2000s. Many architects still look back on that nostalgically. In 2022 a motion was passed in the Dutch Parliament to basically revive the idea.

Our response, which we published in a newspaper opinion piece, was that this no longer makes sense, especially when every task that a new national institute might take on is already being undertaken by a vibrant landscape of existing organizations. We don't need yet another institution, but rather a stronger and healthier ecology of existing organizations with roles that are better defined and coordinated. The idea of a single, centralized clearinghouse is, to me, obsolete. We need multiple players doing multiple things in multiple ways in a coordinated, collaborative manner in order to tackle the complex issues we're talking about. And so, earlier this year, we launched Architectuur Overal ("architecture everywhere"), a coalition of architectural institutions and organizations in the Netherlands that is working on just that: better defining our roles, coordinating our efforts, and collaborating on initiatives to reach policymakers and the public.   I was having similar conversations with other peers in terms of institutional cooperation at various levels. One hindering factor that emerged among institutions, especially those covering similar disciplinary agendas, is competition. They compete because they are operating on this matrix of audience engagement that comes from business planning they are not fit for, added to a popularity contest, which is frankly puerile.   Everywhere I've worked, this idea of competition always comes up, and my response, especially when we're talking about cultural institutions in different geographies, is: competing over what? You're not competing for foot traffic or ticket sales. We're all different; we are all structured differently, we have different mandates, different agendas, different contexts, different constraints and capacities, and different stakeholders. In areas where we do overlap, I would say that the world is big enough for all of us. This also applies to collecting—we're doing a lot of work around networked archives—and to discourse as well. The idea of us being in competition implies that we're all following the same formula, and if so, then that's the problem we should be focusing on.

So, what are the new avenues of collaboration that can be useful across institutions, where they can support and help each other instead?   My answer might be unsatisfying to hear, but it is simply that it depends. Every institution needs to find its own answer to this question because we all have different strengths and needs. We are all context-specific, so the question comes down to how our different contexts and how we use those contexts to shape our agendas and approaches can inform and support each other. The problem is that so many cultural institutions, as we've both indicated, are still weighed down by historical baggage that has left us with cookie-cutter ideas about what they should be.

As an aside, and going back to your question about China, what I found so rewarding about being there was the relative freedom from that baggage that we had. What I loved about the Curatorial Lab at Tongji University when I was there was that it was not about applying Western best practices to China, but instead deriving new or alternative forms of curatorial practice from the conditions of contemporary China. You also know this from your work at Beijing Design Week, Bea.

But whether in China, Europe, or elsewhere, the main point for me is that we need to rethink cultural institutions and our role in society. We are searching for relevance. And the irony here, especially with design museums, is that we were actually founded as instruments for change. The V&A was established with the remit of improving the quality of British manufacturing, albeit within an imperialist framework, which kind of set the agenda for most of the design museums that followed. From the 1930s to the 1950s, MoMA's Good Design initiatives aimed to elevate consumer taste, sometimes in collaboration with department stores, and the Brooklyn Museum's Design Lab created direct links between the museum and industry. There was an explicit mandate to connect with the issues and players of the day. Of course, the issues of those days were mostly about selling more products, but how do we reconnect now with the issues of our day, and who are the partners we should be working with? We lost that tradition, and I would argue that this happened when we became co-opted by art museums and connoisseurship, not that I have anything against art museums or connoisseurship. **Considering the different funding models and cultural policies across major world areas, such as Europe, the USA, and China, which would you say stands on safer ground when thinking through possible future horizons of change?** I think it's more about *creating* safer ground than finding it. In China and the USA, in the absence of robust government support, there is perhaps greater opportunity to tap into private funding in new ways if you're creative enough. I would say this is most urgent in the USA where museums are so dependent on a donor class that is aging, and where the next generation seems more interested in social and environmental philanthropy than in seeing their names on a gallery wall. In Europe, the opportunity lies more in national and EU subsidies. But whatever the case, we have to get a bit more innovative in showing how we can make an impact. For Nieuwe Instituut, I see the testing ground as having the most potential: a cultural institution as an incubator of sorts.

But the question remains: why aren't we experimenting more? Another irony is that we spend our days literally putting on pedestals people from the past who broke rules and pushed boundaries, yet we sometimes seem so incapable of taking the smallest risk ourselves. Perhaps it's because we're all too aware of our precarity, but being motivated by fear rarely ends well.

In so many places in the world today, we are driven by the politics of fear. Fear derives its power from uncertainty and, hence, our instinct to project our worst fears onto what we don't know. Of course, cultural institutions will not single-handedly save the world, but what we can do is make the unknown more knowable. For example, by enacting speculations that show what better alternative futures might look like and how they might actually work. If you make it real, it becomes less scary, and then you confront the fear and, in some small way, the politics.

Part of a generation of initiatives born as a response to the agony of separation imposed by the 2020 Covid outbreak, the Institute for Postnatural Studies has retained a foundational spirit of adaptive sensibility to the "space for vulnerability"[1] that it aimed to shelter and nurture for the professional communities growing around its titular ambit of research. Started as a curated series of online gatherings, it is now operated from a flexible office-cum-workshop space of 300 sqm in Madrid, Spain, where its educational, editorial, and cultural activities continue offering a home to multidisciplinary practitioners and thinkers devoted to eco-critical research in the context of post-anthropocentric politics and the ecological crisis.

The early programs launched by the collaborative efforts of a group led by Gabriel Alonso and Yuri Tuma focused on redefining the terms of a "post-natural conversation" by addressing the very modalities of knowledge production and exchange we have available. By establishing an independent study program dedicated to generating novel understandings, as well as framing the challenges implicated in thinking and working with a planetary paradigm, the Institute is both a networked platform and an embodied project that seeks engagement with the instability of its own subject.[2]

The annual Independent Studies Program has grown into a sustainable financial revenue stream for its expanding operations with Cthulhu Books, the in-house publishing division, and various institutional collaborations in and out of Spain. The program represents the cornerstone of a community-oriented ethos of intimate, non-hierarchical methodologies of collaboration that counter the often extractive approach of traditional institutions, which tend to claim ownership over knowledge and specialized connoisseurship by commodifying them for fast consumption. Alonso is adamant about the importance of safeguarding a "space of thinking" in which fluid intellectual encounters can happen, and a condition of uncertainty can be embraced and absorbed as a place of mediation and active listening.

Its seminars, lectures, symposia, and conversations foster real-time encounters with people and ideas around "decentering the human" through academic and creative practice while allowing this growing field of studies, which encompasses critical geography and anthropology to decolonial practice, to produce its own tools and rules of engagement with the wider cultural infrastructure that increasingly needs to connect with the histories, discourse, and theories of ecological debate.

1   From a conversation between the author and Gabriel Alonso (Madrid, May 23, 2024).
2   See Yuri Tuma, Clara Benito and Gabriel Alonso (eds.), *we? Postnatural Independent Program*, Cthulhu Books, 2023.

Antikythera is a program directed by the writer and philosopher of technology Benjamin Bratton since 2022 under the aegis of the Berggruen Institute, the global think tank established in 2010 by the philanthropist and art collector Nicolas Berggruen. Headquartered in Los Angeles, the Institute operates across continental divides through offices in Beijing and Venice, awaiting the opening of a Scholar Campus designed by Herzog & de Meuron and Gensler in Santa Monica, where its educational activities will be hosted. If the Institute more broadly engages with the emergence of a planetary paradigm in the face of collapsing global systems of governance and the mutating conditions of democratic articulation for future politics, humans, and economies, Antikythera functions as the speculative incubator of its philosophical underpinnings.

The program builds on Bratton's long-standing research and theories around planetary sapience and computation, which look at distributed technological infrastructures (satellites, sensors, servers, user interfaces, etc.) as "forming a new kind of planetary observatory that takes the earth itself as its object,"[1] thus becoming forces heralding new modes of apprehending, building, and governing future living environments.

Its foundational principles can be found in his canon-defining book *The Stack*: *On Software and Sovereignty* (2016), where he unpacks the "accidental megastructure" of contemporary algorithmic governance through six layers—Earth, Cloud, City, Address, Interface, and User. Bratton's ideas had been tested through design-centered queries during his directorship of the now disbanded Strelka Institute for Media, Architecture, and Design (Moscow), where he led two research cycles (2016–21).[2] Both engaged a plethora of transdisciplinary thinkers, designers, and programmers in the speculative development of projects investigating alternative urban futures in the framework of an augmented regime of sensing and building the world made possible by machine learning, imaging, and terrestrial modeling technologies.

Antikythera, which takes its name from an ancient instrument of measuring and navigation, i.e., a computer *ante litteram*, further expands and deliberately complicates ensuing epistemological questions and implications in systemic reorganization by taking computation as its core object of inquiry, more intently targeting software engineers, coders, and interface designers. The studio culture formerly deployed at Strelka is here reactivated under the directorship of Nicolay Boyadjiev to adopt scenario-driven modes of inquiry that, by eschewing solutionism, aim instead to stress-test the theoretical agendas of the program and potentially produce new subjects of research along thematic leads (i.e., planetary sapience, synthetic intelligence, recursive simulations, etc.).

By engaging new partners across academia, the private sector, and civil society, the program also includes lectures, salons, and editorial production such as the digital journal *Antikythera: Philosophy of Planetary Computation* realized with The MIT Press.

Amidst growing anxieties and vulgarizations around the pervasiveness of AI in the management and operationalization of everyday activities and their attendant polarizations across technophilic and technophobic camps, the program brings a nuanced and structured approach to unpacking the depths of our shared lives with machines and natural forms of intelligence. It also opens up critical zones of intervention for design to mitigate both risks and facile solutionism in a post-anthropocentric future.

1   See https://codec.earth/.
    Whole Earth Codec, a 2023 research studio at Antikythera.
2   See more on both via Bretton's website https://bratton.info/.

The Thai entrepreneur Pranitan "Pete" Phornprapha, a third-generation member of a vast family business that includes the Siam Motors Group, established Wonderfruit in 2013 out of a desire to further the environmental and social advocacy work his father had long made central to their corporate culture. By tapping into the well-rehearsed leisure culture of his native country and organizing what was originally a music-focused event, Phornprapha intended to build a connection with the traditions and spiritualism that characterize Thai people's relationship with the land and natural ecosystems, transforming a momentous cultural experience into an ongoing process of co-creation with both locals and visitors.

The Field, the 69 hectares on which the festival takes place, is now dotted with various communal pavilions, each serving different cultural and hospitality functions. These structures have been iteratively built with various designers using natural and locally sourced materials. Wonderfruit's ethos of "serving as a think-tank for connecting mind and nature" finds expression in a dense artistic program aimed at transgenerational audiences, revolving around performative and ritual-centered practices of collective experience. Alongside talks, screenings, shamanic invocations, temporary installations, hands-on workshops, and live acts, the festival encourages active participation in tending to and honoring its natural surroundings.

A participatory rewilding project in the adjacent ancient forest was initiated in 2022 in collaboration with Sugi, a team of biodiversity builders that employ the Miyawaki Method, known for its use of native species only, and a local group of planters from Baan Suan Onsorn. This initiative has since given rise to a series of sound-based programs and sonic interventions exploring the histories and powers of trees' connectivity. The Farm, where rice, papayas, and bananas are cultivated, provides food supplies both during the festival and throughout the year. Knowledge transfer through culinary traditions is also central to the festival experience; seminars, artists' projects, and cooking sessions explore heritage recipes, traditional healing techniques connected to locally grown ingredients and Indigenous forms of conservation, and promote transcultural conversations around diversity and socioeconomic emergencies through the lens of food. Annual reviews of experiments aimed at lowering or controlling environmental impacts, such as waste management and water consumption, are documented in the Wonder Reports, which can be downloaded from the festival's website.

While Wonderfruit remains a temporary experience for the thousands of visitors who find their way there every December, it has organically evolved over the past ten years into its own landscape, both human and natural. It provides employment for local workers, builders, and farmers year-round, and by cultivating an expanding network of like-minded practitioners, local organizations, and regional partners, it is now seeking to activate long-term pedagogical and research-driven programs across the fields of arts, design, and science, informed by the situated knowledge of its eco-social system. An example of this is the collaboration with the Okinawa Institute of Sound and Technology to test the beneficial effects of sound on physiological well-being, connecting science and technology to spiritualism.

The **Transformative Power** of **Speculative** Experience

Director
Brendan McGetrick

I want to start from a project you did a while back titled *Unnamed Design*, which is one of two core sections of the 2011 Gwangju Design Biennale that you curated upon the invitation of Ai Weiwei, who was its co-artistic director with Seung H-Sang.

Quoting something you wrote about it at the time: "[...] in its current form, design projects the values of the free market. It is Western-centric, commodity-driven, and wealth-dependent. [...] Where in the West design is often a tool for exclusion, in Gwangju it can be inclusive, accepting contributors from across cultures and classes. Rather than proposing a single, globalized template for the world to follow, at the biennale, design will become a codeword for the invention of new forms of difference. It expands the boundaries of design to include fields such as bioengineering, virtual communication, capital punishment, premodern technology, and non-violent protest. Ours is an exhibition about the power of ideas, a salvo in honor of the millions of acts of imagination that occur outside the limits of 'design.'"

I find this extremely prescient in terms of the core implications we address in design today. Looking at the state of affairs we live in now, have these notions you provoked taken hold, or where are we today with understanding what design is and does?   Almost 15 years later, I'm still really proud of that show. We were a tiny team, and most of the show was composed of original works that we made simply because we had to. There was no other way to exhibit the "design" of things like political protest, plastic surgery, and improvised explosives without doing it yourself. (Ai) Weiwei initiated the concept but then was arrested; very unfortunately, he missed most of the development of the show. But his spirit infused everything and gave us the courage to be bold and totally unapologetic about our perspective and our choices. He's someone who is very comfortable disturbing conventional wisdom and questioning the fundamentals of any social system. And this attitude fueled everything we did.

That was what *Unnamed* was about, really—disturbing the conventional idea of design and potentially destroying it completely in order for a more generous and inclusive one to emerge. We basically said, "What if you reject the idea that design is limited to a few established disciplines —architecture, fashion, graphic design, industrial design, etc.? What if "design" is actually just a way of thinking and a way of looking at the world? How would that change our understanding of design and of life itself?"

So, then the next question is, what defines this way of thinking, seeing, and ultimately doing? One of our first conclusions was that design has to be functional. It isn't a pure expression of the mind. This is what distinguishes it from art. We felt that drawing a clear line between design and art was essential because too often design exhibitions are just a bunch of contemporary artworks created by designers. But this completely misses the point and, in my opinion, does a disservice to both design and art.

Design is so powerful because it responds to needs that can be identified and articulated. A work of design should play an indefinable role. It should have a practical purpose. Art plays a role, of course, and has an important purpose, but it's ultimately a space of free expression. That's its power. Design has a different kind of power, and the *Unnamed* show was a celebration of that power.

In order to back this up, we needed to show design as a way of engaging with the world and responding to specific challenges and opportunities, and the only way we could do this was by selecting examples from outside the conventionally recognized design disciplines. This was an incredibly fun challenge, not only in identifying examples but even more in finding ways to reveal the design hidden within them.

Through the process of making that show, we had so many fascinating conversations and collaborations with scientists and people in sports, medicine, journalism, and science. They were doing incredibly interesting and important work that was locked away inside their professions. There were no ways to communicate it to a wider public, especially in an exhibition format. So we had to invent techniques for that.

One example was about genetic modification. We were very keen to demonstrate that synthetic biology should be considered a form of design. So we chose a very simple example, a product called Golden Rice. It's essentially a genetically engineered strain of rice that has been bio-fortified to provide vitamin A. It was created in response to the needs of communities that don't eat meat, either for economic or religious reasons, and therefore suffer from iron deficiency and other health problems.

We reached out to them and explained the premise of the show. They were enthusiastic, so we asked if they had any material that clearly showed the steps required to modify the rice and change its essential properties. And they were like, "Absolutely! We've got just what you need!" And then they sent this incomprehensible Power-Point deck that none of us could understand. We had a call, and they said, "See, it's all right there!"

We knew we could never exhibit that, so then we started this really fascinating and inspiring back-and-forth with the scientists. We would sketch our understanding of the process, and they would respond, correcting it and adding to it. Eventually, we arrived at a fairly simple info-graphic that illustrates the design process behind a genetically modified strain of rice.

We had many of these kinds of exchanges for other exhibits, and they all came from the same place: simply needing to prove that something no one considers a design work is actually the product of a very careful process that can be understood as design.

Looking back, I wish we had iterated more on this premise and solidified some visual communication and translation techniques that we established for the show. I think they were really effective and would have been empowering to a lot of people because they weren't high-tech and they weren't dependent on much. But they worked because we knew exactly what we wanted to say and just needed to develop a new language for that.

The exhibition tried to articulate the idea of how a variety of acts of creation in our everyday life are acts of design. **Do you think it is still necessary today to spell out for audiences what design is and what the value of design is?** I think it's good to spell out what design is, only if it's empowering for people. Part of what we were trying to do with *Unnamed* is to say it doesn't matter who the person is or who made the thing. What matters is what they're trying to achieve and how successful they are at achieving it. There's an empowering message that essentially says that the things around you—the experiences, the objects, the systems—are products of decisions. They are designed with intention, and understanding those intentions helps you to better understand and navigate your world.

The title *Unnamed Design* opens up infinite room for interpretation. We tried to make the most of that. For example, we looked at the creation of the Eurozone as bureaucratic and monetary systems design. We showed how its creation was essentially a sequence of treaties that ultimately reimagined a continent in a deeply radical and imaginative way. Regardless of how it might look —a bunch of pictures of old European men sitting around in meetings—the process of bringing the Euro and the entire economic and monetary union into existence was very carefully designed. It had to be in order to succeed.

So, in a sense, "design" provides a very useful metaphor to help people understand that the forces that surround us are acting with intentions. It's in our best interest as citizens and members of a community to understand these intentions and the mechanisms that have been put in place to enact those intentions. Those mechanisms are designed, and recognizing this helps us understand what they are truly trying to achieve.

To me, all of that is valuable, not necessarily for people appreciating design but for appreciating that the world around us is understandable. Experts, including designers, intentionally obscure processes. It's in their interest to keep things a bit magical and mysterious. But Weiwei and I strongly felt that the public deserves transparency. *Unnamed Design* was a kind of manifesto for greater transparency in what design is and what design can do. This reveals hidden beauty and ugliness.   That was also a special historical moment when the premise and promise of an Asia-led century were being shaped, driven by China's hypergrowth, its open-endedness, and its sense of the future; that is, culturally speaking, different notions of how the past and present enter dialogue with what is to come. A reality through which we both lived at the time, and you are currently still embedded in, being based in Dubai.

You once stated something I believe is crucial in our contemporary conversations, and certainly for cultural practice and discourse, which is that globally we have long lived and operated with an idea of the future dominated by American or Western value systems.   I think one important aspect of creativity is in revealing possibilities that are hidden or not yet fully arrived. That's why I said design is a way of seeing. The same has been said about art, of course. Truly great works of art are almost like transmissions from the future; they are expressions of a reality that hasn't yet fully formed but is on its way. In my opinion, we need as many of these transmissions from as many places as possible to get any sense of what is and what can be.

When you talk about the societies that have shaped the future as it is currently imagined, obviously America is probably first on the list because of its technology and popular culture. But the Soviet Union had a radically different understanding of the future, and it produced literature, art, movies, and, of course, a space program that reflected this vision. Now more than ever, it's important to remember how culturally and historically specific the American consumerist vision of the future is. That's not to say it doesn't have value and it isn't inspiring, but it's one voice that often seems to drown out all others.

What's been so interesting, for example, about Liu Cixin's novel *The Three Body Problem* becoming a global sensation and Netflix series, etc., is that it represents for many people a first introduction to a way of thinking about the future that's shaped by Chinese experience and values. For me, its sense of epic scale, with engineering megaprojects that are basically planetary in size, speaks to something really fundamental about the heroism and ambition of contemporary China.

There's a kind of massiveness not just in the book's subjects but in its themes. That's one of the things about China, which you know very well, of course: its comfort with the enormity of its size, its population, its history, its drama. The scale of it is so incredible that it requires a value system and political will to think of big collective efforts. This is important because one of the things that the West has lost is the belief in collective projects —big heroic enterprises that take a long time and require a lot of people and don't deliver right away. In Europe, I'm not sure there is a single leader who can envision a project like that, not to mention mobilize enthusiasm and resources toward it. But that's not the case in the Middle East, and certainly not in Dubai.

The leadership here has a vast multigenerational vision. They are constantly evolving and expanding it. The population is behind it because it's inspiring, but also because the city has accomplished so much over the past 50 years. In 1971, when the UAE was founded, Dubai had only one high school and no universities. It had one hospital and virtually no roads. There were only 45 college graduates in the entire country. So, if you think of that as a starting point and you observe the city's current state, it's not hard to believe that a bright future is possible. It almost feels like an obligation. For Dubai's government, its past success is validation for a culture of hugely ambitious projects and radical transformation.

So, Dubai is a place where the default assumption is that the future will be better. There is an expectation of it and a commitment to work toward it. To me, this is invaluable for the city but also for the wider world. The societies that most shaped the future over the past 100 years —America, Russia, Europe (and I'm including the UK in Europe; I guess I'm being nostalgic in that way), and Japan—are much more pessimistic and, to some extent, intellectually exhausted at the moment.

When we started working on the Museum of the Future, we were deeply aware of this dynamic, especially because it's so obvious in the cultural creations of these places. In the West, we are living in a kind of golden age of dystopian art. If you look at the films and television, literature, and video games produced over the past couple of decades, it seems we have utterly lost the ability to imagine a future that isn't some sort of dystopian hellscape. And in saying that, I'm not criticizing the works themselves. Many are excellent and inspiring to us. But it can't only be *Black Mirror*, *Handmaid's Tale*, and *The Last of Us*. Surely there are other options.

When we started conceiving the museum, we said, okay, we're going to be the anti-*Black Mirror*. What's good about *Black Mirror* is that it very sensitively and intelligently identifies dysfunctional aspects of the present. Then it does something that, to me at least, is an easy out: it extrapolates this dysfunction until it defines society and delivers us into a dystopian future. Our response was to say that we want to be as sensitive as *Black Mirror* in identifying the technologies and trends that are affecting the present and could shape the future, but rather than making them worse and worse, we'd show how, with a different set of values and guidance, these same elements could provide the raw material for a healthier and more empowering future.

Even saying that out loud, I think some people will feel it's a naïve or corny position. But in Dubai, the assumption that the future will inevitably be worse comes across as a lazy, dead-end way of thinking. In Dubai, there isn't really an appetite for it. This is one of the reasons why I think it's so important to amplify voices from this region and others. So, what are the values that you see attached to this different way of understanding the future? You have mentioned that the museum is an embodiment of the idea that "the future matters." Can you elaborate on this expression and how design gets involved in the shaping of this narrative? The MENA region (Middle East and North Africa) has a very young population; the median age is less than 27 years old. More than a quarter of the population is under 18. So, the future matters here by default because the vast majority of the population is going to be around for decades to come. And there's a notion among the current leadership in the UAE, especially, that their legacy is determined by what the next generations are able to achieve. I think that's a really important point of view.

In the museum, we have a quote by a 17th-century Chinese scholar which says, "The ancestors plant the trees, the descendants enjoy the shade." When I talked about imagining a future shaped by different values, this is a good example. That quote feels out of step with our current age of personal optimization, but to imagine a better future, it's essential that we see ourselves as part of a continuum that includes our descendants as well as our ancestors.

It can't be overstated how complex the Middle East's situation is—politically, climatically, culturally, and economically. But that complexity and precarity have created a resilience that's very impressive because you need to be able to think beyond the present to survive.

I think there is also an issue of accountability and responsibility, which has completely waned in Western political institutions, as part of the value system that you referred to earlier in terms of having a collective vision and, therefore, designing the collective effort to get there. It's a big difference. All this said, what is the role of the Museum of the Future, which is a governmental initiative, in this picture? And, more broadly, what do you believe is the role of institutions of culture in articulating the complexities of a renewed collective and collaborative endeavor to move our societies forward? I think it's case by case, but for example, the difference between the Museum of the Future and *Unnamed* was that the latter was all about trying to expose the existing values that produced the material world. So, it wasn't about advocating for values except for the value of curiosity. It was to say this is all based on a value system and choices, and so it was about seeing things slightly differently, which I do think is a massively important role of cultural institutions. Like, for example, at the Tate (London), and I don't know if it still does, for a long time the mantra was "look and think again"—that was kind of what they wanted the effect to be, that you see things and it destabilizes you a little bit, and so you think about the world or yourself a little bit differently. And I think that's a really beautiful aspiration.

What the Museum of the Future is trying to do is say that a better future, which is what we're committed to, requires different values. So, the challenge is how do you define those values, and then how do you weave them into every single touchpoint and kind of creative expression within the museum in a way that you're never lecturing or advocating, but it's just woven into the fabric itself and, through osmosis, you realize it?

For example, our space floor is harnessing solar power and then distributing it so that there's a shared renewable resource for the entire world. So, that's a non-capitalist, non-petro vision of energy. We're not obviously giving a polemic against the petro economy; we're just saying, wouldn't it be amazing to mobilize our best technology and create a multinational project that was dedicated to that?

The difference between a museum where you have a curatorial voice and you advocate for things and make points, and us, is that because what we are doing is really about an immersive experience in a possible future, you have to wrap all of those assumptions into the world itself and then let people explore it at their own pace and draw their own conclusions. So, that's a really different model, but I think both of them are important, and it's a really important role for culture in general: to just help people understand the current system and then imagine and want a different system, a better one.   All of the conversations featured in this book, in fact, depart from this assumption: that in a transformed world, we need transformed institutions, meaning that we can't operate with the same models or narratives that were inscribed in traditional institutional constructs almost 200 years ago.

So, two questions: first, I'd love to hear more about this idea that you do not have a permanent collection but "permanent questions" that you deploy in building the experiences and, therefore, stories you address in the museum. And second, can you elaborate on the idea of experience, given that it is a core factor of engagement for the way the museum is conceived, and at the same time, it is a defining factor in the discipline of design as an expression of the imagination that is intentional, functional, and consequential.   So, permanent questions. We knew from day one there was never going to be a collection. How do you have permanence in an institution knowing that nobody is going to be around forever? How do you define some elements that are fixed, which allow you to generate new things, bring in new partners, and have real flexibility within a certain kind of structure that feels right, appropriate, and kind of timeless?

So, we came up with this idea of permanent questions, which affected, more than anything, the creation of the exhibitions before the opening. We had a big global team of designers and artists coming from different places, with different points of view and signatures, and we wanted to make the most of it all. We wanted everyone to be themselves, but we wanted to make sure that it all felt coherent and cohesive. So, that's really what those questions were; they are the kind of questions that you pose for anyone who is going to present something significant in the museum as a way to ensure a certain set of experiential priorities—and, in a way, almost emotional priorities.

Like I said, I really believe that there's an osmosis effect, particularly if you talk about a museum where you have more than one floor and things are related to each other. At a certain point, if you're doing it well, there's a cumulative effect it has on you, and I think that's an important thing to try to achieve. We have a super broad audience from all over the world, and they have nothing in common, so you have to try to achieve a lot of things which are really almost beyond language and thought; they're more about feeling. One of the ways to achieve that is to make sure that these certain priorities are integrated in a way that feels sincere and legitimate, because a big priority of the museum is to make people feel that the future matters, but also that they matter to the future, and it can't feel passive.

In terms of experience, it kind of extends from it, because experience, in my opinion, is about communication, and the challenge that institutions have now is a communication problem.

For example, I wouldn't want the big encyclopedic museums to change; we need them. If anything, we need them to be more of themselves. There's a real power to these museums that are treasuries of things in their embodiment of a certain mentality, and they exist within a very wide and diverse range of other institutions that can do really different things. In my opinion, experience is about exploring; it is education that allows people to understand ideas or be introduced to ideas in new ways. I think that the struggle that a lot of museums have is that the traditional way, which is a wall text and a label, doesn't resonate anymore, or it resonates for a very particular audience. For other audiences, particularly those who don't go to museums, you really need new ways, and that is where experience comes in. One of the things that I find frustrating, especially about immersive experiences now, is that they don't take advantage of that. They put all their energy into just creating this kind of environment, but there's no reason for it. It's like you've opened the door for people, but then there's nothing behind the door.

Culturally, we have this set of tools, like applications, that can be used to create new kinds of environments, new kinds of interactions, and presentations. A lot of them are only being applied in really superficial ways to almost prove that the technology or technique exists. The reality is that the next step is to go, "This very specific technique exists; the best application of it is to do this," and then that thing becomes why the technique is so valuable. That's why there needs to be more intentional effort on that because, at the moment, it's a lot of smoke and mirrors, a kind of titillation and excitement with no delivery. **Can you give some practical examples of how you effected this large-scale, multi-disciplinary, collaborative endeavor with the various designers, technologists, and scientists you engaged for the creation of the various experiences you present at the museum?** I'll talk about a specific work because it embodies almost everything that you're speaking about. It is inspired by climate change and synthetic biology and the idea of how you could purpose-build, or design, species to play a particular role in repairing a damaged ecosystem. So, could you create a species of fungi, for example, that would detoxify the soil? Or could you create a species of tree capable of withstanding forest fires? In order to do that, you obviously need to speak to experts who are biologists and people working in fields that form the foundation of that kind of effort, such as genetic engineering. To the point that I was making before, the basic premise was that we wanted to create an experience dedicated to new values, so applying new science and technology to repair one of our great tragedies and contemporary crises, which is ecosystem collapse and extinction.

So, what if we applied that to repair our relationship with the natural world? If we could do that, what would that look like as an experience? The defining feature of that floor in the museum is something called the Library, a library of the genetic code of theoretically every species on Earth; in the actual lived reality of the museum, it's 3,400 species. Each has a kind of cylinder with a representation of the species, and you would get a device through which you collect the DNA code, and then there are challenges that you follow to try to create one of these purpose-built synthetic species for a specific goal, like the fire-resistant tree.

In order to do that, we have, on the one hand, biologists who are advisors; on the other hand, we have Superflux, who initiated the idea and are a studio of experimental or experiential futurists. They called it the Vault of Life. Then you have Atelia Bruckner, who are exhibition designers, who take that idea and figure out how to make it into an architectural experience, how to make it spatial and give it a sense of awe. Next to them is Marshmallow Laser Feast, who are mostly working in VR and digital representations of the natural world. They worked on the creation of this device that you use to navigate the space, and they also created the soundscape for it.

I think that one of the most effective things in the museum is that, on the one hand, you mobilize awe because it's a big, expansive space, and then you mobilize that basic feeling of excitement when you see something new —it photographs well, like it ticks those boxes. But in addition to that, it's an active experience where you actually do something. You don't just stand in an infinity room and go, "Wow, awesome." You can use it as a tool and become part of the work of this speculative scientific enterprise. To achieve that, you need biologists, futurists, designers, and architects; you need interaction and sound, and all of these things have to be brought into harmony for that to feel coherent—a resolved experience that almost speaks to you on a deeper level than the mind. It touches you in a way that makes you feel the grandeur of life and the expansiveness of life on Earth is somehow embodied in that space, and that feeling can be channeled toward you actually doing something.

The other thing that I think is interesting is that synthetic biology is a super controversial topic that many people have real objections to for a lot of reasons. So, it's challenging to engage with it in a positive way, and to make that feel like a valid premise, you do have to mobilize experience so that it encourages you to rethink your assumptions. If that's a moving enough experience for you in a convincing way, then it changes the way you think about these things. And then that's kind of all you can do, really. Once you've done that, people draw their own conclusions; in the end, it is totally audience-oriented. It's not really about the work as such but about the work as it affects the people who visit it.   **Let's talk about audiences. You have said before that you're not seeking visitors but participants because of this approach that you just described.**

For many institutions, financial struggles translate into having to secure a constantly growing number of visitors, so ticket sales through exhibitions, which challenge them on the kinds of topics and types of content they offer in order to remain competitive in the fast-consumption economy of today's edutainment. In a museum like yours, which has, in a way, gone all the way into a form of cultural experience not mediated by object-based narratives but "expansive experience," to use your words, what are the metrics of evaluation?

What kind of relationship are you building with your audience, and who are your publics now that you have been open for three years?   We have a very particular challenge in the sense that 30% of our audience has never been to a museum before. That's challenging in some ways, but it's also a privilege. We are aware of our obligation to the audience and do everything we can to make sure that what happens when you come to the museum feels special; that you feel cared for and significant to the experience.

Because of the size of the crowds that we have, we put a great amount of effort into visitor experience. We train our staff in practices that are more typically associated with hospitality than museums of culture in general. We're asking ourselves, what can we learn from hotels, live performance, theme parks, and places where visitor engagement really matters? Museums generally don't care much about that or simply don't invest in it, so you have staff interactions either with volunteers or security. Perhaps the people are friendly and nice, but you don't go to a museum expecting to be cared for in any way. You don't go there expecting to feel that you matter to what's happening.

And all of this matters to us because we are aware that so many of our guests haven't been to a museum before or a museum like this one. So, the quality of their experience will have an influence that stretches long after the visit. If you've intentionally created an experience that is meant to be disorienting and to push people to think beyond the world as it is now, then you should feel some obligation to make the audience feel safe enough to try new things and think new thoughts.

From the earliest days of conceiving the museum, we've said that the highest goal of the experience is to be transformative. We are working to transform passive visitors into participants and ultimately into a community of people committed to making a better future.

In the museum, guests will experience certain settings, objects, or interactions that they never imagined possible. By altering their definition of what's possible, we hope to inspire our audience to see themselves and the world anew. By placing them at the center of a story, we hope to spark feelings of empowerment that propel them far beyond their trip to the museum. Our challenge is not to make the museum of the future but to help create the people of the future.

That sounds nice, although a bit crazily self-aggrandizing when I hear myself say it out loud, but the question then becomes, how do you validate this kind of aspiration? It's easy to say, "we want people to be changed by their visit to the Museum of the Future." What does that mean? How do you know if you're achieving it?

In the 2011 updated edition of *The Experience Economy*[1] originally published in 1999 the authors make the point that the age of experience will be followed by one of transformation. They argue that this requires a fundamental re-evaluation of what you're offering and asking people to pay for. In other words, companies enabling transformations should charge not merely for time but for the change resulting from that time. They should charge for the ends and not only the means of life-changing experiences. I like this idea because it seems almost impossible to think of cultural experiences in this way. But if you can't imagine that your experience could influence people enough to be worth paying for, then you probably shouldn't be using any rhetoric about change, transformation, or anything other than the standard, "we've made something, come buy a ticket and look at it."

I do think there's a space for that, but it requires a fundamentally different understanding of the nature of the institution. At the moment, we are all just trying to make good exhibitions, cool experiences, and all that; and I think we have loftier aspirations, but we have no mechanism for pursuing those. It is definitely an issue with defining or redefining purpose, the need to actually revise one's visions and missions regularly within evolving temporal and territorial contexts.

So, by way of a conclusion, I wanted to talk about your own purpose as an institution that is investing substantially in tech-heavy installations and what kind of position you hold when it comes to digital tech and the evolution of social life in the digital realm. What role do you see for yourself there? Finally, what is your current approach to artificial intelligence and machine learning? So, first, the role of technology: we made a very deliberate decision to show technology as a tool rather than an end in itself. Technology is a means of producing a desired effect. The challenge then is to define what effects we desire. How can technology best serve us—serve society, serve the planet? So, we are not about celebrating the glory of technology, but we are dramatizing its potential.

1   B. Joseph Pine II and James H. Gilmore, *The Experience Economy, Updated Edition,* (1999) Harvard Business Review Press, 2011.

There's so much boosterism in certain parts of the media about "technology." Every year there is a new hype that's meant to be transformational: blockchain, NFTs, Metaverse, AR... If we were to add to the hype cycle when they are peaking in public interest, we'll obviously look naïve when they inevitably crash. So, our approach is to try to understand the deeper potential of an emerging technology, and this often requires ignoring the virtues as they are sold by the tech's biggest advocates, because these are often market-driven, anti-social applications. We consider it one of our responsibilities to expand what the public imagines and expects from tech. This requires placing it into a larger, more emotionally rich story.

Artificial intelligence is the most discussed technology at the moment, and we certainly use AI. We use it for creative ends, for coding, and for basic communication. I'd been sold the promise of generative AI for a while, but I never really got it until ChatGPT emerged. We're an organization with people from around the world, most of whom do not speak English as their native language. This presents a challenge and generally means streamlining language to its bare essentials—sort of like text message brevity as the maximum written form. Then ChatGPT comes along, and suddenly everyone's emails are longer and better written. I'm watching colleagues with no technical background and no prior knowledge of AI and machine learning using ChatGPT for almost everything, especially for learning.

In terms of the exhibition content, we use generative AI for mocking things up, quickly generating images or videos. But that's all process; we aren't interested in exhibiting that as work in itself. What I'm really excited about and waiting for is a bit more advancement in developing digital characters who can interact with our audience. We invest a lot in guest experience, and our staff is truly excellent at helping people understand and feel a part of the future scenarios we're presenting. But it's demanding work that you can never provide enough for, given the size of the audience we have. This is something technology can definitely help with, and I'm excited to work with real-time interactions once the tech is a bit more stable.

When we get to that, we'll see a phase shift in the experience because then you can have digital actors who carry on conversations and give people an intimate one-to-one experience without relying on a human being or a pre-programmed recorded version.

We're always striving for more interactions between the audience and the future worlds we present, because even if they're mediated, personal interactions give the feeling that this future is real, it's populated, and I'm a part of it. Technology will help us achieve this by giving the audience a sense that the world sees them, is affected by them, and wants to better understand and collaborate with them. **Well, why not have them mediated by real people?** Because it doesn't scale, unfortunately. We have 3,400 people visiting every day, and you can't possibly have enough staff to accommodate that. Even if you did, the action would have to be constant, so you'd end up with performers "on stage" for eight hours a day, and it would simply be exhausting. **Now, after three years since opening, do you have conversations with colleagues from other institutions who are starting to understand there's something they perhaps can learn from this different approach of yours?** I think many people as- sume assume what we're doing is very specific and very resource-dependent. It's an extraordinary building with a really significant investment in the exhibitions. So, for artists or institutions that have more limited resources, it may not seem like a particularly relevant model. But I personally feel the work we're doing to develop new forms of communication and experiences that speak to diverse audiences has value beyond the Museum of the Future. I would hope it might have some influence because every- one is struggling with the challenge of creating meaning- ful connections to audiences that often share very little in common and are already highly distracted.

One of the museum's best and worst qualities is the di- versity of our audience. We've had visitors from 177 different countries, and 30% of them have never been to a museum before. Like most contemporary people, many of our guests are taking in the experience with and through their phones. So often, I feel that the challenge is to create an experience that works for those expectations —for selfies, for shareable content, for recorded memories—while staying committed to emotional power and intellectual complexity.

This is much more easily said than done, but it's a fight we engage in every day. The Museum of the Future is one of the world's most active battlefields in that regard, simply because our audience comes from everywhere, has almost nothing in common, and yet has very high expectations and a strong desire to interact with and affect everything they see.

So, we have to constantly review and refine the audience experience and how our ideas are presented. I think of the museum as a kind of laboratory in that sense, where we're actively trying to evolve forms of public experience and communication for the 21st century, following almost a scientific method of trial and error. As I mentioned before, I hope some of the strategies we develop prove helpful to artists and institutions everywhere because none of it is specific to Dubai, the future, or museums, for that matter.

"The Problem" with Design and Its Institutions.

And What Can Be Done About It.

"The problem" at hand might at first sound vapid compared to the hellscape of troubles our societies face now and in the foreseeable future. Minute-by-minute, we are offered reasons for preoccupation, dismay, or frustration—thanks to our trustworthy digital newsfeeds. Our navigation pattern across reality is constantly regurgitated back at us through the masterful trickery of algorithmic design. The medium is the bubble.

Yes, design is everywhere. It's not just in your phone, your house, your workplace, or your street—it is in your habits, what and when you shop, what you choose to eat, and the activist causes you decide to support. It is in your political leanings, or lack thereof.

However seemingly ephemeral, *any solicitation of design work* requires a painstaking ability to observe and deconstruct reality down to its most fundamental units, with the ultimate goal of rewiring it anew. From the scale of bits and atoms that compose computational models and materials to the spatial politics of racial equality and social pluralism, and extending to the geopolitical forces that motivate wars or divestments from ecological projects, design is always entangled with both a poetics and a science of relations that reconfigure the world. Any design choice is a political choice because it invariably impacts collective states or behaviors; it engenders systemic change through individual actions. It can liberate and empower as much as it can subjugate and destroy.

I have long been a strong believer in the power of institutions—whether private or public—to both *celebrate* and constructively engage with this complexity. They can shape forums of public encounter where creativity can come to the rescue, to help us navigate reality in ways that the instant delivery of unmediated politics fails to provide. This failure often reduces reality to a doomscrolling we can easily disconnect from, or worse, completely ignore.

Spaces of culture are machines of collective consciousness. They protend the temperament of their communities by generating publicness through knowledge and empathy. The embodied *practice of celebration* seems a fitting metaphor to imaginatively replenish their power as stages of convergence, inviting an active participatory attitude, an optimistic disposition, and a constructive sense of responsibility within a common human project—particularly in times when we need them the most.

So, "the problem" here concerns the degree and quality of commitment that political, educational, and economic institutions allocate to cultural infrastructures to ensure they continue to serve public interest and remain productive engines of social discourse and civic practice, engaging both professionals and the citizens of the future.

It is not an easy task. Cultural workers that need to deal with chronic underfunding and museums that have been severely affected—some having entirely folded—in the fallout of the Covid crisis are still in a better position than those besieged by misguided administrations, myopic bureaucrats, power struggles, or sheer professional incompetence.

There is abundant resilience, yet surprisingly little innovation in places that have always been devoted to nurturing flights of imagination. What about those devoted to design—the master of all disciplines, capable of making and unmaking your living room as much as a nuclear bomb?

From business planning to program ventures, institutions are, generally speaking, as stagnant in their appearances —architecture, spatial functionalities—as they are in the experiences they offer. "The problem" here is manifold and tied to enduring models that have historically focused on object-oriented collecting (central to financial security) and exhibiting; costly operational models; and sponsorship strategies based on invisible brand consumption, to name a few. Further to this, there is the absolute need for institutions to catch up with the changes at large in our societies and the transformed state of practice itself. Today, the language of design is increasingly articulated through a constellation of gestures predicated on various scales and immaterial domains, along with epistemological questions that concern the very nature of humanity itself, and its role in a radically expanded yet divisive world.

So, "the problem" is: how can we remain faithful to the idea that culture has always been a celebration of unknowns and contradictions? How can we preserve spaces in our public realms where moderated conversations and respectful debates can serve as pedagogical tools to facilitate coexistence and make the future habitable? How do we secure spaces of culture as the ultimate territories where we can co-create the present and imagine what is to come, freed from the economic and political imperatives of power, taste, entertainment, and market penetration?

A good first step would be to change our assessment parameters: museums and their related institutions are often discussed in terms of demographic scale, with their value measured as a return on investment through marketing—that is, communication metrics of unqualified visibility (how many clicks, how many tickets)—instead of ecologies of impact, which would mean more productively fostering economics of innovation and social empowerment that can echo beyond the physical and digital boundaries of their reach.

Can we rewire the relationships among stakeholders in the private, public, and productive sectors through novel paradigms so that institutions of culture can truly remain grounds for intellectual progress, wild dreaming, experimentation, and the practical application of ideas that could inform policy-making and industrial research? This would support innovation for the common good—places where transgenerational conversations are possible, new ecologies of knowledge are explored, and politics of affect are exercised.

The problem ceases to be a problem once we acknowledge the need to take better care of our institutions of culture. This is not merely an insiders' discourse; it is a pivotal topic that could change the way we, as a collective, address the troubles we face in this uncertain era. It is about producing the intellectual framework that will nurture the future for generations to come.

In my professional journey, I have dedicated my efforts to responding to these questions, in places near and far, listening to stories and testing ideas in myriad collaborative configurations with people from all walks of life. Like me, many others have approached this task with earnest dedication—relevant conversations often happen behind closed doors, in informal contexts, far from public view. This editorial project represents a modest but hopefully useful contribution aimed at disclosing the challenges, stories, and, most importantly, concrete propositions that enliven this discourse so that they might inspire others in their own quests.

Beatrice Leanza is a cultural strategist, museum director, and critic with expertise in design, architecture and the visual arts across Asia and beyond. She earned an MA in Asian Studies from Ca'Foscari University, Venice, specializing in contemporary Chinese art, and spent 17 years in Beijing shaping the Chinese creative scene.

Beatrice has served as director of maat—Museum of Art, Architecture and Technology (Lisbon), director of mudac—Museum of Design and Applied Arts (Lausanne), and creative director of Beijing Design Week, where she launched Baitasi Remade, the urban regeneration program of the eponymous historic hutong district. She also co-founded The Global School, China's first independent institute for design and creative practice, founded on pedagogical principles of purpose-driven research.

Her international projects include *Across Chinese Cities*, a research program presented at the Venice Architecture Biennale (2014, 2016, 2018), *Visual Natures: The Culture and Politics of Environmentalism in the 20th and 21st Centuries* at maat (2021–22) and the national pavilion of Saudi Arabia at the 2025 Venice Architecture Biennale. A European Young Leader (Friends of Europe Foundation, Brussels) since 2018, she serves on the advisory board of Design Trust (Hong Kong). Since 2022 she has been an ambassador for Italian Design Day, an international initiative jointly organized by the Italian Ministry of Foreign Affairs and the Ministry of Culture.

@beabiyue

IMAGE CREDITS

COLOPHON

Concept:
Beatrice Leanza

Design:
Offshore, Zurich
with Lea Michel, Zurich

Image processing:
Offshore, Zurich

Illustrations:
Martin Groch, Brussels

Printing and binding:
Graphius, Belgium

© 2025 Beatrice Leanza
and Park Books AG, Zurich
© for the texts: the authors
© for the images: see image credits

Park Books AG
Niederdorfstrasse 54
8001 Zurich
Switzerland
www.park-books.com
+41 44 262 16 62
info@park-books.com

Product Safety
Responsible person according to EU
regulation 2023/988 (GPSR):
GVA Gemeinsame Verlagsauslieferung
Göttingen GmbH & Co. KG
P.O. Box 2021
37010 Göttingen, Germany
+49 551 384 200 0
info@gva-verlage.de

Park Books is being supported by the
Federal Office of Culture with a general
subsidy for the years 2021–2025.

ISBN: 978-3-03860-438-9

This publication was made possible
with support from Golden Goose.

GOLDEN GOOSE